Marital Separation and Lethal Domestic Violence

Marital Separation and Lethal Domestic Violence

Desmond Ellis
LaMarsh Centre for Child and Youth Research, York University

Noreen Stuckless
Department of Psychology, York University / Department of Psychiatry, University of Toronto

Carrie Smith
Department of Psychology, York University

LONDON AND NEW YORK

First published 2015 by Anderson Publishing

Published 2015 by Routledge
2 Park Square, Milton Park, Abingdon, Oxon OX14 4RN

and by Routledge
711 Third Avenue, New York, NY 10017, USA

Routlege is an imprint of the Taylor & Francis Group, an infoma business

Acquiring Editor: Pamela Chester
Development Editor: Ellen S. Boyne
Project Manager: Punithavathy Govindaradjane
Designer: Matthew Limbert

Copyright © 2015 Taylor & Francis. All rights reserved.

No part of this book may be reprinted or reproduced or
utilised in any form or by any electronic, mechanical, or other means, now
known or hereafter invented, including photocopying and recording, or in any
information storage or retrieval system, without permission in writing from
the publishers.

Notices
No responsibility is assumed by the publisher for any injury and/or damage to
persons or property as a matter of products liability, negligence or otherwise,
or from any use of operation of any methods, products, instructions or ideas
contained in the material herein.

Practitioners and researchers must always rely on their own experience and
knowledge in evaluating and using any information, methods, compounds, or
experiments described herein. In using such information or methods they should
be mindful of their own safety and the safety of others, including parties for
whom they have a professional responsibility.

Product or corporate names may be trademarks or registered trademarks, and
are used only for identification and explanation without intent to infringe.

This book and the individual contributions contained in it are protected under copyright by
the Publisher (other than as may be noted herein).

Library of Congress Cataloging-in-Publication Data
Application submitted

British Library Cataloguing in Publication Data
A catalogue record for this book is available from the British Library

ISBN 978-1-4557-7675-7 (pbk)

Contents

List of Figures and Tables ix
Online Resources xi
Introduction xiii

CHAPTER 1 **Marital Separation: Definition and Process** 1
  Marital Separation 1
  Definition 2
  Process: "Untying the Knot" 3
  Separation and Divorce 7
  Definitions: Validity and Utility as Criteria 8
  Protective and Aggravating Effects 9
  Separating from Abusive Male Partners 10
  Comment 10
  Discussion Questions 11

CHAPTER 2 **Lethal Domestic Violence: Definitions and Motives** 13
  Definitions 13
  Homicide 13
  Femicide 14
  Femicide–Suicide 16
  Are Femicide–Suicides Premeditated? 16
  Types of Domestic Violence 21
  Comment 23
  Discussion Questions 27

CHAPTER 3 **Separation and Lethal Intimate Partner Violence** 29
  Sociological Empirical Generalizations 29
  Sex/Gender and Lethal Domestic Violence 31
  Marital Separation 33
  Separation and Homicide–Femicide 34
  Recency of Spousal Femicide and Homicide Following
    Separation 36
  Separation, Divorce, and Spousal Homicide/Suicide 37
  Separation and Femicide–Suicide 38
  Recency of Femicide–Suicide Following Separation 39
  Separation and Suicide 40
  Recency of Suicide Following Marital Separation 40
  Recency of Femicide–Suicide Following Separation 41
  Summary 42

Comment 42
Discussion Questions 43

CHAPTER 4 Theorizing Separation and Intimate Partner Homicide 45
Family as a Stateless Location 45
Homicide as Self-Defense 46
Male Batterers as Their Own Gravediggers 47
Theorizing Intimate Partner Homicide 47
Research 51
Summary 57
Comment 57
Discussion Questions 61

CHAPTER 5 Separation and Intimate Partner Femicide 63
Evolutionary Psychological Theory 63
The By-Product Hypothesis 64
Femicide Adaptation Theory 70
Patriarchy Theory 73
Conflict Resolution Theory 78
Dynamics of Conflict Resolution 84
A Domestic Context-Specific Theory of Conflict Resolution 86
Summary 91
Comment 91
Discussion Questions 97

CHAPTER 6 Separation and Intimate Partner Femicide–Suicide 99
Evolutionary Psychological Theory 99
Sociological Social Control Theory 103
Attribution Theory 104
Masculinity Theory 106
Attachment/Frustration-Aggression Theory 108
Personality Theory 110
Conflict Resolution Theory 114
Comment 117
Discussion Questions 120

CHAPTER 7 Separation and Suicide 121
Social Integration–Regulation Theory 121
Borderline Personality Theory 131
Conflict Resolution Theory 133

		Summary	135
		Comment	136
		Discussion Questions	138
CHAPTER 8		**Preventing Intimate Partner Homicide and Femicide**	139
		Community/Law Enforcement Interventions	139
		Shelters and Domestic Violence Abuse Courts	156
		The Role of Public Policies and Programs in Preventing Femicide	167
		Risk Assessment	174
		Lethality Risk Assessment and Separation	186
		Comment	187
		Discussion Questions	188
References			189
Author Index			213
Subject Index			219

List of Figures and Tables

Table 2.1	Random Effects Meta-Analysis of the Relative Risk of Gun Use in Femicides Followed by Suicides	20
Table 3.1	Relative Frequency of Violent Deaths Reported by 16 U.S. States	31
Table 3.2	Gender and Violent Deaths of Intimate Partners Compared with Males and Females Generally	32
Table 3.3	Marital Status and Lethal Domestic Violence	34
Table 3.4	Femicides and Homicides for Co-residence and Separate Residence Spouses in Legally Registered Marriages	35
Table 4.1	Theories and Causal Mechanisms for the Association between Separation and Intimate Partner Homicide	57
Figure 5.1	Femicide and Femicide-Suicide Risk, Intensity of Conflict, and Months Since Separation	87
Table 5.1	Theories and Causal Mechanisms for the Association between Separation and Intimate Partner Femicide	91
Table 6.1	Theories and Causal Mechanisms for the Association between Separation and Intimate Partner Femicide-Suicide	116
Table 7.1	Household living arrangement decrease in risk of suicide	128
Table 7.2	Theories and Causal Mechanisms for the Association between Separation and Intimate Partner Suicide	135
Table 8.1	Causal Mechanisms in Models for Preventing Femicide	146
Figure 8.1	Process Theory of Interpersonal Power	156
Table 8.2	Summary of Studies Evaluating the Danger Assessment. Entries in Italics Represent Analyses Conducted on Subsamples of a Database Reported in Other Publications	177

Online Resources

Interactive resources can be accessed for free by registering at
www.routledge.com/cw/ellis

Introduction

Most researchers who include marital status in their publications on lethal and/or nonlethal intimate partner violence tend to identify the marital statuses of "separated" and "divorce" as risk factors for these adverse outcomes. The statistical and substantive significance of the association between these variables depends, in part, on how each of them—separation, divorce/lethal, and nonlethal intimate partner violence—is defined and measured *and* whether the meaning of statistical findings (e.g., correlation coefficients) is revealed using qualitative data from investigations of the *process* of separating. Chapter 1 is devoted to an examination of how separation is defined and measured and a description of the process of separating.

Lethal domestic violence—deadly violence that occurs in the specific context of domesticity—is one possible outcomes of separation. Domesticity is defined in terms of the specific arrangement of living or having lived together as a married or cohabiting couple and is differentiated from the more general phenomenon of lethal intimate partner violence. In Chapter 2 we describe the criteria used in differentiating among types of lethal intimate partner violence that occur in both domestic and nondomestic intimate partner contexts, evaluate the differentiation of motives for intimate partner violence in both contexts and, in the concluding segment, answer recurring questions that are asked about the forms or types of lethal intimate partner violence—homicide, femicide, femicide–suicide, and suicide—that are defined in this chapter.

In Chapters 1 and 2, separation and lethal intimate partner violence were discussed independently of each other. In Chapter 3 evidence is presented indicating that they are reliably and strongly associated with each other under certain specified conditions. When these conditions are met the association between these two variables is raised to the level of a sociological empirical generalization. The findings cited in this chapter support the designation of the association between separation and lethal intimate partner violence as a sociological empirical generalization.

Chapters 4, 5, 6, and 7 are similar to each other in that attempts to explain the empirical generalization are derived from theories of lethal intimate partner violence in each of them. At the same time, the chapters are differentiated from each other on the basis of the type or form of lethal intimate partner violence that the theories are designed to explain. Specifically, in Chapters 4, 5, 6, and 7 causal mechanisms explaining the empirical generalization are derived from theories of intimate partner homicide, femicide, femicide–suicide, and suicide, respectively.

In addition to theory and research, prevention is also included in the title of this book. The final chapter—Chapter 8—is devoted to the description and evaluation of three recent innovative national models aimed at preventing femicide as well as an assessment of the contribution made to preventing femicide by women's shelters and the use of lethal domestic violence risk assessment instruments.

Marital Separation: Definition and Process

CHAPTER 1

LEARNING OBJECTIVES

Readers who achieve the learning objectives set for this chapter will be able to demonstrate:
- Awareness of the complexities associated with presenting a valid and useful definition of marital separation
- The ability to critically evaluate metaphors used to describe the process of "his" and "her" separations
- The ability to specify the conditions under which separation is likely to be associated with intimate partner violence

MARITAL SEPARATION

Epidemiological studies of violent deaths are routinely conducted by The Centers for Disease Control and Prevention (CDC) researchers with the objectives of controlling and preventing them. The "circumstances" present at the time of death are regarded as information that is essential to the achievement of both CDC objectives (Barker, 2006). The circumstances referred to by Barker include the marital status of perpetrators and victims. If this information were available to CDC researchers using National Violent Death Reporting System data, perpetrators and victims would be located in one of the following marital status categories: never married, married, widowed, divorced, or separated. Three of these categories—widowed, divorced, and separated—involve the dissolution of intimate partner relationships. The proportion of intimate partner relationships dissolved by death, divorce, and separation varies across Western societies in the same historical period and in the same society during different historical periods.

A review of findings reported by Cherlin (2009) yielded the following conclusion: To a greater degree than at any time in its history, separated has replaced widowed and divorced as the major cause of the dissolution of intimate partner relationships in the United States. Understanding how American families experience this change may be facilitated by the use of a metaphor.

In their book *Metaphors We Live By*, Lakoff and Johnson (1980) refer to a metaphor as a device used to "help us understand and experience one kind of thing in terms of another" (p. 5). Cherlin uses the metaphor of a spinning carousel with people jumping on and off to help us understand and experience separation in the United States. Preserving the metaphor, Weiss (1979) reported that the separated/divorced men and women he interviewed found jumping to separation disrupted the "structure of their social and emotional lives" far more than when they divorced some time later (p. 4). Researchers Bloom, White, and Asher (1979), Holmes and Rahe (1967), Kruk (1993), and Schwartz and Kaslow (1997) include the experience of stress, ambivalence, and emotional distress even by couples who voluntarily jump off together; greater stress, emotional distress, despair, and anger by those who are pushed off by the unilateral decisions of their partners; and hostility between the pushers and the pushed.

Holmes and Rahe (1967) administered their Social Adjustment Rating Scale to a large number of Americans and asked them to assign points from 1 to 100 to life events that required the greatest amount of adjustment. The death of a spouse was ranked the most stressful life event—greatest number of points assigned—and divorce OR marital separation was ranked as the second most stressful life event. These findings are based on perceptions. Weiss (1979) actually interviewed a nonrandom sample of 150 divorced men and women attending his *Seminars for the Separated*. He found that it was "separation, not divorce that disrupted the structure of the individual's social and emotional life" (p. 4).

The emotional distress and other feelings associated with separation may be experienced by individuals who are jumping on and off the marriage-go-round carousel in all Western societies, but compared with family members in societies such as Germany (former West Germany), France, Italy, Norway, Spain, and Sweden, family life in the United States, American family members are likely to experience "frequent [marital status] transitions [and] shorter marriage and cohabiting relationships occur more often" (p. 5). Over a five-year period, almost one-quarter (23%) of all marriages and more than half (55%) of all cohabiting relationships in the United States will be disrupted by separation (Charts 3 and 4, p. 206). Findings reported by Cherlin were based on the analysis of data from a variety of sources, including life tables from Fertility and Family Survey data on selected Western societies (p. 201).

DEFINITION

Marital separation is defined legally and socially. The U.S. Divorce Law Center defines a legal separation as "a court ordered right to live apart, with the rights and obligations of divorced persons, but without divorce" (2009). The rights referred to in this definition include the right to petition for the same outcomes divorcing couples may petition for, including child custody, child support, spousal support, and division of property. Until they obtain a divorce, separated couples cannot legally remarry. For couples who have no intention of ever remarrying and/or who object to divorce on religious grounds or other grounds, legal separations offer an alternative to divorce.

Legal separations are important because they may mediate or moderate the effect of separation on male partner violence by imposing unequal financial, psychological and social costs that are or are perceived to be unfair by one or both of the parties. In cases in which the parties are parents, the best interest of the child or children as perceived by the judge may trump the interests and legal rights of one parent more than the other, or trump the interests of both parties to an equal degree.

The legal separation rate varies across U.S. states with the rate being extremely low in the majority of states that permit the alternatives of no-fault divorce and separation agreements. Separation agreements facilitated by third parties—family lawyers, arbitrators, and mediators—are obtained far more frequently than court-ordered legal separation orders and less frequently than social separations. Social separations are produced by intimate partners themselves, but not all of them are agreed to by both parties.

In the social definition of marital separation formulated by Weiss (1979), separation is defined as "the suspension of vows or agreements (e.g., 'till death do us part')" that "produces the withdrawal of emotional and physical accessibility" (p. 4). Suspension is a subjective term that implies some degree of uncertainty by one or both parties about whether their relationship has truly ended. When at least one of the parties has withdrawn accessibility, moved to a separate residence, and has "no positive plans" to ever live with the other party again, they are, according to Weiss, truly separated. The intimate partners referred to by Weiss are legally married spouses. Spouses may be truly separated even though they have not yet obtained a formal separation agreement. Couples in other intimate relationships who do not want or require a separation agreement may also be truly separated. Consequently, we broaden the definition of intimate partners to include married, common law, cohabiting, and dating couples as well as boy/girlfriends and cheating lovers.

Findings reported by Arendell (1995) do not broaden the Weiss (1975) narrative, but they offer an alternative divorced male partner narrative. Specifically, she reported findings indicating that male partners believe they, and not their wives or third parties such judges and lawyers, are primarily responsible for deciding when they are truly separated or even divorced from the female partners who left them (1995). These findings as well as those reported by the divorced wives studied by Kurz (1995) are reflected in the following modified Weiss definition of social separation: Marital separation is defined as a process characterized by the intentional withdrawal of physical and emotional accessibility by one or both partners that one or both married (legal or common law, de facto) *partners perceive as contingent and temporary or noncontingent and permanent.*

Marital separation is a subset of intimate partner separation. Intimate partner separation is defined as a process characterized by the intentional withdrawal of physical and emotional accessibility by one or both intimate partners that one or both of them perceive as contingent and temporary or noncontingent and permanent. Two case studies illustrating the process of separation involving a married and an unmarried couple follow.

PROCESS: "UNTYING THE KNOT"

In opposition to those who assumed that marriage had the same meaning for both genders, sociologist Jessie Bernard (1972) claimed that the meaning of marriage was different for men and women. "His" and "her" marriages were described in a segment of her book entitled *The Future of Marriage*. This frequently cited segment focuses exclusively on gender differences in the meaning of marriage. We attempt to build upon Bernard's contribution—the meaning of marriage varies with gender—by describing how the meaning/experience of separation varies with the *intersection* of gender and the decision to separate. The decision to separate can be made unilaterally—he alone, she alone—or jointly. Because female partners unilaterally decide to separate in between two-thirds or three-quarters of cases, the modal case of separation is one in which women unilaterally decide to separate (Ellis, 1994). What follows is appropriate for the modal case. It is not appropriate for the second case of his (Bode) and her (Sarah) separation we describe and compare with the separation of Max and Kate.

Two metaphors describing the process of untying the knot of marriage were identified by Thernstrom (2003). An herb (cilantro) that grows rapidly and dies quickly is one of them. A snowfall that gradually becomes an impassable barrier because of the accumulation of small deposits of snow over time is the second one. The second metaphor describes how Kate, age 32 when she married Max, experienced her separation after 11 years of married life. Preserving the snowfall metaphor, the first dusting of snow fell at lunch on their first date. He thought he was being caring when, after lunch, he insisted that she take the leftover spaghetti with her on the jet she was taking to Chicago. Kate "hated leftovers" and felt she was being controlled rather than cared for by Max. But, she said "Fine," took the spaghetti, and threw it in the rubbish bin when she landed. It was "the first of 11 years of things she said 'Fine' to while thinking something different" (p. 40). Other dustings of snow fell when:

- Max, who earned a relatively low salary performing a "socially responsible" job for a nonprofit organization, criticized and showed contempt for the large financial corporation that paid Kate a salary significantly higher than the one received by Max;
- She experienced recurring reminders by a more sophisticated Max of her plebeian and/or unhealthy tastes in food, television, literature, motor cars, wine, music, and the theater;
- Kate became increasingly aware of the fact that their shared interests in bird-watching, baseball, wine, jazz, and theater were really Max's interests;
- Kate's experience of Max's recurring bad moods when she began pursuing her own interests on her own, such as "seeing a friend and playing tennis";
- She experienced recurring occasions when she had no time to herself "going from a crowded office, to a crowded subway to a small apartment where Max was always waiting and annoyed at the late hour she was coming home."

Kate was childless, and the catalyst—a very heavy fall of snow that created an impassable barrier—for her irrevocable decision to separate was an affair she had after a failed attempt to become pregnant at a fertility clinic. Kate reframed her adultery as "a gift to herself" because it made her aware of the "profound absence of … intimacy" in her marriage.

The first metaphor describes how Max, also age 32 when he married Kate, experienced the separation. They fell in love quickly and got married after a short courtship. For Max, marriage involved sharing interests, being with and doing things together, and taking care of Kate. During the course of their 11-year marriage, Kate engaged in a number of activities that angered or annoyed Max such as creating a separate bank account; wanting additional diamonds on her wedding ring; buying a car (BMW), favored by "Republican capitalists"; wanting to spend discretionary time on her own doing what she alone wanted to do; intentionally exposing Max to a sound he hated by "leaving the bathroom door open while she dried her hair"; and criticizing him for the untidy condition of their apartment. However, unlike snowfalls that accumulate, these annoyances were perceived as confetti that blew away with the breezes created by expressions of caring, sharing, and the attempt to have a child of their own or adopt one. Three months after they signed up for an adoption workshop, Kate told Max she was leaving him. Max, who perceived the marriage was working well and progressing to the point of having children to share and care for, was sad, stunned, angry, and determined to "get everything he was legally entitled to under New York's equity sharing laws that required Kate, the higher income earning spouse, to share her income with Max."

From Max's perspective, the separation was climactic, unilaterally initiated, and final. From Kate's perspective, the process of separating was cumulative. Findings reported by a number of researchers indicate that other separating women share Kate's perspective. For example, Anderson and Saunders (2003, p. 176) cite findings indicating that the process of separating involves emotional and physical withdrawal while females are still living with their male partners (e.g., delaying their return to the home from work, accepting jobs or invitations from relatives and friends that entailed spending less time at home, eating meals alone, watching television in separate rooms, sleeping in separate beds). Temporary separations—moving out—and moving back may follow.

Okun (1986) found that the average number of temporary separations preceding the final permanent separation was 2.4. The average number of separations for separated women who sought safety in women's shelters was 5.07. These women did not ever return to live with their former partners (p. 198). Walker (1986) reported findings indicating that abused women will initiate between four and five temporary separations—"the halting of cohabitation by the partners for at least one day in the context of a conflict in the relationship" (p. 198)—before divorcing their partners. Similar findings are reported by Ferarro and Johnson (1983), Landenburger (1998), and Wallace (1986).

The penultimate phase—permanent separation—is the high or low point of a cumulative process that is sometimes preceded by a "tipping point incident or event." How child custody, access, financial support, property division, and collective debt conflicts associated with permanent separation and divorce are settled can increase or decrease the intensity of conflict and consequently the risk of nonlethal and lethal male partner violence during the final post-separation phase (Ellis, 2014).

Max and Kate participated in a collaborative proceeding (mediation) that tends to decrease the intensity of conflict, rather than an adversarial proceeding (litigation), which tends to increase it. In their case, conflict settlement was facilitated by the absence of a zero-sum conflict over child custody—they had no children—and the ability of the mediator to settle the conflict over the amount of money Kate was to pay Max as alimony. Kate perceived the amount of money she paid to Max as "a plundering of her savings." The mediator reframed the payment as "a supplement given to Max for a specified period of time" to cover basic living expenses such as rent (Thernstrom, 2003, p. 43). Had they taken the case to court—Kate's lawyer advised her not to, Max's lawyer advised him to—both of them agreed that "the judge would have [ordered Kate to pay the same amount] and both of them would have felt cheated" (p. 44). Neither Kate nor Max would have chosen the amount of money paid by Kate but both "felt they could live with it, precisely because they did choose it" (p. 44). The risk of intimate partner hostility and violence during the post-separation phase is probably higher for divorcing parties who feel cheated by participating in an adversarial proceeding in which a settlement was imposed on them than it is for those who feel they can live with the mediation agreement they created and signed.

Bode and Sarah

Alpine racing champion Bode Miller, age 36, and ex-Marine firefighter Sara McKenna, age 27, were introduced to each other by an upscale dating website in San Diego. With marriage in mind, they met sometime in April 2012 and dated each other for about six weeks. According to Sarah, Bode wanted a large family, "at least four babies from you." To this end, they had sex once. Sarah was (presumably) unwilling to give him four babies by having more sex because she did not want a large family. Consequently, Sarah left California and Bode. A few weeks later, they agreed to meet in Florida. They had sex one more time. Sarah reported that "he never offered to use a condom [because] he assumed I was ready to get pregnant." When she was 7 months pregnant she moved from California to New York. About 2 months later, she gave birth to a boy she named Samuel. She also filed for temporary custody of her son who she and her lawyers felt Bode was not interested in establishing a caring relationship with.

One of the reasons Sarah left San Diego was that Bode was dating a volleyball player named Morgan Beck. They got married in October 2012, about 2 months after Sarah and Bode separated. The marriage significantly escalated the intensity of the conflict between Bode and Sarah to the point where they could not even agree on a name for their child. In fact, Bode applied to the court in San Diego to include Nathaniel among his names and he called him Nate while she called him Samuel. In January, Morgan gave birth to a stillborn child. Within days, Bode, who now wanted to be a father to son Nate/Samuel, filed for joint custody of his son in a family court in San Diego. He was awarded primary custody because Bode's lawyer persuaded the judge that pregnant Sarah left California for New York because family court judges in New York were more likely to award custody to mothers. Bode contested the temporary custody order made by a family court judge in New York. In May 2013, a family court referee in New York refused to award temporary custody to Sarah, castigating her for "appropriating the child while it was in utero" and returned the case to the family court in San Diego even though Samuel was born and lived in New York. Shortly after, on September 4, 2013, Bode and his wife arrived at her apartment in New York and, according to Sarah, "took the baby out of my arms, dropped it in a car seat and drove away."

In November 2013, an appeals panel in New York roundly criticized the referee for his refusal to award temporary custody to Sarah, returning the case to San Diego, and implicitly suggesting that it was appropriate for a woman who got pregnant after only a "brief romantic relationship" should obtain permission from the father for moving from one state to another. Family courts in two states were now involved in a jurisdictional conflict and their "custody battle" widened after the submission of an *amicus* brief supporting the rights of pregnant women "to make life decisions about where they work, live, go to school." The battle for custody fought in family courts has been ongoing for about 1 year.

On December 9, 2013, Bode and Sarah appeared in a family court in New York and left the court with the following agreement in hand: During the next four months they would spend an equal amount of time being with and caring for Samuel/Nate (Burns, 2013; Gabriel, 2013; Nye, 2013).

Unlike Kate and Max, who met during the course of living their everyday lives and who lived together as man and wife for a number of years, the meeting between Bode and Sarah was arranged through a dating website and they cohabited briefly before separating. Third parties were involved in the process of separating but the proceedings each couple participated in were different. Kate and Max participated in a collaborative proceeding (mediation) and Bode and Sarah participated in an adversarial proceeding (adjudication). Until Bode achieved what he wanted, albeit temporarily—joint custody of Samuel/Nate—participation in the adversarial proceedings widened and escalated the intensity of the conflict. Participation in a collaborative proceeding did not widen and may have decreased the intensity of conflict between Kate and Max.

Compared with living in a common law relationship or cohabiting, marriage with its legal rights and obligations complicates the formal process of divorcing. For married couples with children, participation in this process yields fateful outcomes for parents and children. In addition to findings reported by other researchers, findings based on four years of observing family court proceedings by fourth-year students enrolled in a conflict resolution course taught by one of the authors indicate that parenting plans about the primary residence of children and/or access to them by "noncustodial" parents are a modal and most important source of conflict between parents. The formal process of separating is complicated and more fateful for an increasing proportion of common law and cohabiting couples because 41% of the children born in the United States are now born to unmarried couples (Ryan, 2013).

SEPARATION AND DIVORCE

Unmarried couples (Bode and Sarah) can separate, but only married couples (Kate and Max) can divorce. All U.S. states have rules permitting "no fault" and "fault" as grounds for filing for divorce. U.S. states vary in the number of faults they specify as grounds. For example, Illinois specifies the following 11 fault grounds: adultery; cruelty or violence; willful desertion for 1 year; drug/alcohol addiction for two years; impotency; unexplained absence; conviction of crime; venereal disease; undissolved prior marriage; attempted murder of spouse; and two-year separation by irreconcilable differences. Florida has only one: "mental incapacity of one party for preceding period of at least three years." Most states specify cruelty/violence and adultery as fault grounds. All states include "irreconcilable differences/irretrievable breakdown" and separation as no-fault grounds for filing for a divorce.

Most divorces are preceded by separation. Analysis of data published by USLegal (2014) yields these findings: For a randomly selected sample of U.S. states ($n = 26$), the period of required separation (living separate and apart) ranges from 2 to 36 months; the median number of months required is 22; and the mean number of months required is 16.7 months. In Chapter 3, the association between months-since-separation and lethal intimate partner violence is investigated.

DEFINITIONS: VALIDITY AND UTILITY AS CRITERIA

The validity of definitions in social science is usually established by consensus among theorists and researchers who specialize in studying the family. In the case of marital separation, consensus among those who publish books on the family is difficult to assess because, unlike divorce, separation is rarely defined. Specifically, it is defined in only one (Weiss, 1979) of the 24 family texts we reviewed that were published between 1987 (Skolnick, *The Intimate Environment*) and 2009 (Cherlin, *The Marriage-Go-Round*). Alternatively or additionally, the validity of definitions can be established by couples who have experienced the process of separating from an intimate partner one or more times. Because the Weiss definition we modified was derived from interviews with from *Parents Without Partners*, it represents consensus among members of this separated–divorced group. We hypothesize that there is also consensus on our definition among a random sample of men and women in the United States who have separated from married or cohabiting partners.

The definition we offered is also useful because it can be put into operation by measuring physical and emotional accessibility when the partners are separated and also while intimate partners are still living together and are in the cumulative process of separating (e.g., minimal or no communication, sleeping in separate bedrooms, living in separate residences). Interview data may reveal phases and other complexities in the process of separating that are not published in the U.S. Census and other official statistics (Hetherington, Law, & O'Connor, 2001; Jacobson & Portuges, 1978). Included among these complexities is the contribution made to separation effects by the independent or interaction effects of such factors as domestic violence, infidelity, the age group of the intimate partners who are separating, age difference between them, and the presence and ages of children and stepchildren (Block, 2000).

PROTECTIVE AND AGGRAVATING EFFECTS

Male partner violence is a function of opportunity and motivation. Opportunities for men to use violence against women who are living with them are available 24/7 and decrease significantly after their female partners start living in separate public or private residences (Ellis & Stuckless, 2006). Shelters for abused women are public residences. One of the major reasons for establishing them is to eliminate opportunities for sublethal and lethal male partner violence (Ellis, Sakinofsky, & Stuckless, 2012). Living in separate private residences decreases opportunities and therefore the risk of sublethal violence but it appears to increase the motivation for lethal male partner violence (Wilson & Daly, 1994).

Separated/divorced male partners include meanings attached to unilateral female partner–initiated separations in their narratives (Arendell, 1995). To the extent that subjective construals of events have objective consequences (Cross & Madsen, 1997; Thomas, 1996), subjectively constructing a female-initiated separation as an "utter abandonment," "an ultimate challenge to male partner control," or "a betrayal" is likely to increase the risk of lethal male partner femicide and femicide–suicide while jointly constructing it as a "a relief," "an opportunity for a new life," or "in the best interest of the children" is likely to decrease the risk of these lethal outcomes.

For some male partners, the female partner's decision to separate may be anticlimactic because of the degree and duration of the withdrawal of physical and emotional accessibility when they were living together (Bernard, 1972; Gottmann, Murray, Swanson, Tyson, & Swanson, 2002). For other males, the female partner's decision to separate may be climactic because it is a total, most unwelcome surprise. Anticlimactic separations are likely to decrease the risk of lethal male partner violence. Climactic separations are likely to increase the risk of lethal male partner violence, especially when the female partner is leaving to live with a man she has been sexually involved with during the time she was living with the man she is separating from (Koziol-McLain et al., 2006).

Separations and divorces may be willingly agreed to by both parties (willing separations). They may also be initiated by one party and contested by the other (unwilling separations). Unwilling separations may involve conflict over fact of separation and/or issues associated with separation, especially issues related to parenting plans and financial support. These separations, as well as those in male partner violence, female partner infidelity, and "leaving to live with another man" are implicated, tend to more strongly associated with lethal male partner violence than separating for reasons such as "personal development," "communication problems," or "problems with in-laws."

In addition to the phases described earlier, separation also has temporal phases. The *acute* phase refers to the days and weeks immediately before the male partner becomes aware of the female partner's intention or decision to leave him permanently. The *proximal* phase refers to the three- to six-month period immediately following the female partner's move to a separate residence and the initiation of formal separation proceedings. The *distal* phase refers to the period of time—more than six months—following participation in formal separation and divorce proceedings. These phases build upon and modify those suggested by Ide, Wyder, Kolves, and De Leo (2010). They are important to note because the risk of lethal male partner violence varies with them.

SEPARATING FROM ABUSIVE MALE PARTNERS

Two-thirds of the 129 separated/divorced women interviewed by Kurz (1995) reported experiencing violence one or more times during their marriages and more than one-third (37%) reported experiencing "frequent and serious violence while they were married" (p. 53). Among newlywed couples ($n = 56$), Rogge and Bradbury (1999) found that separations peaked in the fourth year following marriage and the use of violent means of settling conflicts early in the relationship made a statistically significant contribution toward their early dissolution. The National Survey of Families and Households is administered in waves (1987–1988 wave 1 and 1992–1994 wave 2). DeMaris (2004) investigated the effect of using two different conflict resolution tactics by 3,508 couples who had been married for at least 20 years of separation during the wave 1 survey period on separation during the wave 2 survey years. Physical violence by male partners made a significant contribution toward separation/divorce by reducing the quality of the relationship between couples. Findings reported by a number of other researchers (Walker, Logan, Jordan, & Campbell, 2004, p. 158) also indicate that physical abuse by male partners is strongly associated with separations initiated by female partners.

The process of separating from abusive male partners is a "normal, non-pathological process" that is "complex and multifaceted" (Rhatigan, Street, & Axsom, 2006, p. 342). Unlike theories predicting "violent relationship termination" that pathologize the process of decision-making by abused female partners (e.g., Walker's Battered Women's Syndrome/learned helplessness theory), a theory conceiving of the process of separating as "reasoned action/planned behavior" more reliably predicts intentions to separate and separation. Male partner violence does influence decisions to separate that go through different phases—denial/minimization of the violence, acknowledging male partner violence, control and marital conflicts and thinking about separating, preparing/making plans to separate, separating, and taking action to survive financially, socially, and psychologically as a separated person or parent—but it elicits cost–benefit calculations regarding the merits of staying or leaving rather than eliciting nonrational decision-making suggested by the alternative theories of learned helplessness, psychological entrapment, or traumatic bonding (p. 339).

COMMENT

A review of the content presented here elicits two comments.

First, compared with research on separation as an outcome, descriptions of the actual *process* of separating are relatively rare. Anderson and Saunders (2003) made a contribution to closing the gap between outcome and process research by referring to a number of studies describing the process of separating from abused partners. Still, descriptions of the process of separating remain relatively rare compared with studies in which "separated" is treated as an outcome.

Second, publications describing/explaining the effects of participation in collaborative and adversarial separation and divorce proceedings on femicide, femicide–suicide and suicide are even rarer than descriptions of the process of separating and divorcing. Members of the public are aware of these lethal outcomes because they are newsworthy, but these reports rarely link them with participation in separation and divorce proceedings because investigating police officers—the main source of information for the media—rarely record information on either marital status as an outcome or participation in the proceedings that resulted in this outcome.

DISCUSSION QUESTIONS

1. Describe and critically evaluate the metaphors used to describe the separation between Max and Kate.

2. Describe and critically evaluate the validity and utility of the definitions of separation described in this chapter.

3. Was intimate partner violence was not associated with the separation of Max and Kate because they are two civilized middle-class individuals?

4. Evaluate this statement: The presence of children and participation in adversarial separation proceedings increase the intensity of conflict between separating couples. Do you agree or disagree? Give reasons for your answer.

CHAPTER 2

Lethal Domestic Violence: Definitions and Motives

LEARNING OBJECTIVES

Readers who achieve the learning objectives set for this chapter will be able to demonstrate:

- An awareness of the complexity involved in defining types of lethal intimate partner violence
- The ability to use the criteria of validity and utility in evaluating different definitions of lethal intimate partner violence
- The ability to create a rationale for defining homicide, femicide, femicide–suicide, and suicide before attempting to theorize the association between separation and each of these four types

DEFINITIONS

Lethal domestic violence refers to violence that occurs in the context of domesticity. Context-specific definitions are useful to theorists, researchers, and practitioners, but we attempt to increase their validity and utility by engaging in the process of differentiation. Specifically, we differentiate domestic from nondomestic contexts, differentiate among different types or forms of lethal violence, and evaluate hypothesized differences in major motives for intimate partner violence in both domestic and nondomestic contexts.

Using the criterion of "living arrangement" (joint versus separate residence) we differentiate between lethal violence involving intimate partners who are/were in a married or cohabiting relationship from lethal violence involving couples who are dating and lovers whose partners may or may not be married or cohabiting. Using the criteria of gender, relationship status, and perpetrator/victim role, we differentiate among the following types or forms of lethal violence: intimate partner homicide (female kills male intimate partner); intimate partner femicide (male kills female intimate partner); intimate partner femicide–suicide (male kills female intimate partner and then himself); and suicide (male or female partner kills self).

HOMICIDE

In the *Uniform Crime Reports* published by the Federal Bureau of Investigation (FBI), murder and manslaughter are defined as "the willful killing of one human being by another" as determined exclusively by police investigation (2011, p. 1). In the *Supplementary Homicide Reports* published by the FBI, homicide is defined as "the killing of one human being by another" (2011). This wide definition includes "justifiable homicides" (e.g., killings by police officers in the line of duty), "excusable homicides" (e.g., killings in self-defense or the defense of another person), and "criminal homicides." In the *Uniform Crime Reports* (2011) published by the FBI, criminal homicides are defined as "the willful nonnegligent killing of one human being by another." This definition applies to murder and nonnegligent manslaughter, but unlike homicide statistics published by Statistics Canada that include the Canadian Criminal Code offenses of murder and manslaughter (*Homicide Survey*, 2011), homicide statistics published in the FBI, *Supplementary Homicide Reports*, refer only to murder.

After discussing some of the difficulties associated with defining homicide, especially the issue of intent, Daly and Wilson (1988) adopt a pragmatic approach to defining homicide. Specifically, they defined homicide in a way that enabled them to use homicide data reported by Statistics Canada and the Detroit police force. To this end, they defined homicides as "those interpersonal assaults and other acts directed against another person (for example poisonings) that occur outside the context of warfare, and that prove fatal" (p. 14). In this definition and all the other definitions of homicide we reviewed in official (police) statistics published in the United States, Britain, Australia, and Canada, we found that the sex/gender of victims was not included in definitions of homicide. That is to say, both males and females are included as perpetrators and victims. We did find references to sex/gender in dictionaries—Oxford English and Webster's. However, the reference to Homo (man) in the sense 2 definition in both sources does not indicate whether the man is a perpetrator or a victim. For the purposes of this text, we define homicide as *willful or nonnegligent conduct by a female that causes the death of a male* and intimate partner homicide (IPH) as *willful and nonnegligent conduct by a female that causes the death of a male intimate partner or ex-partner.*

FEMICIDE

Unlike the gender-neutral concepts of murder and homicide, the gendered concept of femicide is not included as a crime in the FBI *Uniform Crime Reports* or *Supplementary Homicide Statistics*, *Homicide Trends in the United States*, published by the Bureau of Justice Statistics, *Surveillance for Violent Deaths Reports* published by the National Violent Death Reporting System, or in any of the other official crime statistics published by governments in Britain, Canada, or Australia.

One of the earliest references to femicide was made by researcher Diana Russell when she testified at the International Conference on Crimes Against Women held in Belgium in 1976. Here, she grounded femicide in misogyny and created awareness about it but did not define it. Sixteen years later, Russell and Radford edited a book entitled *Femicide*. In this book, Radford (1992) defined femicide as "the misogynous killing of women by men" (p. 3). This definition grounds misogyny in patriarchy, which includes the motivation for femicide and extends it beyond legal definitions of murder to include deaths from "botched abortions, unnecessary hysterectomies and clitorectomies and other surgeries as well as infanticides" involving female children as victims (p. 7).

Six years later, Campbell and Runyan (1998) defined femicide as "all killings of women, regardless of motive or perpetrator status." In this definition, femicide is broadly defined to include men and women perpetrators; misogyny is excluded as a motive and patriarchy is excluded as the societal context. Patriarchy as the societal context, motive, and perpetrator status (sex/gender) are restored in Russell's (2001) definition of femicide as "the killing of females by males because they are females." Relationship status (married/cohabiting/dating) was included in Stout's (1993) definition of intimate femicide as "the killing of women by male intimate partners." Dawson and Gartner (1998) broadened Stout's definition by including "current or former legal spouses, common law partners or boyfriends" as perpetrators. This wider definition of intimates is one we adopt because it is grounded in findings indicating that femicides involving dating and cohabiting partners and ex-partners as victims occur more frequently than femicides involving spouses and ex-spouses as victims (Block, 2000; Browne & Williams, 1993, pp. 81, 91).

Accidental killings by current and former intimate partners are included in the Stout and Dawson and Gartner definitions of femicide, but they are excluded in the definition of femicide presented by Johnson and Dawson (2011). These authors define femicide as "the killing of women by men [that] incorporates the crimes of murder and manslaughter" (p. 4) but murder and manslaughter are excluded from the Dawson and Gartner definition of intimate partner femicide they cite and support "killings of women by current and former legal and non-legal partners and common-law partners" (p. 128). Evidently, accidental killings of women by men are excluded from Johnson and Dawson's definition of femicide but not from their definition of intimate partner femicide.

In 2008, the World Health Organization and other agencies held a conference in Washington, DC on *Strengthening Understanding of Femicide: Using research to Galvanize Action and Accountability*. At this conference, Monique Widyono (2008) presented an article in which she reviewed a number of the definitions of femicide and intimate partner femicide presented here as well as definitions used by researchers in different countries. She found variations in definitions of intimate femicide with respect to the inclusion of female partners, incest perpetrators, and family members other than past or present male partners and "little consistency in the terminology used by researchers and service providers" (pp. 8–9). Our attempt to generate consistency takes the form of offering for consideration the following definitions of femicide, intimate partner femicide, and family femicide.

Femicide refers to *willful and nonnegligent conduct by men that causes the death of women*. Intimate partner femicide refers to *willful and nonnegligent conduct by men that causes the death of past or present female intimate partners*. An example of nonnegligent (criminal) conduct causing death of a female intimate partner is provided by the case of a man who is driving his wife to the airport when they resume arguing about her decision to leave him. He expressed his anger at her refusal to change her mind by driving dangerously in the direction of the airport increasing his speed to twice the speed limit, tailgating, and changing lanes recklessly, despite her fearful cries and protests. As he approached a bridge near the airport, he lost control of the car and it smashed into one of the stone bridge supports on the passenger side, killing his wife and breaking his legs.

Family femicide refers to *willful and nonnegligent conduct by family members that causes the death of wives, mothers, and daughters*. In the highly publicized Sharia case, two of his daughters and his wife were murdered in the name of "family honor" by husband/father Sharia, his common law female partner, and his son (Wiseman, 2010).

FEMICIDE–SUICIDE

Femicide–suicide refers to *femicides that are followed by the suicides of male partner perpetrators who are motivated by their intention to commit suicide*. Homicide–suicide refers to *homicides that are followed by the suicides of female partner perpetrators who are motivated by their intention to commit suicide*.

Researchers vary in the meaning they attach to "followed by" in the definition of femicide–suicide. In some definitions, the femicide must be immediately followed by the suicide (Cavan, 1928; Johnson & Hotton, 2003; Milroy, 1993). In other definitions, the latter must follow the former "within 24 hours" (Banks, Crandall, Sklar, & Bauer 2008; Barber et al., 2008; Flynn, Swinson, & While, 2009; Large et al., 2009), "3 days or fewer" (Barraclough & Harris, 2002), or "within 7 days" (Liem & Nieuwbeerta, 2010; Marzuk, Tardiff, & Hirsch, 1992).

In the absence of clear evidence of the intention to commit suicide after the femicide (e.g., a suicide note), researchers appear to rely on the time since the femicide as an indicator of intention or motive. The underlying assumption seems to be the shorter the time-gap between the femicide and the homicide, the greater the likelihood that the femicide and the suicide constitute a single act by a perpetrator of femicide–suicide who intended to commit suicide (Cavan, 1928). The longer the time-gap between the femicide and the suicide, the more difficult it becomes to attribute intention or motive to the suicide that follows it. On the other hand, femicide–suicides are rare events and researchers can include a greater number of these cases by increasing the size of their samples. Sample size can be increased by including longer time-gap cases in the samples they select. Larger samples provide more stable findings and a fairly large sample was used by Dawson to answer the interesting question that follows.

ARE FEMICIDE–SUICIDES PREMEDITATED?

The answer published by Dawson (2005) was based upon the multivariate statistical analysis of information from the following sources: a subset of 703 solved homicides including 194 (28%) femicide-suicides reported by police forces in Ontario between 1974 and 1994. The sample included only perpetrators who were "current or former legal spouses, common law partners, or boyfriends." Data on individuals in the sample were collected from the death records (homicide and suicide files) stored in the Office of the Chief Coroner for Ontario cross-referenced with reports of police officers investigating the homicides included in the files and the files of crowns prosecuting the cases, the trials of some defendants, and newspapers and magazine articles on the perpetrators.

In the United States, federal law (Title 18, US Code section 1111) defines premeditated murder as a criminal act that "wrongfully causes the death of another person(s)" after rationally considering the timing or method of commission in order to increase the likelihood of success or to evade detection or apprehension. "Rational consideration" involves planning and deliberation. Premeditation was measured by one person (Dawson) using a modified version of an index of premeditation created by another researcher. Eight indicators of premeditation were identified. "Waylays victim as she leaves home/workplace" was the first one. The seven remaining indicators were: "breaks into victim's home, victim was sleeping when she was killed, perpetrator previously threatened to kill the victim and/or himself, perpetrator brought a gun to the location of the crime, perpetrator left a suicide note indicating he intended to kill himself and/or his partner" and "other indicators" (e.g., changing a will, making funeral arrangements, and taking out life insurance). Dawson coded the data to produce a dichotomous variable: evidence of premeditation versus no evidence or possible evidence of premeditation. The dependent or outcome variable also a dichotomous variable: femicide versus femicide–suicide.

Perpetrators were located in three categories on the basis of their motivation: jealousy, including jealousy associated with separating and being separated; ill health; and motivations that could not be subsumed under jealousy or ill health. Variables known to be associated with femicide–suicide (e.g., age, presence of children, employment, and criminal record) were included in the analysis as control variables.

Multivariate statistical analysis (logistic regression) of the data yielded three major findings. First, a statistically significant association with premeditation was found for only two of 19 variables, "ill health or failing health" and "gun use" (p. 86). Second, femicide–suicides are more likely to be premeditated than femicides. Third, among perpetrators of femicide–suicide the degree of premeditation varies with "type of suicidal" with the sick or in failing health type demonstrating the highest degree of premeditation.

Polk (1994) reported findings indicating that 73 femicide cases could not be differentiated from the 15 femicide–suicide cases he studied on the specific basis of premeditation because premeditation/planning characterized both types of homicides (p. 23 & p. 44). The findings reported by Polk are based on a comparison between femicides and femicide–suicides involving aging male partners experiencing a "depressive crisis" as perpetrators. Polk's perpetrators of femicide–suicide would probably be classified as the "sick/ill health" type of suicidal killer by Dawson. In Polk's study, this type of killer is as likely to demonstrate premeditation as perpetrators of femicide. In Dawson's study, they are far more likely to do so.

Findings on premeditation were revealed by Harper and Voight's use of NVivo to analyze qualitative data on 30 homicide–suicides from the following multiple sources: "… newspaper articles … police incident reports … interviews with police officers with first responders … and interviews with family members, friends, and relatives of victims and perpetrators" (p. 302). Like Polk and Dobash and Dobash, they used "preset analytical categories" or filters, such as age, ethnicity, and victim-offender relationship, to analyze the data. Unlike familicides, which were planned, Harper and Voight (2007) found intimate partner femicide–suicides involving perpetrators and victims whose average ages were 29 years were not premeditated. Instead, these cases were "characterized by extreme conflict and violent outbursts immediately preceding the brutal homicide-suicide event" (p. 305).

In a study conducted by Ellis, Sakinofsky, and Stuckless (2012), the interview schedule administered to 50 incarcerated perpetrators of femicide and femicide/attempted suicide ended with the following open-ended question: *Is there anything else you would like to say?* Their answers were analyzed using computer-assisted qualitative data analysis software NVivo 9.2. Spur-of-the-moment killings of female partners was found to be a main mode identified by NVivo analysis of qualitative data from perpetrators of femicide and femicide-suicide. In Dawson's study, perpetrators of femicide were more likely to perpetrate spur-of-the-moment or nonpremeditated murders involving intimate female partners as victims.

Unlike Dawson, Polk, or Harper and Voight, Adams (2007) collected interview data from perpetrators themselves. Specifically, he interviewed 31 men convicted of murdering female intimate partners. Included among the 21 were four cases of femicide–suicide. He reports that stalking—a fairly reliable precursor of femicide that suggests premeditation—characterizes femicide but not femicide-suicide (pp. 184–194). Stalking is not identified as an indicator of premeditation in Dawson's (2005) study. As a result, the demonstration of premeditation by perpetrators of femicide may be underestimated.

Findings reported by Easteal (1993) reveal that premeditation is strongly associated with the methods used by perpetrators to murder their partners. Three-quarters (75%) of the cases in which firearms were used were premeditated compared with 21.9% of the cases in which knives were used and 11.1% of the cases in which assaults caused deaths. Conversely, 15% of the cases were not premeditated (spontaneous) when firearms were used, 46.9% of the cases were not premeditated when knives were used, and 40.8% of the cases were not premeditated when assaults were used. The base for these percentages is 40 firearms cases, 32 knife cases, and 36 assault cases (p. 41). When we calculated the relative odds of firearms use when premeditation was present and the odds for firearms use when premeditation was absent, we found that firearms were 17.3 times more likely to be used when premeditation was present ($p < 0.0001$). The comparable figure reported by Dawson is "twice as likely" (p. 86).

Easteal's findings support the findings reported by Dawson, but they also raise a question. If the proportion of femicide–suicides in which guns were used (75%) is 1.2 times greater than the corresponding proportion reported by Dawson (62%), why are guns much more likely to be used when premeditation is present in the Australian femicides–suicides studied by Easteal than in the Canadian femicide-suicides investigated by Dawson? One reason may be different methods of statistical analysis (bivariate versus multivariate). Different ways of measuring premeditation is another. Easteal does not reveal how she measured premeditation. Dawson used a modified index of premeditation but, as she classified cases on her own, we have no way of knowing whether Easteal would have produced the same results if she (or another researcher) had classified Dawson's cases. Still, the strong association between gun use and femicide-suicide in the cases reported by Easteal and Dawson suggests homogeneity. We analyzed a larger number of studies to test this hypothesis.

A random effects meta-analysis was conducted on the relative risk of a femicide culminating in a suicide when a firearm is used by the perpetrator (see Table 2.1). Only five studies reported frequencies broken down in this manner. Analysis revealed that the relative risk of perpetrator suicide is 3.79 (95% confidence interval: 1.95–7.4) times higher when the murder is committed with a gun rather than some other method. At the same time, there was evidence of significant heterogeneity ($Q(4) = 37.7878$, $p < 0.0001$) suggesting that further investigation is clearly warranted. An important contribution toward lines of further investigation could have been made by Dawson if she had concentrated on the factors known to be strongly associated with gun use while regressing femicide-suicide on premeditation.

The answer to the question that forms the subheading of this segment is that premeditation is only one of a number of factors known to be associated with gun use, and the independent contribution made by premeditation to femicide-suicide can be validly assessed quantitatively only when the association between premeditation and femicide-suicide is analyzed while controlling on other factors also known to be associated with gun use (Ellis, Sakinofsky, & Stuckless, 2010, pp. 41–42; Kellerman et al., 1993; Koziol-McLain, et al., 2006). If/when this is done, we could then state that, via its effect on gun use, premeditation explains a smaller or larger proportion of the variation in femicide–suicide.

Our confidence is this answer would be increased if it was supported by findings based on the qualitative analysis of interview data from survivors of femicide-attempted suicides. Interview data with survivors may also yield findings suggesting that Dawson's findings do not apply to all femicide–suicides but only to femicide–suicides that are really "extended suicides." They may also suggest that extended suicides constitute a majority of the cases included in Dawson's sample and all other samples that conflate femicide–suicides that are primarily femicides with femicide–suicides that are extended suicides.

Dawson is confident enough in her answer to the premeditation question to suggest that "premeditation measures" (questions) be included in domestic violence risk assessment instruments designed to assess the risk of femicide–suicide and that interventions derived from subscores on premeditation should be implemented (pp. 88–89).

Suicide

Like femicide–suicide, suicide is a contested concept. For example, Durkheim's paradigmatic sociological theory of suicide was grounded in the definition of suicide as "all cases of death resulting directly or indirectly from a positive or negative act of

Table 2.1 Random Effects Meta-Analysis of the Relative Risk of Gun Use in Femicides Followed by Suicides

		N Femicide w/ Suicide	Total N Femicide		
Chan et al., 2010	China	19	85		0.22 [0.13 , 0.31]
Adinkrah, 2008	Ghana	13	60		0.22 [0.11 , 0.32]
Chimbos, 1998	Greece	10	49		0.20 [0.09 , 0.32]
Sela-Shayovitz, 2010	Isreal	36	174		0.21 [0.15 , 0.27]
Mathews et al., 2008	South Africa	69	360		0.19 [0.15 , 0.23]
Cooper & Eaves, 1996	Canada	14	39		0.36 [0.21 , 0.51]
Dawson, 2005	Canada	194	703		0.28 [0.24 , 0.31]
Eke et al., 2011	Canada	7	30		0.23 [0.08 , 0.38]
Farden, 1996	Canada	5	40		0.12 [0.02 , 0.23]
Banks et al., 2008	United States	46	124		0.37 [0.29 , 0.46]
Barber et al., 2008	United States	60	151		0.40 [0.32 , 0.48]
Block & Christakos, 1995	United States	191	1271		0.15 [0.13 , 0.17]
Bossarte et al., 2006	United States	134	438		0.31 [0.26 , 0.35]
Brewer, 1999	United States	40	191		0.21 [0.15 , 0.27]
Frye et al., 2005	United States	122	447		0.27 [0.23 , 0.31]
Koziol-McLain et al., 2006	United States	67	219		0.31 [0.24 , 0.37]
Lund & Smorodinsky, 2001	United States	74	155		0.48 [0.40 , 0.56]
Moracco et al., 1998	United States	76	293		0.26 [0.21 , 0.31]
Richards et al., 2011	United States	80.7	299		0.27 [0.22 , 0.32]
Taylor et al., 2009	United States	41	150		0.27 [0.20 , 0.34]
RE model					0.27 [0.23 , 0.30]

Proportion

the victim himself, which he knows will produce this result" (1897, p. 200). Baechler (1980) rejects this definition on the grounds that it does not include genuine attempted suicides and nonrational or unreflective suicide cases in which the victim does not fully know that his behavior will result in his/her death (p. 72). Coroners/medical examiners—not pathologists who use different criteria of proof of suicide as the cause of death—are the main if not exclusive source of medical evidence indicating that the manner of death—how he/she died—was suicide. Why he/she died may be revealed by reading individual biographies (Taylor, 1982, pp. 89–90). Based on his review of the evidence, including evidence from his study of Persons Under Trains (Taylor, 1982) concluded that "there may sources of systematic biases in the (official) statistics on suicide—an aggregate of individual suicide cases—which could well provide alternative explanations of the positive correlations found by students of suicide rates" (p. 93). Based on their analysis of individual cases, Atkinson (1971) and Douglas (1967) reject official suicide statistics on the ground of their invalidity.

Notwithstanding the positions adopted by those who are skeptical about or reject official statistics grounded in information on individual cases collected, analyzed, and actually used by coroners, the Centers for Disease Control and Prevention (2012) define suicide as *death caused by self-directed injurious behavior with any intent to die as a result of the behavior*. Not infrequently, suicidal ideation is a precursor of suicide. Suicidal ideation is defined as *thinking about, considering, or planning for suicide* (Centers for Disease Control and Prevention, 2012).

This definition of suicide is a revision of an earlier definition undertaken as part of the Centers for Disease Control and Prevention's effort to create "uniform definitions and recommended data elements" as guidelines for researchers collecting self-directed violence surveillance data. Perhaps an expansion of their efforts to include other directed violence surveillance data will follow because "consistent (other-directed violence) data (will also) allow researchers to better gauge the scope of the problem, identify high risk groups, monitor the effects of prevention programs and policies" (p. 10) and "provide insights about why (femicide and femicide–suicides occurred)" (National Violent Death Reporting System, 2012, p. 1).

One step toward answering definitional, theoretical, and melioristic questions was taken by researchers who were assigned the task of differentiating among types of "domestic violence."

TYPES OF DOMESTIC VIOLENCE

In 2006, one of the authors of this book was invited to participate in the Wingspread Conference on Domestic Violence held in Racine, Wisconsin. A subgroup of participants was asked to meet in order to discuss differentiating among types of violence that hitherto had been defined as gender-neutral "domestic violence" or gendered (male partner) battering. Subsequently, an article on this topic was published by Kelly and Johnson (2008). Four different types of domestic violence were identified. They are coercive controlling violence (CCV), violent resistance (VR), situational couple violence (SCV), and separation-instigated violence (SIV).

CCV refers to "a pattern of emotionally abusive intimidation, coercion, and control coupled with physical violence against partners" (p. 478). This is a gender-neutral definition. However, the example they cite indicates that the violence referred to in the definition refers to a male pattern of violence and abuse against female partners. Specifically, coercive controlling tactics are broadly defined to include all the violent and nonviolent tactics identified in the gendered Pence and Paymar Power Wheel (1993). In cases in which patterns of male or female power and control are thoroughly effective, the actual use of physical violence may be relatively low. Finally, the motive of control is indicated by the name of this type of violence.

VR is defined as "an immediate (violent) reaction to an assault that is intended primarily to protect oneself or others from injury" (p. 484). This definition "meets the common sense definition of self-defense." That is to say it "reflects realities in the lives of abused female partners." The authors also state that "the resort to self-protective violence may be almost automatic and surfaces almost as soon as the coercive controlling violent partner begins using physical violence himself" (p. 484). This statement suggests that conflict is the usual context for VR.

Unlike the legal definition of self-defense that requires the apprehension of immediate harm and an immediate and proportional response to it, VR also includes "varieties of violent resistance that have little to do with the legal meanings of self defense" (p. 484). When self-defense is more broadly or socially defined—as it is by researchers and women's advocates—VR should be classified as self-defense. An exemplary case of socially defined self-defense is provided by the case of Nicole Ryan, a 39-year-old school teacher who weighs 98 pounds. Here is what she reported her hard drinking, 6 ft., 3 in., career soldier husband did to her over a period of time:

- killed the family dog;
- threatened to kill her;
- held a gun to her head on several occasions;
- demanded sex regularly;
- when she told him she was thinking of leaving him, he threatened to "destroy" her and their daughter if she actually carried out her plan to divorce him;
- asked the police to intervene on many occasions but they were unwilling to intervene in domestic disputes.

Ryan responded by searching for an individual who, for a fee, would kill the abusive husband who terrified her even after she separated from him. The male "contract killer" she eventually hired turned out to be an undercover Royal Canadian Mounted Police Officer. He arrested her for "counseling murder," an offense under the Canadian Criminal Code. She was acquitted. The Nova Scotia Court of Appeal upheld the lower court's decision. The Supreme Court of Canada did not affirm the decision of the lower court, stating that it was unclear as to whether she could claim self-defense and she could not claim she was under "duress" because she had committed a crime. Still, eight of the nine judges ordered her release without the prospect of facing a retrial (MacCharles, 2013; Makin, 2013). In sum, self-defense—socially rather than legally defined—is the motive for VR and when VR occurs it is usually used as a conflict resolution tactic.

SCV is gender-neutral and grounded in "arguments between partners that escalate on occasion into physical violence" (p. 485). As recurring conflict is (1) endemic in intimate partner relationships and (2) is more frequently associated with physical violence and abuse than any other type of intimate partner violence (Ellis & Stuckless, 1996; Stets & Straus, 1990), it is difficult to understand why this type of violence is defined as "situational couple violence" rather than "conflict instigated violence." Of greater concern to us is the unqualified statement that compared with CCV, SCV is "… more likely to stop after separation." The National Violence Against Women Survey and other findings they cite in support of this assertion do not apply to lethal domestic violence. Moreover, the identification of CCV and SCV as types of violence prevalent in different kinds of victim samples is challenged by findings indicating both types are present in the same (shelter) sample and are positively associated with each other (Ellis et al., 2012). Finally, situational or "common couple violence" must refer to nonlethal violence because intimate partner homicides and femicides are most uncommon.

SIV is instigated by the unilateral decision to separate. The perpetrator is almost invariably the person who is being left, or less charitably, dumped. As it was defined by Mahoney (1991), SIV referred to as separation-instigated assaults by male partners with view to preventing female partners from leaving or persuading them to return. The control element is absent in the Kelly and Johnson description of SIV and replaced by outbursts you would expect from dumped male partners who "just go nuts" (p. 487). As defined by Kelly and Johnson (p. 487), SIV comes close to resembling Simmel's "nonrealistic conflicts" where expressing anger or distress is the motive for engaging in the violent acts instigated by events such as the totally disorienting and unanticipated experience of actually being dumped (Simmel, 1955, pp. 32–34). Lethal intimate partner violence was not referred to in the definition of SIV.

COMMENT

The comments that follow are presented in the form of answers to two recurring questions about lethal intimate partner violence. The first answer deals with definitions of femicide–suicide and the second with whether sublethal and lethal violence should be located at different points of the same continuum on conceived of as distinct categories.

Femicide–Suicide: Femicide or Extended Suicide?

The definition of femicide–suicide as "extended suicide" is ignored by compilers of official crime statistics who define femicide–suicide as homicide and contested by researchers who define femicide–suicide as femicide. Researchers in this group define femicide–suicides as femicides that are primarily motivated by the loss-of-control over female partners who or are believed to be guilty of infidelity and/or deserting them. In these accounts, suicide is either ignored or treated as a secondary or disassociated outcome that can be explained by ad hoc factors, such as fear of consequences, guilt, remorse, and/or revenge (Allen, 1983; Bancroft, 2002; Black, 2004; Campbell, 1992; Caputi & Russell, 1992; Cooper & Eaves,1996; Mahoney, 1991; Morton, Runyan, Moracco, & Butts, 1998; Serran & Firestone, 2004; Wilson & Daly, 1992).

Other researchers conceive of femicide–suicides as "extended suicides," which are perpetrated mainly by a relatively few male partners who are often depressed, extremely dependent emotionally on their intimate female partners, who perceive desertion as abandonment, and who have thought about, planned, or attempted suicide (Adler, 2001; Banks et al., 2008; Brodsky, Malone, Ellis, & Mann, 1997; Cavan, 1928; Dutton & Kerry, 1999; Koziol-McLain et al., 2006; Liem & Roberts, 2009; Lund & Smorodinsky, 2001; Marzuk et al., 1992; Milroy, 1998, Palermo, 1994; Palmer & Humphrey, 1980; West, 1966).

Academic interest is one reason why competing definitions of femicide–suicide ought to be investigated. Two socially significant reasons for investigating them are worth noting. First, the effectiveness of interventions aimed at prevention will vary with the reliability, validity, and utility of definitions of femicide–suicide. If femicide–suicide is found to be an extended suicide, then violence risk prevention/assessment instruments aimed at preventing suicide should also prevent femicide. Second, femicide-suicide accounts for a significant proportion of femicides—55% in Arizona, 51% in Houston, 40% in Florida, 46% in British Columbia—(Ellis et al., 2012; Koziol-Mclain et al., 2006) and a disproportionately high number of cases in which the perpetrator's own children are killed. Stack (1997) found that killing "own children" was associated with a 10-fold increase in the odds of suicide following femicide.

Lethal and Nonlethal Intimate Partner Violence: Categories or Continuum?

The application of natural selection thinking led Daly and Wilson (1988) to conclude that murder-suicide is "spiteful" in the sense that "the actor plans and carries out a course of action that is devastating to his own interests, just for the sake of inflicting damage on others" (p. 219). Such a plan and course of intentional action "must somehow be a byproduct of his more adaptive … *proprietary jealousy* … concerns." Although the perpetrator or femicide-suicide has "lapsed into futile spite he is acting out his vestigial agenda of dominance to no useful end." By killing his partner, the perpetrator has "called the shots and exerted his authority."

For Daly and Wilson, femicide–suicide clearly "illustrates why adaptation must be sought at a more psychological level than that of direct behavioral optimization and fitness maximization" (p. 215). The man who perpetrates femicide–suicide is engaging in behavior that is maladaptive—that is to say, it "oversteps the bounds of utility" (reproductive failure) but it is adaptive psychologically because it is motivated by the male partner's proprietary interests. Nonlethal violence aimed at settling conflicts and controlling infidelity and desertion by wives differs from lethal male partner violence aimed at the same ends only by its far greater frequency (Wilson & Daly, 1992, p. 93).

In this evolutionary psychological account, lethal violence is located at one end of the severity continuum and nonlethal violence at different points on the same continuum depending upon the severity of the injuries inflicted. Following his review of an alternative evolutionary explanation for homicide (homicide ideation) presented by Buss (2005), Durrant (2009) concluded that actual or perceived infidelity and desertion "tend to evoke high levels of emotional arousal and motivate behaviors to punish or control, which may, very occasionally, include homicide" (p. 379). The evidence from which this conclusion was derived supports the Daly and Wilson/Wilson and Daly continuum definition over the Buss separate categories definition.

Findings reported by a number of social science researchers who identify male intimate partner violence as a risk factor for femicide implicitly support a continuum definition. Most of them are referred to in reviews by Aldridge and Browne (2003), Eliason (2009), Ellis et al. (2012), Garcia, Soria, and Hurwitz (2007), and Walker et al. (2004). Grounded theorists, such as Ogle and Jacobs (2002), conceive of battering by male partners to be a "slow homicidal process" that frequently ends in femicide "at the climax of a battering incident, when the female partner attempts to end the relationship" or "when the victim attempts to utilize other social resources to end the battering" (p. 77).

On the other hand, most if not all theorists and researchers (e.g., Browne, 1987; Easteal, 1993; Ogle & Jacobs, 2002) who define intimate partner homicide as self-defense implicitly support a separate categories definition because sublethal violence by women against male intimate partners is rarely if ever identified as a risk factor for intimate partner homicide.

A separate category definition is explicitly supported by Mahoney's (1991) definition of "separation assaults"—male partner assaults and femicides that are not preceded by male partner violence. This definition is also supported by findings on perpetrators of femicide reported by Dobash, Dobash, Cavanagh, and Medina-Ariza (2007), Dutton (2006, p. 298), and Goussinsky and Yassour-Borochowitz (2012), and on perpetrators of femicide–suicide by Showalter, Bonnie, and Roddy (1980, p. 125).

Dobash et al. (2007) compared 122 men convicted of using nonlethal violence against their female partners with 106 men convicted of murdering their female partners (femicides). Multiple sources of individuals, situational, and circumstantial (case file) data on the men were analyzed with identifying risk factors in mind. They reported findings indicating that 59% of the men who perpetrated femicide had and 41% had not previously used violence against the partners they murdered. The comparable had/had not figures for men who previously used sublethal violence against their partners was 100% and 0%, respectively (p. 342).

This finding "do not support the notion of a simple progression from lethal to non-lethal violence" (p. 329).

Goussinsky and Yassour-Borochowitz (2012) found that premeditation differentiated nonlethal male partner violence from femicide. Dutton reported findings indicating that "spousal homicide may not be necessarily be predicted by ... nonlethal violence" and Showwalter, Bonnie, and Roddy found that 11 of the 13 perpetrators they interviewed "lacked recorded histories of assaultive ... behavior."

Finally, Gelles (1991) is included among those providing a separate category definition because "discontinuities in the data on (child) violence, abuse, and homicide" led him to conclude that these were different kinds of behavior. Homicide in particular was a "distinct form of behavior requiring a distinct explanation" (p. 69).

The decision to locate lethal and nonlethal intimate partner violence on a continuum or in separate categories is an important one because of its implications for theory, research, and prevention. First, description of the circumstances surrounding nonlethal and lethal intimate partner violence makes an important contribution toward specifying special design conditions for these two forms of intimate partner violence generally as well as the violence that follows separation.

Second, the separate category definition requires at least two theories, one for each category, whereas the continuum definition requires only one, albeit one that accounts for the fact that very few female partners who are battered kill their batterers in self-defense, and very few men who are deserted by their female partners kill them in a fit of jealous rage or for some other reason.

Third, risk factor researchers using separate categories and continuum definitions should avoid including risk factors in risk assessment/prevention instruments that are inconsistent with their definition (and therefore theory) of intimate partner violence. For example, "recent increases in the frequency and severity of violence" or "history of intimate partner violence" would not be included as risk factors in risk assessment instruments created by researchers locating nonlethal and lethal male partner violence in separate categories. Conversely, special design conditions for separation associated femicide, such as those described by Duntley and Buss (2008) (absence of agnatic kin or effective third party guardians, child bearing age of female partners, unwilling separation), would not be included in risk assessment instruments created by researchers using separate category definitions that inform their theories.

Finally, the nature and timing of interventions aimed at preventing lethal intimate partner violence also vary with continuum and separate category definitions of this phenomenon. Early intervention aimed at preventing nonlethal violence is clearly called for by those using the former definition. Changing situational and other design conditions eliciting lethal violence by couples most likely to encounter all or most of them would be called for by researchers using separate category definitions.

DISCUSSION QUESTIONS

1. Formulate a definition of femicide and then defend it on the grounds of its validity and utility.
2. Femicide–suicides are extended suicides. Do you agree or disagree? Give reasons for your answer.
3. Describe and critically evaluate the Kelly and Johnson (Wingspread) definitions of types of intimate partner violence.
4. Describe and critically evaluate the definition and measurement of the marital status category of "separated" in official U.S. (FBI/Bureau of Justice) homicide statistics and the U.S. census.

CHAPTER 3

Separation and Lethal Intimate Partner Violence

LEARNING OBJECTIVES

Readers of this chapter who achieve the learning objectives set for it will be able to:

- Differentiate between sociological empirical generalizations and theories designed to explain them
- Demonstrate awareness of the problems associated with specifying separation as a cause of lethal intimate male partner violence
- Assess the significance of the recency of lethal domestic violence following separation for an explanation of the empirical generalization that forms the title of this chapter
- Answer the question, "How do we know that separation is strongly associated with lethal intimate partner violence?"

SOCIOLOGICAL EMPIRICAL GENERALIZATIONS

Merton (1957) defines a sociological (empirical) generalization as "an isolated proposition summarizing observed uniformities of relationships between two or more variables" (p. 95). If the isolated proposition "lethal intimate partner violence is positively and strongly associated with separation" is supported by findings cited in this chapter, then this proposition will have achieved the status of a sociological empirical generalization. The strength of a relationship or association between these two variables (separation/lethal intimate partner violence) can be expressed statistically (e.g., Chi square or a correlation coefficient), but the dynamic conduct (action, reactions, interactions) that produce the statistics is usually described qualitatively. The case study briefly described in the next paragraph is the reality we keep in mind when constructing tables with numbers.

In 1994, Randall Iles, age 35, started living in a common–law relationship with Arlene May, age 34. Randall brought to this relationship a history of three previous dissolved marriages, four children from them, and criminal convictions for a variety of crimes that included threatening with a weapon, stalking, breach of probation, harassing phone calls, and custody disputes in family court. Arlene became pregnant early in 1996, and Randall assaulted her on more than one occasion during her pregnancy. She delivered a stillborn infant in the autumn of 1995. Shortly afterward, on November 14, 1995, Randall assaulted Arlene again, and Arlene left him to seek safety in a women's shelter. Following advice she received from shelter staff, Arlene reported the assault to the police. Randall appeared in criminal court on February 29, 1996. He was ordered to leave the jurisdiction of the court. There was a warrant for his arrest on another matter in an adjacent county. The court ordered Randall not to communicate with Arlene, and he breached the order by doing so. On March 6, 1996, another warrant was issued for his arrest. On March 7, Randall's lawyer informed him about the warrant for his arrest. At this point, he decided to commit suicide after killing Arlene. To this end, he bought a gun, rented a van, drove to Arlene's home, and waited for her to return home. When she arrived, he forced her to enter her home, ordered her three children to go to a local corner store, and call the police. When they left, he shot Arlene to death and then used the gun to kill himself (Synopsis of the May-Iles Inquest. Deputy Chief Coroner Dr. Bonita Porter, Toronto, July, 1998).

As we indicated earlier, an empirical generalization is not an explanation, but requires explanation. The starting point for our attempt to describe and evaluate explanations of the empirical generalization is the investigation of the relative frequency of homicide, femicide, femicide–suicide, and suicide. The main but not exclusive source of information on the strength of the association between separation and each of these four types of lethal violence is the latest National Violent Death Reporting System (NVDRS) *Surveillance Summaries* (Logan et al., 2008). NVDRS collects data on homicides, homicide–suicides, and suicides from police investigation and medical examiner/coroner reports. Researchers using NVDRS data are able to link any given violent death with a wider variety of characteristics than can researchers using other sources of official data, such as the FBI's Uniform Crime Reports and Supplementary Homicide Statistics, or Bureau of Justice Statistics. Moreover, NDVR researchers can corroborate the accuracy of information included in police investigation reports by examining more detailed information on the same incident included in death reports completed by coroners or medical examiners.

In addition to gender, marital status, and other background factors, NDVRS *Surveillance Summaries* also include information about the circumstances preceding violent deaths. Precipitating circumstances are defined as "events that preceded and therefore might have contributed to the infliction of the fatal injury" (2009, p. 7). Events on which they collected information include alcohol ingested at the time of death, depression, mental health problems, and recent, stressful life experiences. The starting point of our investigation of background factors and precipitating events is a description of the relative frequency of the deaths with which they are associated.

Relative Frequencies

The relative frequencies of different types of violent death are presented in Table 3.1.

Findings presented in Table 3.1 indicate that deaths by suicide are reported more frequently than deaths by homicide, and far more frequently than deaths by homicide–suicide. Specifically, the ratio of suicides to homicides and homicide–suicides is 2.5:1 and 43:1, respectively. The ratio of homicides to homicide–suicides is 18:1.

Table 3.1 Relative Frequency of Violent Deaths Reported by 16 U.S. States*

Type of Violent Death	Violent Deaths§		Rate per 100,000¶
	#	%	
Homicides	4057	28.5	5.0
Homicide–suicides	229	1.6	0.9
Suicides	9949	69.9	12.2
Total	14,235	100.0	

*NDVRS *Surveillance Summaries*, 2009.
§Deaths for which intent was determined.
¶U.S. population aged 18 and older.

SEX/GENDER AND LETHAL DOMESTIC VIOLENCE

NDVRS *Surveillance Summaries* include information on linkages between sex–gender and four types of violent death. This information is presented in Table 3.2. Family femicides are not included in this table because they are not included as a type of violent death in any of the *Surveillance Summaries* we reviewed.

Findings presented in Table 3.2 indicate that the strength of the association between sex–gender and violent deaths varies with gender and the relationship between the parties. Thus, the ratio of intimate partner femicides to intimate partner homicides is 5:1 and the ratio of female to male homicide deaths is 3:1. Similarly, the ratio of male to female suicide deaths is 4:1 and the ratio of femicide–suicides to homicide–suicides increases to 16:1. Gender differences reported in this table are supported by findings reported by most researchers, who have investigated the link between gender and lethal domestic violence. Many references to research demonstrating the strength of this link are included in reviews published by Aldridge and Browne (2003), Brownridge (2006), Garcia, Soria, and Hurwitz (2007), and in books published by Easteal (1993), Dobash and Dobash (1979), Johnson and Dawson (2011), and Radford and Russell (1992). A few frequently cited findings for each type of lethal domestic violence follow: women in the United States are more at risk to be killed by a male partner than by all categories of persons outside the partnership, combined (Browne & Williams, 1993, p. 81); male partners are at greater risk of being killed by their current married female intimate-partners (one man per million couples), whereas female partners face a greater risk of being killed by their ex-intimate partners (39 per million couples) (Hotton, 2001, p. 1); in 1998, women were nearly three out of four victims of the 1,830 murders attributable to intimate partners (Rennison & Welchans, 2000); an examination of homicide–suicide episodes occurring in Yorkshire and Humberside between 1975 and 1992 showed that 95% of the assailants were male (Milroy, 1998, p. 62); all 74 perpetrators of homicides followed by suicides that occurred in Los Angeles in 1996 were male (Lund and Smorodinsky, 2001, p. 453); spousal homicide–suicides are a

*Table 3.2 Gender and Violent Deaths of Intimate Partners Compared with Males and Females Generally**

Type of Violent Death	Violent Deaths		Rate per 100,000
	#	%	
Homicides, male	3076	21.0	7.7'
Homicides, female	981	6.7	2.4
Intimate partner homicides	84	0.6	0.2
Intimate partner femicides	410	2.8	1.1
Femicide–suicides	187	1.3	0.4
Homicide–suicides	12	0.1	0.0¹
Suicides, male	7827	53.2	5.1
Suicides, female	2122	14.4	19.5
Total	14,699	100.1	

*NDVRS Surveillance Summaries, 2009.
§ Deaths for which intent was determined.
¶ U.S. population aged 18 and older.
¹rates are not reported for cases involving less than 20 cases/incidents.

male-driven phenomenon, as only 3% of all spousal homicide victims ($n = 857$) were male killed by a female spouse (Aston & Bunge, 2005, p. 61); men were almost five times (4.8) more likely to commit suicide as women (RR = 4.45 95% CI = 3.62,5.47) (Kposowa, 2000, p. 256) and Chi square 1972.9, $p < 0.0001$ (Wyder, Ward, & De Leo, 2009, p. 210).

The findings reported here indicate that the violent deaths identified in Table 3.1 vary so strongly with gender as to constitute a robust empirical generalization that demands an explanation at both individual and aggregate levels of analysis (Browne & Williams, 1993, p. 91).

Findings reported in almost every study of violent deaths involving majority group intimate partners as perpetrators and victims support the gender-asymmetric pattern favoring males as killers of female intimate partners described here (Aldridge & Browne, 2003; Block, 2000; Brownridge, 2006; Garcia, Soria, & Hurwitz, 2007; Walker, Logan, Jordan, & Campbell, 2004). Findings reported in studies of violent deaths involving members of minority groups as perpetrators and victims reveal different patterns. A review of violent deaths involving First Nations peoples in Canada (1988–1990) revealed the presence of a spousal sex ratio of killings (SSROK) favoring females as killers of male intimate partners (SSROK = 32 female killers/21 male killers). The SSROK for Canada (1981–1989) was 238 male killers/69 female killers (Ellis & DeKeseredy, 1996: Tables 3–8, p. 86). Block (2000) reported findings for Chicago indicating that between the years 1965 and 1993, "the risk of being killed by an intimate partner was roughly equal for men and women" (p. 502). When race/ethnicity was taken into account, the risk of being killed by an intimate partner was higher for male than for female partners. Specifically, the victimization rate for female and male African-American intimate partners was 3.9 and 5.8, respectively (pp. 502–503).

MARITAL SEPARATION

We start this segment with the observation that marital separation is a neglected marital status, and when it is not neglected, its frequency is seriously underestimated. In the U.S. Census, respondents are given the option of checking Separated only if they are legally married but not living with their spouse. In the 2000 Census, 2.2% of 81,665,080 persons aged 15 and older checked Separated. Separation is not included as a distinct Census marital status category for millions of individuals who are involved in common law, cohabiting, girlfriend/boyfriend, or lover-pair relationships, and separation is also not identified as a marital status category for these individuals in death in certificates completed by coroners/medical examiners, in official police statistics, and frequently, in police narratives that accompany incident reports.

Serious underestimation occurs when separated individuals who were not legally married are classified as Never Married, and Married persons who divorced, subsequently became involved in a cohabiting relationship, and then separated are classified as Married. Similarly, widowed persons who become involved in a cohabiting relationship and separate are classified as Widowed. Individuals who will not divorce for religious reasons but will separate are classified as Married. As a result, we are left with the following paradox: The single most frequent cause of the dissolution of intimate partner relationships in the United States that has been identified as a risk factor for lethal domestic violence by almost researchers investigating lethal domestic violence (Ellis, Sakinofsky, & Stuckless, 2012) cannot included in the "high-quality ... comprehensive surveillance data ... on the magnitude and characteristics on violent death at the national, state and local levels" (2012, p. 2) collected by NDVRS.

In the U.S. Census (2010), the marital status of the population age 15 years and older is distributed across the marital status categories of Never married (30.4%), Married (58.0%), Divorced (9.0%), and Widowed (2.7%). In the NVDRS *Surveillance Summaries* (2012), violent deaths are linked with only four of the five marital status categories included in the 2010 Census. In this Census, the marital status of the population age 15 years and older is distributed across four marital status categories as follows: Never married (30.4%), Married (58.0%), Divorced (9.0%), and Widowed (2.7%). Table 3.3 describes the distribution of types of violent deaths across these marital status categories.

One way of understanding the findings presented in this table is to compare the distribution of each type of violent death across marital status categories with the distribution of the U.S. population across the same marital status categories. When this was, done two major findings emerge. First, divorced persons are overrepresented among victims of all four types of fatal violence, with the degree of overrepresentation varying from a low of 5% among homicide victims and a high of 20% among victims of suicide. Second, married persons are underrepresented among victims of homicide and femicide (17%) and suicide (20%).

Table 3.3 Marital Status and Lethal Domestic Violence

Type of Violence	Violent Deaths #	Marital Status*		
		Married %	Never Married %	Divorced %
Homicides	3346	54.3	22.8	14.4
Intimate partner homicides/femicides	494	41.4	30.3	19.7
Homicide–suicides	198	46.3	26.6	17.7
Suicides	9949	38.3	23.7	29.0

*N = 229,000 (1000).

The findings presented in Table 3.3 seriously underestimate the number of separated persons among victims of lethal domestic violence, not only for the reasons described earlier, but also because "the relation of the suspects to the victims was not known" in approximately 46% of the homicides, femicides, and femicide–suicides. (p. 10). Additionally, Wilson and Daly (1993) note that in the absence of the category "separated/de facto unions" in the forms that investigating police officers are required to complete, victims may be classified as "friends or acquaintances" (p. 6). When separation is included as a distinct marital status category in official homicide statistics (separated/married and separated/common law (e.g., Homicide Surveys, Center for Justice Statistics, Statistics Canada)) and in investigating police officer narratives, its association with femicide and femicide–suicide has been found to be strong (Aston & Bunge, 2005; Hotton, 2001; Johnson & Dawson, 2011).

SEPARATION AND HOMICIDE–FEMICIDE

One of the most frequently cited cross-national studies of the link between spousal homicide and separation was conducted by Wilson and Daly (1993). This study is important for two reasons: First, it is a cross-national study comparing three countries with "different census practices and overall homicide rates" (p. 5). Second, within each country they make a number of comparisons (e.g., co-residing vs separate residence victims involved in legally registered and de facto unions) that make a significant contribution to the corpus of knowledge on linkages between separation and spousal homicide.

Three major findings were reported by Wilson and Daly. First, among legally registered married couples separation greatly increases the risk of spousal homicides with the risk being significantly greater for wives than for husbands. Relevant findings are presented in Table 3.4.

Findings presented in this table indicate that the per–separated men rate for femicides is three, six, and seven times greater than the co-resident rate in Chicago, New South Wales, and Canada, respectively. The separated-men rate for homicides is significantly lower than the comparable rate for femicides in all three countries,

Table 3.4 Femicides and Homicides for Co-residence and Separate Residence Spouses in Legally Registered Marriages*

Location	Femicides		Homicides	
	Co-resident Rate	Per Separated Men[§] Rate	Co-resident Rate	Per Separated Men Rate
Chicago	30	100	23	45
New South Wales	7	43	2	2
Canada	7	47	1	4

*Source: Figure 1 in Daly, Singh, and Wilson (1993).
[§]Rates per million separated women are lower than the rates per million men, but they also reveal significant differences in the elevation of risk for female spouses following separation.

and the co-resident/separated men homicide rate differential is not as great as the co-resident/separated men femicide rate in any of the three countries.

In interpreting this finding, we noted that *estranged* husbands and wives still living together were not being compared with *estranged* husbands and wives living apart. Instead (presumably happy) husbands and wives living together were being compared with (presumably unhappy) estranged husbands and wives living in separate residences. It is also relevant to note that factors or variables mediating the effect of estrangement on femicide were not identified. This gap is closed in Chapter 5, where we identify "intensity of conflict" as a mediating factor.

In a later study of 1,886 spousal homicides recorded in Canada (Homicide Survey) between 1974 and 1992, Wilson and Daly (1994) compared spousal homicide and femicide rates between 727 co-residing and 226 separated couples. They found a femicide rate (husbands killing wives) of 7.2 for co-residing and 45.2 for separated couples, and a homicide rate (wives killing husbands) of 1.9 for co-residing and 5.7 for separated couples. These findings indicated that separation entailed a 6-fold increase in femicides and a 3-fold increase in homicides (p. 8).

Findings indicating the presence of a strong association between separation and femicide have been reported by a legion of other researchers. The Canadian Homicide Survey, 1991–1999, included data on rates of homicide and femicide for intimate partners who were married, lived common law, and were separated. The femicide rates (per 100,000) for women in these three marital status groups were 4.5 (married), 26.4 (common law), and 38.7 (separated). These findings indicate that separation entails a 9-fold increase in the risk of femicide for married women who separate. The homicide rates for men in these three marital status categories are 1.1 (married), 11.5 (common law), and 2.2 (separated). Separation entails a 2-fold risk of homicide for married men who separate.

Spousal homicide rates for men and women living common law who separated from their partners were not calculated by Hotton (2001) because "there were no reliable estimates for separated common law partners from the Canadian census" (p. 7).

Hotton did calculate the rates of femicide and homicide per million Canadian couples who were victims of spousal femicide and homicide between 1991 and 1999. She reported findings indicating that the rate for separated women who were killed by their ex-partners was 39 per million couples. The comparable figure for men killed by their female ex-partners was two men per million couples (pp. 6–7).

Adding two years to the same coroner/police investigator generated data set used by Crawford and Gartner (1992) and Gartner, Dawson, and Crawford (1999) investigated the killings of 1,206 women in Ontario who were age 15 and older. When they compared the percentage of women identified by Census Canada interviews as married or separated with the percentage of married and separated femicide victims, this is what they found: separated women were significantly overrepresented among femicide victims. Specifically, women separated from the men they were married to (registered marriages only) represent 3% of the population of women aged 15 in Ontario and 16% of the victims of intimate femicide. In interpreting this finding we noted—as the authors did—that "separated" is defined differently by Census Canada and Gartner et al. The former limits its definition of "separated" to women who are separated from their legally registered marriage partners. Gartner and Dawson define "separated" more broadly to include killers who were "current partners or former legal spouses, common law partners or boyfriends of their victims" (p. 10). As a result, the proportion of intimate femicide victims who were separated in their sample is greater.

Similar findings were reported by a number of researchers including Block (2000), Block and Christakos (1993), Campbell and 17 associates (2003), Dobash, Dobash, Cavanagh, and Medina-Ariza (2007), Garcia, Soria, and Hurwitz (2007), Kurz (1996), Dutton and Kerry (1999), Sev'er (1997), Hall Smith, Moracco, and Butts (1998), Kposowa, Singh, and Breault (1994), McFarlane, Campbell, and Watson (2002), Wallace (1986), and Websdale (1999).

RECENCY OF SPOUSAL FEMICIDE AND HOMICIDE FOLLOWING SEPARATION

The second major finding reported by Wilson and Daly (1993) indicated that the risk of spousal homicide varied with recency of separation. Findings on recency of separation were available for only 52 cases—New South Wales ($n = 32$) and Chicago ($n = 20$). Twenty-five of the wives and six of 11 husbands were killed within two months of separating. Almost 60% (31 of 52) of the spousal homicide victims were killed within two months of separating. Recency of separation data for Canada may not have been available to Daly and Wilson because they did not use police narrative data in Homicide Surveys, which may have contained this information.

The Wilson and Daly findings on the recency of separation have been supported by a number of researchers using a variety of data sources, covering different periods, and all three types of lethal domestic violence. Hotton (2001) investigated a total of 1,056 homicides recorded in annual Canadian Homicide Surveys between 1991 and 2000. Police narratives were available for a subsample of 73 homicides. Analysis of these cases revealed that 49% (n = 36) occurred within two months following separation and 74% (n = 54) occurred between two and six months after separation.

Canada has three Domestic Violence Death Review Committees (DVDRCs). One of them is located in Toronto, Ontario. The Toronto/Ontario DVDRC was established in 2003. The DVDRC mandate is to "assist the Chief Coroner of Ontario investigate and review deaths involving domestic violence … and reduce domestic violence in general." One of its eight specific objectives is to "identify … risk factors … from the cases reviewed and make recommendations for effective intervention and prevention strategies." Sources of information on the cases reviewed are coroner death reports and reports of police investigators. Toronto/Ontario DVDRC Annual Reports (2003–2008) consistently identify "actual or pending separation" as the highest-ranked risk factor, a precursor in 78% of the 111 cases reviewed by DVDRC members. Recency of separation is identified as the period of highest risk in the 2008 Annual report. On page 69 of this report, we discover that 45% (18) of 40 homicides occurred within three months after separation and 68% (27) occurred between three and six months after separation. Stout (1993) reported findings indicating that over half (52%) of the men who killed their female partners had been separated from them for less than one month.

SEPARATION, DIVORCE, AND SPOUSAL HOMICIDE/SUICIDE

The third major finding reported by Wilson and Daly (1993) indicated that the association between separation and spousal homicide/femicide is far stronger than the association between divorce and spousal homicide/femicide. This conclusion is based on the following specific finding: Of the total number of registered marriages/estranged spousal homicide victims in all three countries (n = 517) only 15% (n = 69) were divorced (p. 7).

Crawford and Gartner (1992) investigated 551 intimate femicides that occurred in Ontario between 1974 and 1992. During this period, 551 female partners and 62 children were killed by male partners and 39% (210) of the male partner perpetrators committed suicide or attempted to do so (7%). Divorce was found to be unrelated to femicide or femicide–homicide. Specifically, divorced women were not found to be involved as victims in a single femicide or femicide–suicide (Table 3.4, pp. 42–43). Impending estrangement (separation) was found to be the precursor for 455 of the intimate femicides where a motive could be established (n = 73) (p. 44).

Kowalski (2005) analyzed 788 spousal homicides recorded in Canada between 1995 and 2004. Spousal homicides were defined as homicides that "involve persons in legal marriages, those who are separated or divorced from such unions and those in common law relationships" (p. 52). Compared with separated persons who account for 4% of the Canadian population age 15 and older and account for 235 of spousal homicide victims, divorced persons represent 8% of the same population and account for only 2% of spousal homicide victims (p. 53). Easteal (1993) reported findings indicating that 53% of the 42 intimate partner homicides she investigated occurred between one and three months after separating and 63% occurred within six months of separating (p. 62).

Liem, Postulart, and Nieuwbeerta (2009) investigated 103 homicide–suicides that were reported to have occurred in the Netherlands between 1992 and 1996. They found that "almost all" the 52 intimate partners who were involved as victims and perpetrators were estranged but not necessarily divorced (p. 117). Similar findings are reported by Alderbigee (1997), Liem and Roberts (2009), and Stack (1997), and all the researchers we identified reported findings indicating that homicides, femicides, homicide–suicides, femicide–suicides, or all of these, occurred within three months of separating.

SEPARATION AND FEMICIDE–SUICIDE

Wilson and Daly (1993) did not include femicide–suicide as an outcome in the cross-national study they conducted (1993). A number of other researchers have investigated the link between separation and femicide–suicide involving intimate partners as perpetrators and victims. One of the most frequently cited researchers is C. M. Milroy. Milroy (1998) examined coroner inquest data on 52 cases that occurred in England (Yorkshire and Humberside specifically) between 1975 and 1992. Findings based on his analysis of coroner inquest data revealed that separation "accounted for 50% of all homicide-suicide episodes" (p. 63).

Moving from England to California, Lund and Smorodinsky (2001) studied 181 homicide and 181 intimate-partner homicide and femicide–suicide cases. Information on these cases was obtained from multiple sources, including the California Department of Justice Homicide File and law enforcement case records. Findings from a logistic regression analysis indicated that separation was significantly associated with femicide–homicide ($p < 0.05$) and entailed a 3-fold increase in the odds of dyadic death (OR 2.9 95% CI 0.9, 9.0) (p. 455).

Morton, Runyan, Moracco, and Butts (1998) obtained data on 119 victims of femicide–suicide from medical examiner files on 116 homicide–suicide events that occurred in North Carolina between 1992 and 1998. In this study, "victim separation from the perpetrators" was found to be the most common factor or life event preceding femicide–suicide. Specifically, 45% (39) of the victims were separated or separating from the perpetrator (p. 96). In Hong Kong, Chan, Beh, and Broadhurst (2003) studied 42 femicide–suicides and 14 homicide–suicides that occurred between 1989 and 1998. Information on these dyadic deaths was obtained from coroner and police investigation reports. Findings reported by these researchers indicated that the majority of them 39% (22) were "motivated by separation," with spouses and lovers accounting for 46% of the victims (p. 167).

In Australia, Easteal (1993) analyzed "in-depth data" on 150 cases of homicide involving "sexual intimates" as victims and perpetrators collected by Polk and Ransom (1991) in an earlier study. A comparison between 102 co-residing and 48 separate-residence sexually intimate partners revealed a highly significant difference ($p < 0.01$) in the number of perpetrators who committed suicide afterward

(15% vs 35%) (p. 193). Homicide–suicide in Australia was also investigated by Carcach and Grabosky (1998) using homicide case records submitted by each police service (state and territorial) to the Australia's National Homicide Monitoring Program. Information was obtained on 2,226 homicides that occurred between 1989 and 1996. Homicide–suicides accounted for 144 (6.5%) of the cases but only 128 were analyzed because 16 suicide pact cases were excluded. Logistic regression revealed that the association between separation and homicide–suicide was highly significant ($p < 0.01$), and killing a former spouse entailed a 5-fold increase (4.6) in the risk of the perpetrator committing suicide. Killing a current spouse entailed a 3-fold increase (3.2) in the risk of the perpetrator committing suicide (p. 5).

Between 1965 and 1990, 16,245 homicides were analyzed by the Chicago Police Department, and the results were kept in its homicide files. Stack (1997) obtained access to files that also included 267 homicide–suicide cases. Multivariate logistic analysis of 265 homicide–suicide cases—two suicide pact cases were excluded—and 16.245 homicide cases revealed a 13-fold increase (12.68) in the risk of homicide–suicide involving former spouses and lovers as victims, compared with an 8-fold increase in the risk of homicide–suicide involving current spouses as victims (p. 466). As 97% of the perpetrators were males, the vast majority of the homicide–suicides were actually femicide–suicides.

Using data from coroner death reports and police investigation files, Crawford and Gartner (1992) obtained information on 969 femicides and 551 intimate femicides that were recorded for Ontario between 1974 and 1990. The 551 femicides accounted for the death of 767 persons. Most of the perpetrators were males whose female partners were leaving or had left them (p. 48).

A nontrivial association between separation and femicide–suicide has been reported by a number of researchers using samples of cases that varied in size and type, time periods, study designs, and methods of analysis. Included among them are Barraclough and Harris (2002), Bourget, Gage, and Moamai (2000), Buteau, Lesage, and Kiely (1993), Dutton and Kerry (1999), Koziol-Mclain et al. (2006), Logan et al. (2008), Rosenbaum (1990), Violence Policy Center (2006), and West (1966).

RECENCY OF FEMICIDE–SUICIDE FOLLOWING SEPARATION

Based on findings from the retrospective study of medical examiner records of 119 victims of femicide–suicide, Morton et al. (1998) found that most of the 39 victims were female intimate partners who "had recently separated from the perpetrator, expressed intent to leave or were in the act of leaving" when they were killed (p. 96). In the modal femicide–suicide case described by Milroy (1998), the man who commits suicide after killing his wife "kills his spouse when she attempts to leave the relationship ... or after she has left" (p. 63). Logan and associates (2008) found that 191 femicide–suicide perpetrators used a firearm in the femicide–suicide incident, and of these, the immediate precursor in 39% (75) of these incidents was a "divorce request or breakup" initiated by their female partners (p. 1060).

Findings reported in the NVDRS *Surveillance Summaries* (2012) are consistent with findings reported by these researchers, because 71% of the 198 femicide–suicides they investigated were preceded by "relationship problems" (conflicts) that could have been associated with the female partner's actual or impending separation or a "personal crisis within the preceding or impending two weeks" that could have been associated with separating or communicating the intention to separate (p. 14 & Table 29).

SEPARATION AND SUICIDE

Using data from the National Longitudinal Mortality Study, 1979–1989 and two linked additional data bases, epidemiologist Kposowa (2000) investigated the association between marital status and other characteristics (age, sex, race/ethnicity, household income, education, and region of the country) on the 545 suicides that were reported during this period. Three major findings were reported. First, compared with married persons, divorced/separated individuals were twice as likely to commit suicide (RR = 2.08, 95% CI 1.58, 2.72). Second, compared with married men, divorced/separated men were 2.5 times more likely to commit suicide, net of the effect of the seven other characteristics identified earlier RR = 2.47 (5% CI = 1.84, 3.30). Third, compared with married women, divorced/separated women were equally likely to commit suicide. These findings led Kposowa to conclude that divorce/separation has a net effect of death by suicide "but only for men" (p. 258).

Between 1994 and 2004, 6026 individuals in Queensland, Australia, committed suicide. The use of two separate data sets (registries) enabled researchers Wyder et al. (2009) to "isolate the variable 'separated' with great reliability" (p. 1). Specifically, they were able to include separations from registered marriages and de facto unions. Findings on the relative risks (RR) for suicide for marital status, age, and gender indicate that separation and divorce are far more strongly associated with suicide than the marital statuses of single, widowed, and married across all age groups and for men and women. For example, among males age 15 to 24—the highest-risk-for-suicide age group—the relative risk for married, divorced, separated, single, and widowed was 7.57, 20.69, 91.62, 4.55, and 10.73, respectively (p. 210, Table 3.3) (Kolves et al., 2006).

RECENCY OF SUICIDE FOLLOWING MARITAL SEPARATION

The 2012 NVDRS *Surveillance Summaries* include information on 9,949 suicides that occurred during 2009. "A crisis of some kind in the preceding two weeks" was reported for more than one quarter (27%) of the suicide cases. In a substantial minority of these cases (31%), the crisis may have involved intimate partner conflicts over an impending separation (Table 7). Using psychological autopsies as a source of data, Kolves, Varnik, Schneider, Fritze, and Allik (2006) conducted a cross-national study of 56 suicides in Tallinn, Estonia, and 163 suicides in Frankfurt, Germany. One of their major findings was that "life events," such as separation that occurred during the preceding three months, were more strongly associated with suicide than the same events that occurred more than three months earlier.

Psychological autopsy data are often incomplete, and for social reasons may be systematically biased (Paykel, Myers, Klerman, Lindenthal, & Pepper, 1969). These concerns were acknowledged but not addressed by the authors. Still, support for their findings is provided by life-event researchers Heikkinen, Aro, & Lonnqvist (1992), who used other data collection methods such as interviewing partners of suicide victims (Heikkinen et al., 1992). Ide, Wyder, Kolves, and De Leo (2010) undertook a critical review of 52 articles using a variety of data collection techniques on recent life events and suicide. Findings suggested that the risk of suicide varied with phase of separation, with the odds of suicide being highest for individuals during the "acute–immediate/recent phase" of separation.

RECENCY OF FEMICIDE–SUICIDE FOLLOWING SEPARATION

Annual Homicide Surveys published by Statistics Canada include a narrative segment that is supposed to be fully completed by police officers investigating spousal homicide–suicides in Canada. Between 1991 and 2002, 257 spousal homicide–suicides were recorded. Close to complete police narratives were available for 86% (222) of them. Information on recency of separation was available for 13% (29) of the 222 close-to-complete narratives. Almost one-third (18) of the femicide–suicides occurred within three months after the women separated from their husbands, and nine of the 18 femicide–suicides occurred during the first two weeks after separation (Aston & Bunge, 2005, p. 62).

Kolves et al. (2006) compared individuals in Tallinn who committed suicide with the same number of comparison (matched) subjects who did not. Logistic regression analysis was used to estimate the independent contribution made by "life events" such as family conflict, financial problems, separation, and illness (mental and physical) to suicide. Of the 11 life events occurring during the preceding three months that were included in the first model, seven were found to be statistically significant predictors of suicide.

Psychological autopsy data are often incomplete and systematically biased (Paykel et al., 1969). These concerns were acknowledged but not addressed by the authors. Still, support for their findings is provided by life event researchers Heikkinen et al. (1992), who used other data collection methods such as interviewing partners of suicide victims. Ide et al. (2010) undertook a critical review of 52 articles using a variety of data collection techniques on recent life events and suicide. Findings suggested that the risk of suicide varied with phase of separation, with the odds of suicide being highest for individuals during the "acute–immediate/recent phase" of separation.

SUMMARY

1. Gender differences in lethal domestic violence expressed as ratios:
    a. Intimate partner femicide/intimate partner homicide 5:1;
    b. Femicide–suicide/homicide–suicide 16:1;
    c. Male/female suicide 4:1.
2. Compared with co-residence, separation entails an average:
    a. 6-fold increase in femicides;
    b. 2-fold increase in homicides;
    c. 7-fold increase in femicide–suicides;
    d. 5-fold increase in suicides for men.
3. Recency (average months after separating)
    a. Femicide
        - 47% within three months;
        - 74% between two and six months.
    b. Femicide–suicide
        - 62% within three months;
        - 50% within first two weeks.
    c. Suicide
        - Odds highest during most recent months after separating.

COMMENT

Five comments on limitations of the studies described here seem warranted. First, none of the studies we reviewed included information on whether the separations they referred to were the result of joint or unilateral decisions, and if the latter, by which partner. We assumed that the separations referred to by the authors were unilaterally initiated by female partners and contested by their male partners. Grounding this assumption in data would confirm its validity.

Second, separation includes both the process of separating while the partners are living together and when they are living apart. Yet, in the studies we reviewed, in only one of them was separation defined broadly enough to include both co-residing and separate-residence phases of the process.

Third, counts of the number of separated persons who were involved as perpetrators and victims of violent deaths vary greatly because the "intimate partner" from whom one could separate is broadly defined to include current and former spouses, common–law partners, cohabiting partners, boyfriends/girlfriends, and lovers in some studies, and narrowly defined to include only ex-spouses in others. For example, Block (2000) identifies 14 different intimate partners from whom a partner could separate (p. 99), but in the U.S. Census the only intimate partners classified as separated were ex-partners who no longer reside with the persons they are still legally married to.

Fourth, an investigation of the lived lives and sometimes multiple intimate partner relationships of women suggest that separating from men who regarded them as "their closest or only intimate partner" may be more hazardous than separating from male partners they are married to, living with, or dating, and who do not regard them in the same way (Block, 2000, p. 56). Information on the closeness and/or exclusivity of the relationship between the perpetrators of lethal domestic violence and their victims was not revealed in any of the sources of data (census, police narratives, coroner reports, or inquests) used in the studies we reviewed.

Fifth, social selection variables are rarely measured and included in statistical analyses even though they may also help explain why separation and homicide/femicide occur together or in fairly close temporal proximity to each other. For example, if infidelity by female partners and battering by male partners are found to be reliable precursors of both separation and femicide/homicide, they may also help explain why separation and femicide/homicide are so strongly associated with each other (Wilson & Daly, 1992, p. 94). Another example: Some individuals may possess "pathological personality traits" that reliably select them "out of marriage" and "into" the relatively small group of perpetrators of femicide–suicide (Repetti, 2001).

Extant models (e.g., co-twin control design) can differentiate separation effects on femicide, homicide, femicide–suicide, and suicide from the effects of selection variables and intervening variables (Sbarra, Law, & Portley, 2011, p. 464). Findings based on the use of such a design would probably indicate that sociological, social psychological, and psychological mechanisms identified in the four chapters that follow explain a greater or lesser amount of the variation in lethal domestic violence associated with separation depending on the amount of the variation explained by selection factors. A seesaw model may be applicable. When selection mechanisms are stronger, post-selection/life experience mechanisms are weaker, and when selection mechanisms are weaker, post-separation/life event mechanisms are stronger.

DISCUSSION QUESTIONS

1. Why are separated wives more likely to be killed by their husbands than wives who are living with their husbands?

2. Evaluate this statement: Femicide following separation is simply an escalation of violence by male partners with a history of using violence against their wives. Do you agree or disagree? Give reasons for your answer.

3. Why is marital separation more strongly associated with femicide than divorce?

4. Describe and critically evaluate findings cited in support of the empirical generalization that forms the title of this chapter.

CHAPTER 4

Theorizing Separation and Intimate Partner Homicide

LEARNING OBJECTIVES

Readers who achieve the learning objectives set for this chapter will be able to:

- Demonstrate the ability to evaluate self-defense definitions of intimate partner homicide using the criteria of validity and utility
- Derive causal mechanisms underlying the association between separation and intimate partner homicide from the theories of intimate partner homicide described in this chapter
- Demonstrate awareness of the contribution made by separation, conflict, and conflict resolution to intimate partner homicide

Our objective here is to theorize separation and intimate partner homicide by building on the contributions made by researchers investigating the association between these two variables. The contributions are characterized by the following conception, definition, and conclusion. The domestic context is conceived of as a "stateless location." Intimate partner homicide is defined as self-defense. The conclusion is that males who repeatedly and seriously assault their female partners are digging their own graves.

FAMILY AS A STATELESS LOCATION

In Black's Theory of Self-help (1983, 1988), stateless locations are defined as places where "lower-status people of all kinds ... enjoy less legal protection ... when complaints are made ... and ... when conflict erupts among them." The domestic context is included as a stateless location because "People in intimate relationships ... find that legal officials are relatively unconcerned about their conflicts" (p. 41). Findings reported by numerous researchers (e.g., Browne, 1987; Goetting, 1987; Jensen, 2001; Jones, 1994; Ogle & Jacobs, 2002; Totman, 1978) support the inclusion of the private domestic context as a stateless location but expand the definition of stateless location. The expanded definition includes neighborhoods in which officials who control financial, housing, social, and psychological resources for victims of intimate partner violence are relatively indifferent to their plight.

The neighborhoods in which "people in intimate relations" reside may also vary in the degree to which they provide or deny resources to victims of domestic violence. Sampson, Raudenbush, and Earls (1997) used the concept of "collective efficacy" to refer to the degree to which neighborhoods were characterized by a high or low degree of social cohesion among residents and their willingness or unwillingness to intervene in the lives of residents for the good of the community as a whole. Intimate partners who reside in disadvantaged neighborhoods are living in a private stateless location within a public-local stateless location, where, compared with their counterparts in advantaged state locations, collective efficacy is weak because of the relatively high proportion of transient residents and recent immigrants with language difficulties. Consequently, neighbors and other residents in low–collective efficacy neighborhoods are less likely to intervene in ways that help victims of domestic violence (Pinchevsky & Wright, 2012). Thus, when Kim (who subsequently killed Billy) was kicked and punched in a restaurant and again in its parking lot, "people averted their eyes from Kim's injuries or pretended they were not there and refrained from intervention (or even from calling the police or ambulance) during public attacks" (Browne, 1987, pp. 148–149 & 156).

HOMICIDE AS SELF-DEFENSE

Self-defense is broadly defined to include intimate partner homicides grounded in a reasonable belief that a deadly assault or serious injury would be inflicted by a male partner imminently, immediately, or sometime during the next few hours or days and that killing the partner was a necessary and sufficient condition for personal survival and/or the survival of a child, children, or other loved ones. In the incident described next, Kim kills Billy in self-defense—broadly defined.

> Billy first assaulted Kim in January, 1979, about three months after they started living together. This and many subsequent assaults usually started when Billy (and sometimes Kim) was drinking and they began to argue. The last time Billy beat and injured Kim was in February 1983. During the five years they lived together—not continuously because she left him and returned to live with him on many occasions—Billy threatened to kill her if she ever gave him a reason, such as arguing with him; pointed a handgun at her head and fired at her but high; beat her in front of his relatives and in public places; would plead with her and promise to change if she would return after leaving him and then increase the severity of his beatings when she did return; severely beat her in the parking lot of a local restaurant and only stopped when he was confronted by the restaurant owner holding a loaded shotgun; sexually assaulted her; deliberately drove his truck at high speed and in a manner consistent with his intention to throw her out, and when she survived his attempt to kill or seriously injure her, he stopped the truck, forced her to have oral sex and choked and banged her head against the dashboard; and shot and killed her kittens. Early in February 1983, Billy, who had been drinking, severely beat Kim, who had also been drinking, ignoring her pleas to stop. The next thing Kim remembers is standing in the living room facing Billy with a rifle at her shoulder. She fired once, killing him. Kim was charged with murder.
>
> **Browne, 1987, pp. 154–155**

MALE BATTERERS AS THEIR OWN GRAVEDIGGERS

The case of Billy and Kim is one of many, if not most, of the cases described by Browne (1987) and Jones (1994) that illustrate a process that culminates in the death of a male batterer. Findings reported in the research segment that follows indicate that male partner violence that is increasing in frequency and severity is strongly associated with intimate partner homicide. This is why male batterers are said to be digging their own graves when they batter their female partners.

THEORIZING INTIMATE PARTNER HOMICIDE

In New South Wales, Australia, the ratio of intimate partner femicides to intimate partner homicides associated with separating/separated is 25:1 (75–3). In the United States, the same ratio among African-American spouses is 1:1 (Block, 2000; Ellis & DeKeseredy, 1996, p. 86). Wallace (1986) suggested that this significant difference may be explained by the fact that African-American wives were more assertive and economically independent. As a result, they were more likely than wives in New South Wales to kill rather than be killed by their male partners during conflicts associated with separation. Historical and cultural factors were called on to account for differences in the assertiveness and independence of African-American and Australian female partners.

In the societal context of gender inequality favoring men generally and male partners in particular, Browne applied the "social judgment theory" created by Sherif and Hovland (1961) to the problem of explaining intimate partner homicides perpetrated in self-defense. More specifically, Browne (1987, pp. 128–130) used principles derived from the social judgment theory created by Sherif and Hovland to explain why some battered female partners used lethal violent resistance in self-defense while others did not and why those who did kill their male batterer partners did not when they experienced male partner violence on earlier occasions.

Browne focuses on the *contrast* between the last threats or violent acts of male batterers and the violence to which female partners have become assimilated. Female partners believe that when any given violent threat or violent act falls, or is perceived to fall, within the range of what their male batterer had done in the past, lethal violent resistance is not believed to be necessary for their survival. Lethal violent resistance is believed to be necessary for the survival of female partners who experience recent increases in the frequency and seriousness of actual and threatened violence, a life-threatening attack, and/or credible threats to harm or kill children or relatives that had never been made before. Evidence of this kind is a "turning point" for the decision to kill their male partner to survive and/or to protect loved ones from serious injury or death.

In a 1992, a publication titled "Till Death Us Do Part" by Wilson and Daly presented an explanation of intimate partner femicide in which conflict and conflict resolution figure prominently. Specifically, abusive male partners who attempt to control their partners by using coercive control-motivated violence against them also attempt to settle conflicts with female partners over their suspected or actual desertion and/or infidelity. Not infrequently, attempts to settle conflicts through arguments escalate to the use of physical force and sometimes, albeit infrequently, lethal force. The typical scenario is described in these terms: "Men … strive to control women, albeit with variable success; women struggle to resist coercion and maintain their choices. There is brinkmanship and risk of disaster in any such contest, and homicides by spouses of either sex may be considered slips in a dangerous game" (p. 93). Given sex differences in strength and size, men are better able to settle such conflicts by using physical force (strangling, choking, hitting, kicking, head-butting). Consequently, female partners tend to make up for differences in physical resources by using weapons (knives, guns) during and following conflicts when they believe their (or their children's) survival to be at stake.

Support for the Wilson and Daly scenario is provided by Browne, who found that the typical intimate partner homicide was "unplanned and occurred in the midst of an attack against the woman" who believed that her death "was inevitable within a certain time-frame" (1987, p. 135). The case of Hans and Hilde is the sort of situation Browne has in mind.

> The police had been called to the home of Hans and Hilde on many occasions when arguments had escalated in physical assaults by Hans. Hilde worried every day that Hans would kill her. She alleged that he stabbed her on one occasion. On the night of the killing, Hilde drank two bottles of wine and was intoxicated. So was Hans when he returned home later that night. He woke Hilde and they started arguing over her refusal to provide him with more beer. At one point, Hans jumped her in the kitchen, threatening to kill her and calling her "a rubbish [expletive]." In the course of the conflict, she struck Hans, causing him to fall against a table and cut his head. Verbally abusing Hilde, Hans went into the bathroom. Hilde picked up a knife from the kitchen and followed Hans into the bathroom. The opening door caused Hans to fall into the bathtub. As Hilde approached him, he kicked her in the groin and lower abdomen. Hilde stabbed Hans in the lung, killing him.
>
> Easteal, 1993, pp. 70–71

In the patriarchy theory formulated by Easteal (1993), wife battering is conceived of as "an act of domination which cannot be seen as isolated from the patriarchal society in which it takes place" (p. 186) and a reliable precursor of both intimate partner femicide and intimate partner homicide. Battering is proactive and increases in its frequency and severity to culminate in intimate partner femicide. Intimate partner homicide is reactive. That is, it is a reaction to battering that increases in frequency and severity to the point where the battered a wife who is currently experiencing a lethal attack or one to come "going forward" believes she will be killed. She kills in self-defense to survive. Easteal hypothesizes that women experiencing battered women's syndrome are overrepresented among wives committing intimate partner homicide.

The notion that "characteristics of the incident itself may be the primary risk factor" for intimate partner homicide is implicit in Browne's theory and explicit in Block's (2000) assumption that intimate partner femicide and homicide can be prevented by "preventing one particular incident of intimate partner violence, the incident resulting in death" (p. 269). According to Block, the significance of the characteristics of the incident for prevention varies with the degree to which they reveal reasons for the homicide. The "incident itself" is more likely to reveal reasons in cases where there has been no prior violence against the women who killed their male partners and the partners were interacting immediately prior to the homicide (p. 241). Reasons are less likely to be revealed in cases where there has been no prior or ongoing interaction between the partners immediately preceding the homicide (p. 241).

Block identifies two patterns of violence: the regular and the irregular. In the former pattern, recurring intimate partner violence increases in intensity and "eventually leads to a fatal incident." In the irregular pattern, "something different happens in the fatal incident" compared with what has happened before (p. 269). The irregular pattern is the one that includes the tipping points identified by Browne and Block.

The situational circumstances that "surround … the last altercation between the husband and wife" are also the focus of Grant's (1983) "encapsulation/conflict resolution theory" of intimate partner homicide. Lofland (1969) used the concept of encapsulation to refer to a period during the course of an interaction when one or both of the parties who are intoxicated or high on drugs or in a state of religious ecstasy are, as it were, fully and completely contained in a capsule that shields them from awareness of the short- and longer-term consequences of the violent actions associated with being intoxicated or high. Abused female partners who are encapsulated by alcohol or other drugs are primed to use intimate partner homicide rather than separation as a conflict resolution tactic under the three conditions specified in Felson's (1989) routine activities model (co-presence of motivated perpetrators, vulnerable victims, and the absence of effective guardian(s) willing to intervene) and:

- long-standing increasing frequent, serious, and recent abuse;
- previous threats to kill her by the male partner; and
- repeated prior unhelpful experiences with officers who responded to her calls for intervention.

In the "strain theory" of intimate partner homicide formulated by Ogle, Katkin, and Bernard (1995), structural (gender inequality), cultural (patriarchal elements), and social conditions (e.g., gender role expectations and stereotypes) are identified as sources of strain for women. Agnew (1992) hypothesizes that strain produces anger that seeks release. Cultural norms inculcated during socialization proscribe the external expression of anger directed toward the source of the strain. As a result, anger is internalized and experienced as "guilt and hurt." Conformity with cultural norms and a subordinate position contribute toward the proliferation of females with "overcontrolled personalities" who function in a variety of social situations.

Included among them is the situation of being involved in a long-term abusive relationship with a male partner where, because of their couple's relative isolation, lack experience in expressing aggression directly and physically and consequently lack opportunities to learn rules regulating the expression of anger; overcontrolled female partners react explosively with lethal violence against abusive male partners during or following conflicts, beatings, the discovery of infidelity, and/or sexual assaults on their children, when they "experience intense anger amounting to rage" (p. 186).

Ogle and Jacobs (2012) offer a "new social interaction theory" in which structural, cultural, situational, and personal (physical) factors influence interaction between intimate partners involved in an ongoing cyclical battering relationship that escalates to the point of ending in intimate partner homicide as an act of self-defense. More specifically, intimate partner homicides preceded by battering are conceived of as "a long term survival process" (p. 6) because the "battering process is a homicidal process" and the female partner's ultimate homicidal reaction is "a reasonable response to the long-term homicidal process" (p. 71).

Clearly, Ogle and Jacobs believed that the emphasis placed by Block and Grant on the characteristics of the last fatal incident is misplaced. Battering is defined as "a relationship that involves two socially and physically unequal combatants with intimate knowledge of each other developed over a long period of time, participating in an on-going long-term (cyclical) confrontation" (p. 4). During the cyclical process, violence escalates in frequency and seriousness in a "spiraling process of reciprocal exchange" (p. 6). Separations and attempted separations by female partners that escalate the seriousness of threatened and/or actual violence by male partners figure prominently as precursors of both intimate partner femicide ("separation attacks") and intimate partner homicide (lethal reactions to separation attacks believed to be necessary for survival).

Gender inequality is the major source of intimate partner homicide in Jensen's (2001) theory of homicides committed by female partners. She identifies two types of inequality: economic (educational and occupational) and social (gender roles, identities, expectations, and stereotypes). Intimate partner homicide rates are positively associated with increases in both types of inequality and negatively associated with changes in the direction of greater economic and social equality. Greater economic equality decreases the risk of intimate partner violence by providing abused women who are gainfully employed outside the home with economic power resources (money), which facilitates leaving their abusive partners or choosing effective, nonviolent ways of settling conflicts if they continue to live with them.

Greater social equality also provides normative support for women to leave unhappy marriages generally, to leave marriages with abusive partners in particular, and to cohabit with male partners before marriage or as an alternative to it. Cohabitation decreases the likelihood of intimate partner homicide because it is a nontraditional marital status characterized by the absence of relatively inflexible gender roles and expectations that are a major source of conflict in traditional marriages and greater normative support for leaving the relationship than is provided for partners who end their marriages (pp. 110–111).

Gender equality can also decrease the rate of intimate partner homicide by delegitimating the use of violence by male partners and consequently decreasing the necessity of women's use of fatal violence in self-defense (p. 51). Moreover, economic and social equality increases economic normative support for separation and divorce by married couples, and separation increases the risk of serious and lethal violence because it threatens male partner dominance (pp. 48–49). Contested gender inequality may be one of the reasons why "conflicts and quarrels [are] ... the most common motive for women's homicide" (p. 47).

RESEARCH

Like homicide squads in other cities, Philadelphia's homicide squad keeps files on all homicides they investigate; the files of 588 criminal homicides that were investigated between January 1, 1948, and December 31, 1952, were analyzed by Wolfgang (1958). Just over one-quarter (150, or 26%) of these homicides were victim precipitated (VP); that is, they were cases that met legal requirements for mitigation of the charge from murder to manslaughter and/or a criminal homicide to an excused homicide. Wolfgang defined VP cases as cases in which "the victim was the first to use physical force directed against his subsequent slayer ... to show and use a deadly weapon, to strike a blow in an altercation-in short, the first to commence the interplay or resort to physical violence" (p. 389). His definition is illustrated by the following case:

> A husband accused his wife of giving money to another man, and while she was making breakfast, he attacked her with a milk bottle, then a brick, and finally a concrete block. Having a butcher knife in her hand, she stabbed him during the fight.

Findings reported by Wolfgang indicate that almost three-quarters (73.5%) of the 136 "family relationship/VP" cases involved a "spouse" as a victim. Because none of the cases described by Wolfgang involve female intimate partners and most of the spousal VP victims reported by other researchers (e.g., Barnard, Vera, & Newman, 1982; Goetting, 1987; Totman, 1982) were males, it may be reasonable to assume that the majority of the spousal VP victims were husbands.

A social definition of "self-defense" is not the same thing as the legal definition of "victim precipitation." The former broadens the requirements for intimate partner homicide in self-defense in ways that were indicated earlier. The latter narrows VP intimate partner homicides to cases in which the following criteria were met: "adequate provocation"; the homicide immediately followed the provocation and the perpetrator was "in the heat of passion" when he/she killed the victim; and the provocation caused the heat of passion, which caused the intimate partner homicide (p. 388). If heat of passion is broadened to include emotional arousal associated with fear of a violent death and the requirements were broadened to homicides that occur before, during, and shortly after a reasonable battered woman believed she would be killed, then many more of the intimate partner homicides in self-defense described by Browne (1987) may also be defined as VP.

CHAPTER 4 Theorizing Separation and Intimate Partner Homicide

About five years before Daly and Wilson defined "homicide" as the ultimate conflict resolution tactic (1988, p. ix), Grant (1983) included homicide and separation among the variety of conflict resolution options that may be available to intimate partners for settling conflicts between them (p. 59). The data she analyzed were collected from a nonprobability sample of 21 female penitentiary inmates serving time for killing (murder 1 and 2 and manslaughter 1 and 2) their male partners and from 293 resident intake forms administered by women's shelter staff to residents when they entered the shelter. She reported findings indicating that the choice of homicide over separation to settle conflicts varied:

- positively with drug use by female partners ($\chi^2 = 151.22$, $p < 0.05$);
- inversely with the educational level of the husband—the lower his level of education, the greater the likelihood that his female partner would use homicide rather than separation to settle conflicts between them ($\chi^2 = 29.10$, $p < 0.05$) (p. 77);
- positively with the number of times the male partner had been married previously—the greater the number of previous marriages, the more likely that his female partner would use homicide rather than separation ($\chi^2 = 110.2$, $p < 0.05$) (p. 80);
- with economic dependency on the male partner—compared with employed women, unemployed women were more likely to use homicide rather than separation to settle intimate partner conflicts ($\chi^2 = 19.0$, $p < 0.05$) (p. 83);
- positively with the frequency of male partner abuse—the greater the frequency, the more likely it was that the female partner would settle conflicts by killing rather than separating from her abusive partner ($\chi^2 = 2.57$, $p < 0.05$) (p. 89);
- with threats made by male partners—female partners were more likely to kill than to separate from a male partner who made threats to harm her ($\chi^2 = 98.5$, $p < 0.05$);
- curvilinearly with the number of times the police had previously been called to their residence—when no calls were made and when calls were made eight or more times, the more likely it was that female partners were to use homicide rather than separation to settle conflicts ($\chi^2 = 32.5$, $p < 0.05$) (p. 91).

A year later, Wilbanks (1984) published findings based on his analysis of 569 homicides that occurred in Miami during 1980. Information on motives and circumstances was obtained form 269 arrested offenders. The data he analyzed were collected from multiple sources (medical examiner files, FBI *Uniform Crime Reports*, criminal court records, and a newspaper, the *Miami Herald*). He reported the following findings:

- The most frequent motive for homicide was arguments (56%) (p. 52).
- Wives were far more likely than husbands to kill during a domestic argument (the ratio of homicides to femicides was almost 6:1, 64.2% vs 10.8%) (p. 172).
- Fifty-seven percent of the victims of the 569 Dade county homicides were engaged in such "risky activities" as drinking, arguing, and engaging in a criminal act at the time of their death (p. 37).

- Intoxicated victims, especially those involved in domestic or other arguments, were six times more likely to have precipitated their deaths than were those who were not intoxicated and involved in arguments (p. 40).
- Seriously intoxicated victims were six times more likely to be involved in domestic and other arguments (p. 40).
- An equal proportion of offenders and victims were drinking or had been drinking at the time of the homicide (p. 39).
- In almost every case, where traces of alcohol were found, they were likely to be found in both victims and offenders (p. 39).

The New South Wales (Australia) police homicide files include information on 1,393 individuals (85% males and 15% females) who were charged with homicide between 1961 and 1983. Spousal homicides accounted for 296 (21.2%) of the total number of homicides. More in-depth information on the "life circumstances of the accused" was obtained from court records (pp. 27–28). Information from both sources was analyzed by Wallace (1986). One of her major findings was that the following characteristics—sex (gender) differences, legal vs de factor unions, duration of the relationship, employment status, alcohol consumption, urban vs. rural residence, separation, jealousy, child custody—were "characteristics of cases in which marital conflict led to (lethal) violence" (pp. 83–104).

Another noteworthy finding has to do with separation. Wallace found 76% of those who were killed were separated or in the process of separating. Gender differences in separation-associated spousal homicides were significant: only three of 75 perpetrators of separation-associated homicides were female spouses (pp. 98–99). Perhaps this is why Wallace speculated on the causes of intimate partner femicide but not of intimate partner homicide. Still, a theory is implicit in her findings, and we shall attempt to build on it.

In analyzing data on 110 homicide cases collected from multiple sources (coroner's courts, offices of the directors of public prosecutions, and the Supreme Court) and 150 homicide cases collected from the National Homicide Monitoring Program files, Easteal (1993) reported findings indicating that separation was the most frequently identified precursor to "the 106 homicides between adult sexual intimates" that occurred between 1998 and 1990. Specifically, separations preceded homicides in 38% of the cases, followed by alcohol/drugs (31%) and battering (27%). Proportions of the population who were separated (or who imbibed alcohol/drugs or male batterers) were not identified, so it is not possible to specify the degree to which separated couples were overrepresented among intimate partner homicide perpetrators, but findings for Canada indicate that it varies between 6% and 8% (Totton, 2001). Moreover, Easteal states that the figure of 38% underestimates the actual number of separation-associated homicides because police investigators either do not record the information or do not accurately identify major contributing factors (p. 68).

The same caveat applies to fights reported as a primary contributing factor for 9% of the cases. Conflict and conflict resolution (arguments and/or fights) are implicated in the modal homicidal incident described by Easteal (e.g., pp. 52, 53, 57, 69, 71, & 72) and in 77% of 56 non-Aboriginal and 97% of 36 Aboriginal homicides.

In 1987, Browne published the results of her qualitative comparative study of when battered women kill their male intimate partners. Her findings were based on a judgmental (nonprobability) sample of 42 physically abused women who were convicted of killing or seriously injuring their partners and of 205 physically abused women who did not kill or attempt to kill their partners. Seven factors were found to distinguish the former from the latter group of abused women:

- Escalation of threats
- Perception of entrapment
- Failed alternatives to lethal violence
- Male partners used drugs more frequently
- Became intoxicated more frequently
- Used threats and assaultive behavior more frequently
- Threatened to kill others other than themselves more frequently

Block (2000) compared female partners who were victims of male partner violence during the past 12 months who were *victims* of intimate partner femicide ($n = 49$, or 65%) with abused female partners who were *perpetrators* of intimate partner homicide ($n = 26$, or 35%). These 75 homicides and femicides were selected for analysis because questionnaire data and official statistics were available for this subset of the 87 intimate partner homicides and femicides that were recorded for 1995 and 1996 (p. 221). Compared with victims of male partner femicide, Block (pp. 220–276) found abused female perpetrators of intimate partner homicide:

- experienced violence more frequently and/or forced sex during the preceding 12 months (Exhibit 101, p. 236)
- were more likely to believe their lives were in danger (Exhibit 101, p. 236) (59% vs. 45%)
- were more likely to be involved in long-term legally registered marriages
- were less likely to have financial, educational, or social support resources enabling them to leave the relationship and/or power resources they could use to change the behavior of abusive male partners prior to reaching the point of believing they were going to be killed by them
- were less likely to have tried to leave or asked the abusive male partner to leave
- were less likely to have tried to separate or separated during the 12 months preceding the homicide
- were far more likely to have experienced a violent attack or incident during the four weeks preceding the homicide
- were more likely to have contacted the police because male partner threats or violence were more serious

Although findings reported by some researchers indicate that "coercion and control [are] important for both sexes" (Flynn & Graham, 2010, p. 248), none of them report finding cases of coercive control-motivated intimate partner homicides. Block does report cases of coercive control-motivated intimate partner femicides and sudden unprovoked male partner "explosive rage," but the majority of intimate partner femicides and homicides reported by Block appear to be conflict instigated. The following finding supports this conclusion: "Some type of violent physical interaction immediately preceded the homicide (and femicide) in all 35 cases about which information on heterosexual intimate partner interaction immediately preceding the femicide or homicide was known. The male partner was the first one to use violent conflict resolution tactics in 30 of 35 cases. In four additional cases, male partners who may have used threats to kill as a conflict resolution tactic during attempts to settle conflicts were killed by the female partners against whom the threats were uttered" (p. 222).

Other researchers who report findings indicating that intimate partner homicides often occur in the context of intimate partner conflicts include Barker (2006), Centers for Disease Control and Prevention (2012), Chimbos (1976), Easteal (1993), Goetting (1987), Grant (1983), Jensen (2001), Jurik and Wynne (1990), Kellermann and associates (1993), Silverman and Kennedy (1993), Wilson and Daly (1992), and Wallace (1986).

Finally, unlike the association between separation and intimate partner femicides, where 74% of the femicide victims tried to leave or left during the 12 months preceding the homicide, the association between separation and intimate partner homicide is weaker. During the preceding 12 months, 58% of the female partners who killed their male partners tried to leave or left. Moreover, trying to end or ending the relationship was found to be "an immediate precipitating factor in 38% of the intimate partner femicides [female partner victims] but only 13% of intimate partner homicides [male partner victims]." Based on findings reported earlier, the dynamic in the latter case may have involved a conflict about her leaving or having left, during which the male partner assaulted or otherwise physically injured her and she responded by killing him (Block, 2000, p. 272).

Coroner's files in Quebec include information on all 276 spousal (legally married and common law) homicides that occurred between 1991 and 2010. Bourget and Gagne (2012) found that intimate partner femicides accounted for 85% (234) of them and intimate partner homicides for the remaining 15% (42). Information in these files was subjected to a "retrospective clinical review." One of the major findings reported by these authors was that "only 28% of female offenders ... had previously been subjected to violence by their victim" (p. 7). The authors concluded that this finding did not support the hypothesis that "most female perpetrated spousal homicide occurs in self defense or in reaction to long-term abuse" (p. 1). A second major finding reported by Bourget and Gagne was that intimate partner homicides they investigated occurred spontaneously and were unpredictable.

Consensus on the conception of intimate partner homicide as exclusively reactive and in self-defense has been challenged by critics such as Dutton (2006), who cite findings indicating that this conception is grounded in research using nonprobability samples (shelters and self-selected abused women) that are not representative of women in community probability samples, where female partners were more likely than male partners to instigate violence by "striking the first blow." Taken together, findings from the six studies he reviewed led him to conclude that women "use violence against male partners repeatedly ... for reasons other than self defense" (pp. 118–119). Dutton's challenge may not be relevant to intimate partner homicide because none of the findings he cites are about intimate partner homicide. All of them refer to nonlethal intimate partner violence.

Findings reported by other researchers indicate that some intimate partner homicides cannot easily be defined as violent resistance/self-defense. For example, Dee (2003) reports findings indicating that homicides by wives following the implementation of a new divorce law regimen were economically motivated. Belknap and associates (2012) investigated heterosexual intimate partner homicides perpetrated by a sample of 117 heterosexual homicides (1991–2009) that were recorded by the Denver Metro Domestic Violence Fatality Review Committee. In 10 homicides where motive could be discerned, only five of them were unambiguously classified as self-defense cases and three of them were motivated by "sexual proprietariness" (p. 370).

Gauthier and Bankstron (2004) selected a sample of cities with 100,000 or more residents in which 157 spousal homicides and 140 dating homicides were recorded between 1984 and 1996. The results of ordinary least squares regression indicated that cultural variables as indicated by the percentage of the population who are black and age 15–34 were strongly and positively associated with rates of femicide and homicide but more strongly associated with femicide than with homicide (p. 112). Matrilocal residence, the matriarchal family structure of disadvantaged black people, and female partner retaliation against abusive male partners were cited as reasons for the association between increases in the spousal sex ratio of killings favoring female killers and increases in the percentage of black disadvantaged households in their sample of cities. Given relatively high rates of male partner infidelity (Oliver, 2006), an unknown proportion of homicides by black female partners may have been motivated by "sexual proprietariness."

Sexual proprietariness also seems to motivate white females to kill or attempt to kill men they want to possess. For example, Ruth Ann Steinhagen shot Eddie Waitkis, who played first base for the Philadelphia Phillies baseball team. Prompt medical intervention saved Eddie's life and reduced the charge against Steinhagen from murder to attempted murder. Ruth's explanation follows.

> As time went on, I just became nuttier and nuttier about the guy. I knew I would never get to know him in the normal way, so I kept thinking. I will never get him and if I can't have him, nobody else can. Then I decided I would kill him.
> **Associated Press, 2013**

Findings indicating that black female intimate partners are as or more likely to kill their male partners than are male intimate partners are to kill their female partners have been reported by a number of authors (Block, 2000; Ellis & DeKeseredy, 1996; Mercy & Saltzman, 1989; Wilson & Daly, 1992). If high rates of black male partner sublethal violence against female partners are found to be strongly associated with homicides by black female partners, the case for classifying a significant proportion of them as self-defense homicides would be stronger.

SUMMARY

A summary of the causal mechanisms explaining the empirical generalizations that are derived from or implicit in the theories described here are presented in Table 4.1.

Table 4.1 Theories and Causal Mechanisms for the Association Between Separation and Intimate Partner Homicide

Theory	Causal Mechanism
Conflict resolution	Self-defense/miscalculation
Femicide adaptation theory	Homicide ideation
Self-defense	Fear of a violent death
Female personality	Over-controlled
Gender	Inequality
Loss of control	Encapsulation

COMMENT

The theories described here elicit a number of comments. First, Grant's theory precludes the possibility of explaining the empirical generalization—Why does intimate partner homicide vary with marital separation?—because separation is not treated as an independent variable. Specifically, choice of conflict resolution tactic—homicide or separation—was treated as the dependent variable. Encapsulation was invoked to explain the choice of homicide as a conflict resolution, but it was inferred, not directly measured by interviewing perpetrators. Two-by-two tables were used to present findings on factors influencing the choice of one of the two conflict resolution tactics. The small number of cases precludes the possibility of using multivariate statistical procedures in analyzing her data. Data on type of marital separation—female initiated/contested, female initiated not contested, male initiated/contested, and not contested—was almost certainly not available to her, and the small number of cases would make it difficult to control on even one variable, such as this one or being drunk or high at the time of the homicide, to determine its effect on choice of conflict resolution tactic if separation had been used as an independent variable.

The independence/assertiveness explanation offered by Wallace for variations in intimate partner homicide is really just another characteristic of cases where female partners use lethal violence as a means of settling conflicts with male partners, including conflicts associated with separation. Most, if not all, of the separations associated with intimate partner femicides and homicides in New South Wales were probably unilaterally initiated and contested, but the coroner and court data analyzed by Wallace do not differentiate one type of separation (e.g., unilateral male, unilateral female, or joint) from another or whether the separation actually involved the spouse or another person "who felt emotionally closest to him/her" (Block, 2000). This information does not seem to be available to researchers using official statistics (census, police, coroner, court) in any country (Block, 2000).

Browne's use of social judgment theory is creative, and findings derived from interviews with abusers revealed important information about the dynamics underlying intimate homicide. However, the contrast mechanism (turning points) she calls on to explain why some abused women killed their male partners while other abused women did not seems to be inferred rather than demonstrated even in the 11 cases she chose to describe in detail. In one case (Molly and Jim), the contrast effect was clearly revealed when Molly stated that "he had never threatened the baby [Kevin] before" but Molly also made statements revealing the presence of cues (e.g., laughing inappropriately, drinking) indicating that serious violence against her was forthcoming. Furthermore, although separation effectively discriminated abused female partners who killed their male partners from abused female partners who did not (46% of the former and only 9% of the latter were separated at the time of the homicide) and figured prominently as a precursor of intimate partner homicides, an explanation of the association between separation and intimate partner homicide was not offered. Instead, Browne presented an explanation of intimate partner homicide.

We also noted that the malign "turning points" she identified as the major reason for the difference between two groups she compared—abused female partners who experienced them killed their partners while abused female partners who did not did not kill their partners—may, to some degree, reflect the greater frequency of benign "turning points" among women who did not kill their male partners. Specifically, their partners may have accepted responsibility of their violent conduct and made a firm decision to stop the violence after participating in a court-mandated program for abusers or when they made a credible decision to leave them or following the birth of a child (Bowker, 1983, p. 123; Shaheen, Thakor, & Stewart, 2012).

Finally, Browne refers to separation as "one of the most dangerous times for partners in a violent relationship … and even discussions [of separating] and attempts to separate could set off a violent attack" (pp. 115–116). Yet, separation is not included among the seven factors distinguishing female partners who kill their abusive partners from those who do not. Perhaps all of the women in the two groups were separated and those who killed their partners were high on drugs or intoxicated at the time of the homicide.

In the conflict resolution theory formulated by Wilson and Daly (1994), coercion control-motivated and conflict-instigated violence are related to each other sequentially. The scenario they describe may well be a modal scenario in which either partner could be the perpetrator of lethal violence. However, a conflict scenario about a conflict over the *female* partner's unilateral decision to end the relationship that includes a description of specific circumstances under which a *female* partner is most likely to end the conflict by killing her male partner would make a greater contribution toward theorizing the strong association between separation and intimate partner homicide perpetrated in self-defense.

Conflict and conflict resolution (arguments and fights) and separation figure prominently in the findings reported by Easteal, but they are not integrated in a theory that explains or attempts to explain the empirical generalization. Instead, she calls on "the patriarchy" to explain wife battering, a reliable precursor of intimate partner homicide by battered women experiencing the battered women's syndrome. Her support for using the battered woman syndrome to prove self-defense in such cases represents an attempt to obtain acquittals by broadening the criteria needed to prove self-defense by battered women experiencing the syndrome who kill their batterers.

The battered woman syndrome and "learned helplessness" associated with it (Walker, 1978; Walker, 1979) have been subjected to criticism by a number of academicians and practitioners because of the adverse consequences for women who use battered woman syndrome to prove self-defense. Instead of being perceived as battered women acting reasonably in self-defense under a specific set of life- or serious injury–threatening circumstances, they tend to be perceived by judges and juries as psychologically damaged passive individuals who cannot make rational choices among the alternatives facing them or act independently, rationally, and assertively (Browne, 1987, pp. 176–177; Schecter, 1982; Schneider, 1986).

Attributes of Block's (2002) study—longitudinal study design, valid, useful, and inclusive definitions of major concepts such as marital status, aggregate- and individual-level data collection, and a relatively large sample—represent a closer approximation to an ideal case-control field study involving the selection of large samples of intimate partners who were victims and perpetrators of homicides and femicides and many years of follow-up observations than do most investigations of intimate partner homicide and femicide conducted in the United States. At the same time, it is an atheoretical study conducted with the aim of identifying risk and protective factors. It was not intended to be an investigation designed to test propositions (and melioristic interventions) derived from a deductive theory of intimate partner homicide or femicide. As a result, neither separation nor conflict is included in an integrated deductive theory of intimate partner homicide formulated by Block or by any of the other researcher/theorists whose contributions we attempted to build on in the deductive theory presented at the conclusion of this segment.

The theory formulated by Ogle and associates (1995) is noteworthy for at least three reasons. First, it is a general theory that integrates strain theory and personality theory. Second, the concept of "overcontrolled" does not refer to an outcome of extreme male partner control over female partners but rather to a female personality dimension (Megargee, 1966) associated with women's reaction to interpersonal, situational, cultural, and structural conditions and sources of strain or stress. Third, intimate partner homicide is not motivated by self-defense.

This theory is also noteworthy—but not in a good way—for treating females with a specific personality (overcontrolled) as a category rather than females who may be placed on a continuum of a self-control personality dimension as they would be if the dimension was one included in Costa and McCrae's Five Factor Personality Inventory (1992). If female partners were placed on such a continuum in this interesting and creative theory, we may find that the proportion of abused overcontrolled women in Browne's homicide sample was significantly higher than the proportion of these women in her nonhomicide abused sample and that most of the overcontrolled women killed their male partners during an outburst of explosive rage. Neither Ogle, Katkin, and Bernard nor Browne reported such findings, and Chimbos reported findings indicating that "the last fatal act was rarely sudden and explosive … but rather the end result of a long-standing series of conflicts" (1976, p. 589).

Ogle and Jacobs (2002) presented a valid and useful conception of battering as a cyclical process with a relatively long history, but their theory was not designed to explain the empirical generalization referred to in the title of this chapter. Instead, they presented a theory designed to provide a sounder basis than the battered women's syndrome for "a self defense for battered women who have killed their partners in confrontational and non-confrontational situations" (p. 6). Findings supporting their theory took the form of presenting a case study. One obvious limitation of this theory is inability to explain "separation homicides." Following Mahoney (1991), these are intimate partner homicides against nonviolent male partners who reacted with threats or attempts to kill female partners who decided to separate from them.

Jensen (2001) makes an important contribution to a conflict resolution explanation of the empirical generalization by identifying gender inequality as a societal condition that influences the manner in which conflicts are settled by female partners in general and battered women in particular. More specifically, gender inequality decreases the availability of resources that would enable battered women to safely remain in a relationship with intimate partners (Bowker, 1983) or safely leave the relationship before conflicts over separation and other issues escalated to the point where intimate partner homicide is believed to be the necessary and sufficient for survival. On the other hand, her contribution stops at this point because she does not integrate conflict resolution and separation in a theory that accounts for the strong association between separation and intimate partner homicide. Instead, her theory is deigned to explain intimate partner homicide. The aggregate homicide data she analyzes to test her theory are heir to a variety of measurement and other limitations of which she is fully aware (pp. 143–152) and Sampson (1989) has addressed.

Bourget and Gagne (2012) do not attempt to theorize the association between marital separation and intimate partner homicide. In fact, information on the marital status of perpetrators and victims was not analyzed because it was unavailable or difficult to classify (p. 613). Data collected by coroners are primarily collected with the professional interests and objectives of coroners in mind. The same considerations govern data collection by police officers. Consequently, social science researchers using police and coroner data routinely confront a "missing data" problem; that is, data of significant theoretical or practical interest to researchers are not collected or collected on a few or some cases.

Researchers Bourget and Gagne analyzed a secondary (coroner) data set that included information provided by police officers. Police officers investigating homicides in Quebec must be more diligent in collecting data on domestic violence and the marital status of perpetrators and victims than their counterparts in Toronto because our experience of collecting data from coroner files in Toronto revealed that neither the domestic violence box (yes/no) nor the marital status box was checked by investigating police officers in the majority of cases. Our experience with coroner file data suggests that the relatively low percent of female perpetrators with a past history of domestic violence reflected the investigative behavior of Quebec police officers rather than the nonviolent behavior of the male partners who were killed.

The research reviewed here demonstrates consensus on two findings. First, compared with the number of men who kill female partners who separate or try separate from them, very few women kill male partners who do or try to do the same thing. For example, 38 men (88%) and only five women (12%) killed intimate partners from which they were estranged (Easteal, 1993, p. 61). Perhaps the very small number of intimate partner homicide perpetrators accounts for the relative lack of academic interest in theorizing the *association* between marital separation and intimate partner homicide. Instead, most of the theories we described attempt to explain intimate partner homicide. The 3-fold increase in the risk of intimate partner femicides associated with separation does not appear to be accompanied by a 3-fold increase in publications devoted to explaining the association between separation and intimate partner homicide.

Second, separation, conflict, and conflict resolution—using lethal tactics in self-defense—figure prominently in the findings reported by a majority of researchers. All or most of the researchers would probably agree that conflict is endemic in relationships between intimate partners and that conflicts over the end of the relationship itself are likely to be far more intense and "dysfunctional" (i.e., involve the mutual use of violent conflict resolution tactics) than are conflicts over other issues (Coser, 1956, pp. 73–74; Wilson & Daly, 1992).

Based on the theory and research reviewed here, we identify "fear of a violent death" in the specific context of intense conflict over the female partner's unilateral decision to separate as the mechanism underlying the association between separation and intimate partner homicides committed in self-defense.

DISCUSSION QUESTIONS

1. Critically evaluate the definition of intimate partner homicide as self-defense using the criteria of validity and utility.
2. Compare and evaluate causal mechanisms explaining the association between separation and intimate partner homicide that can be derived from Brown's "social judgment theory" and Ogle and Jacobs' "new social interaction theory."
3. The causal mechanism underlying the association between separation and intimate partner homicide is "encapsulation." Discuss.
4. Evaluate this statement: Fear of a violent death is the causal mechanism explaining the association between separation and intimate partner homicides committed in self-defense. Do you agree or disagree? Give reasons for your answer.

Separation and Intimate Partner Femicide

CHAPTER 5

LEARNING OBJECTIVES

Readers of this chapter who achieve the learning objectives set for it will be able to:

- Demonstrate awareness of how deductive theory can be used to identify causal mechanisms that explain the association between separation and intimate partner homicide
- Derive different causal mechanisms accounting for the association between separation and intimate partner femicide from the two evolutionary psychological theories of intimate partner femicide described in this chapter
- Derive different causal mechanisms underlying the association between separation and intimate partner femicide from the patriarchy and conflict resolution theories described in this chapter
- Demonstrate awareness of choosing/using different self-help and third party methods of settling conflicts over separation to intimate partner femicide during and after separation

The primary objective of this chapter is to derive a deductive theoretical explanation of the association between separation and intimate partner femicide from one or more of the theories that are frequently used to interpret findings on this association. Specifically, we reviewed evolutionary psychological, patriarchy, and conflict resolution with a view to discovering whether a testable deductive theory could be derived from them.

EVOLUTIONARY PSYCHOLOGICAL THEORY

Buss (2002) conceives of evolutionary psychology as a discipline grounded in the following "core premises":

1. Manifest behavior depends on underlying psychological mechanisms … in conjunction with external and internal inputs that trigger their activation.
2. Evolution by selection is the only known causal process capable of creating such complex mechanisms.
3. Evolved psychological mechanisms are functionally specialized to solve adaptive problems that recurred for humans over deep evolutionary time.
4. Selection designed the information processing of many evolved psychological mechanisms to be adaptively influenced by specific classes of information from the environment.

5. Human psychology consists of a large number of functionally specialized evolved mechanisms, each sensitive to particular forms of contextual input that get combined, coordinated, and integrated with each other to produce manifest behavior.

The opening segment of this chapter will be devoted to describing two evolutionary psychological theories that have been used to explain the association between separation and intimate partner femicide. Acceptance of the core premises identified by Buss is evident in the publications of theorists who created the two theories. Their publications also reveal acceptance of the following fundamental criterion or "only requirement" for their evolutionary psychological explanations of recurring contemporary behavior: "The same behavior in ancestral times assisted the survival of genes promoting it" (Dawkins, 2009, p. 400). At the same time, Duntley and Buss (2008), who formulated the homicide adaptation theory (HAT), and Wilson and Daly, who formulated an evolutionary by-product ("male sexual proprietariness"; MSP) hypothesis, identify different evolved psychological information processing mechanisms motivating the use of femicide as a solution for adaptive problems facing our ancestors. That is to say, they accept premise 1, but identify different evolved psychological mechanisms.

THE BY-PRODUCT HYPOTHESIS

In 1979, Stephen Jay Gould and Richard Lewontin published a paper entitled "The Spandrels of San Marco and the Panglossian Paradigm: A Critique of the Adaptationist Paradigm." In this paper, a spandrel was defined as "a secondary epiphenomenon" (p. 584). An evolutionary phenomenon is any behavior or biological feature such as wings on birds "that is selected for by the process of natural selection." An epiphenomenon is any behavior or biological attribute that is a by-product of an evolutionary phenomenon. The former is directly selected; the latter is indirectly selected (Gould, 1992, pp. 124–138). Daly and Wilson (1988) define coercive violence against females by their male partners as a by-product of cognitions underlying the evolved psychological mechanism they refer to as "MSP" (pp. 12–13).

MSP refers to "an encompassing mind-set … and a pervasive attitude" toward relationships in which intimate female partners are thought of as property men are entitled to own in the same way that slave owners were entitled to own slaves, parents are entitled to own children, and Marxian capitalists were entitled to own the instruments of production. Men are sexually proprietary in their relations with women. Specifically, they tend to think of women as sexual and reproductive "property" they own and can exchange. Violations of MSP rights are associated with a state of emotional arousal defined as "sexual jealousy." Wilson and Daly (1992, p. 302) define sexual jealousy as "the state of being concerned that one's sexual exclusivity is or might be violated" (1992, p. 302). Institutions and cultural norms and practices reinforce MSP in male–female relationships generally and in male–female intimate partner relationships in particular.

The information-processing psychological mechanism (MSP) that motivates coercive control violence against female partners today evolved among our ancestors because it was a specialized functional solution (adaptation) to specific recurring problems they faced. Desertion by female partners was one of the recurring problems faced by our male ancestors. Desertion was significant for them because it negatively impacted their reproductive success. Specifically, it entailed not only "the total loss of [current] reproductively relevant resources" but also future opportunities to acquire new reproductive resources because desertion decreased the chances of obtaining another female partner. Additionally, it resulted in a loss of status among men (Kaighobadi & Shackleford, 2009).

Infidelity was another recurring problem faced by our male ancestors because of "paternity uncertainty." Unlike our female ancestors who knew that the children they gave birth to were theirs (maternity certainty), fathers can never be certain that the children they are helping care for and control are really their offspring (paternity uncertainty). The emotion of male sexual jealousy solves the problem of paternity uncertainty by "preventing partner infidelity and outright desertion" through deterrence (Kaighobadi & Shackleford, 2009). Deterrence is a function of the anticipated severity of punishment—silent treatment, confinement in the dwelling, threats of violence, assaults resulting in minor injuries, assaults resulting in major injuries, and (albeit rarely), femicide—multiplied by the certainty of being punished. Effective deterrence results in paternity certainty or a relatively close approximation to it. Consequently, it serves the evolutionary end of reproductive success.

For Wilson and Daly, the inclusion of femicide among the sanctions administered by male partners is "paradoxical" because it is simultaneously conceived of as a serving and not serving the evolutionary end of inclusive fitness. As a "manifestation of proprietariness" that is motivated by jealousy—"If I Can't Have You No One Can" (Wilson & Daly, 1992, p. 86)—femicide serves the end of inclusive fitness. As "dysfunctionally extreme by-products" and "overreactive mistakes" of an evolved psychological mechanism (MSP) that "overstepped the bounds of utility" (Daly & Wilson, 1988, pp. 12–13; Wilson & Daly, 1992, p. 93), femicides may serve the end of demonstrating male domination but not the end of inclusive fitness.

Research

In a segment entitled "Wives as Commodities," Daly and Wilson (1998) cited historical and cross-national evidence indicating that (1) wives were commodities exchanged by men (p. 188), (2) marriage entails the acquisition of proprietary rights to a woman's reproductive capacity (p. 190), and (3) a "reasonable man" who was provoked by his wife's adultery was justified (legally excused) in killing her (pp. 193–194), especially when he was actually witnessing it. None of the evidence cited was directly related to desertion that, like infidelity, also entails a loss of control over the wife's reproductive capacity.

"Conjugal Jealousy and Violence Around the World" was also investigated by Daly and Wilson. Specifically, "all societies they could find with a sample of homicides" were studied. They found that "most [spousal homicides] arise out of the husband's jealous, proprietary, violent response to his wife's [real or imagined] infidelity or desertion" (p. 202). Our review of the evidence they cited indicates that males kill partners who have left, are leaving, or are suspected of wanting to leave, but a minority of them were motivated by jealousy-possessiveness (13 of 59 in one study, 11 of 32 in another. No motive was stated for the 34 spousal homicide cases in four aboriginal Indian societies) (pp. 202–203).

In a third research segment, Daly and Wilson reported findings on "spousal homicide and sexual jealousy" in Philadelphia, Miami, Detroit, and Canada. In Philadelphia, conflict resolution was the most frequently attributed motive for intimate partner homicides, with jealousy being the most frequently identified source of conflicts that were settled by homicide (Wolfgang, 1958).

Daly, Wilson, and Weghorst (1982) investigated 58 sexual jealousy conflicts leading to homicide in Detroit in 1972. Of the 690 homicides recorded in 1972, 512 were closed (solved) cases. Sixty-six percent ($n = 339$) of the closed cases were coded as "social conflict homicides" and 17% ($n = 58$) were coded as "jealousy conflicts." Forty of the 58 cases were found to be "love triangle" cases. In the remaining 18 cases, 16 jealous men killed their female intimate partners, one jealous female killed a male partner, and one jealous person killed his/her partner because he/she had "taken exception to the other's terminating the relationship" (p. 15). If it is reasonable to assume that some or many of the 40 love triangle killers believed that their female partners were thinking or planning to leave them for the men they were sexually involved with, then sexual jealousy elicited by suspected impending desertion was not a potent cause of conflict settled by homicide because this happened in only one case.

In 1984, Wilbanks published findings based on his analysis of 526 homicides and 43 spousal homicides recorded in Miami during 1980. Conflict resolution was the motive attributed to 17 of the 43 spousal homicides and male sexual jealousy was the motive attributed the 17 of them, with female sexual jealousy as the motive attributed to four cases. Other motives were attributed to the remaining five cases. No findings were reported identifying male sexual jealousy as the motive for killing wives who had separated or were suspected of wanting to separate. Other findings reported by Wilbanks (pp. 37–40) suggest that wives were far more likely to settle conflicts over separation in the same way they settled conflicts over other issues—by killing husbands who were intoxicated at the time. The ratio of conflict-instigated homicides to femicides was 6:1 (p. 172).

Between 1974 and 1983, investigating police officers attributed motives for 1,006 spousal homicides that were recorded in Canada during this period. Conflict resolution (arguments escalating to homicide) accounted for 51% ($n = 513$). More than two-thirds (69%) of the perpetrators were male partners, with the motive of jealousy was attributed to 21% ($n = 214$). This finding indicates that the motive of jealousy was attributed to approximately one-fifth of the conflict-settling spousal homicides for which motives were attributed (Daly et al., 1982, p. 198). The fraction of jealous husbands who settled conflicts over separation by the killing wives who initiated the conflicts was not reported. It was reported by Dobash, Dobash, Cavanagh, and Medina-Ariza (2007).

Dobash et al. (2007) found jealousy-possessiveness to be the motive/attitude that differentiated 122 males convicted of a nonlethal violent crime against a female intimate partner from 106 males convicted of murdering a female intimate partner. They also found that although this motive/attitude "… was an important source of conflict for lethal violence, it did not constitute the source of conflict in a considerable proportion [about two-thirds] of the murders" (p. 16).

In 1992, Campbell published the results of her investigation of police files on all homicides "involving women as either perpetrator or victim" ($n = 73$) occurring in Dayton, Ohio, between January 1974 and December 1979. Fifty-seven cases involving spouse killers (28 male and 29 female) were analyzed. She presents findings indicating that none of the women were killed because *they* were jealous, but that 18 of the 28 male killers were motivated by jealousy (1992, p. 105), with one extremely jealous perpetrator stating, "If I can't have you, no one can." This finding was interpreted as supporting the "jealousy connotes ownership" (MSP) hypothesis formulated by Daly et al. (1982). However, we do not know how many of the 18 perpetrators of intimate partner femicide were jealous because of their partner's infidelity—another man was controlling or suspected of controlling their reproductive capacity—or because of their actual or suspected desertion—losing control of their reproductive capacity.

Campbell's findings were based on the attributions of motives by the investigating police officers. Adams (2007) actually interviewed 31 men convicted of murdering their female partners. He reports findings indicating that 42% ($n = 13$) were motivated by jealous rage (p. 41). Although homicides generally and femicides in particular are motivated by a variety of factors (Dobash et al., 2007), only one motive—jealousy—was attributed by police officers in the Campbell study. Wolfgang (1958) also studied police attributions of motive. The findings he reported indicated that conflict resolution was the most frequently attributed motive for homicide. Jealousy was the third most frequently attributed motive after "altercations" and "quarrels."

Based on their review of a number of studies, including their own 1994 study, Wilson and Daly concluded that the ranking of motives reported by Wolfgang are supported by findings reported in "many studies" using police attributions of motives as the source of data (1992, pp. 86–87). Collectively, they provide evidence indicating that possessiveness/jealousy is the primary motive for femicide (pp. 88–89). However, our review of the same studies does not support the conclusion that jealousy was the only—or even the primary—motive for femicide. Examples are given in the following paragraphs.

In Guttmacher's (1955) study, "pathological jealousy" is referred to as an "apparent motivational factor" for only four of 36 killers of female partners he interviewed. Femicides perpetrated by 25 of the 41 males were, according to Wilson and Daly, "motivated by sexual proprietariness" because promiscuity and actual or suspected adultery were identified as apparent motives. Guttmacher's findings are presented ambiguously but he did not subsume killings preceded by promiscuity and adultery as indicators of jealousy—pathological, morbid, or amorous.

Findings cited by Chimbos (1978) are also interpreted as supporting MSP. Chimbos identified "sexual matters" (infidelity and refusals) as the source of conflicts resulting in femicide by 29 of 34 male partners (29 men and five women). Unfortunately, he did not identify the gender of the spouses having or suspected of having affairs. As a result, we do not know how many of the conflicts that resulted in the murder of female partners were preceded by the promiscuity of *male* partners.

Empirical support for the Wilson and Daly hypothesis that males who kill their female partners of reproductive age are motivated by possessiveness/jealousy would appear to be provided by the authors of the Annual Report (2011) of the Oklahoma Domestic Violence Fatality Review Board. Findings presented in this report are based on the analysis of 1,000 homicides identified as domestic violence homicides by the Domestic Violence Fatality Review Board. Forty-three percent of the perpetrators were reported to have been motivated by "morbid jealousy" (p. 6). Morbid jealousy was indicated by "the behavior and words" of the perpetrators before the homicide. The behavior and words of the perpetrators may have revealed *why* they were morbidly jealous, but if they did, this information was not revealed in the Annual Report. Consequently, we do not know how many of the 434 (43%) perpetrators were morbidly jealous because of the actual or suspected infidelity of their female partners compared with the number of perpetrators who were morbidly jealous because their partners were leaving or suspected of wanting to leave them.

Using the method of "retrospective case review," the Denver Metro Domestic Fatality Review Committee (2012) collected data on 117 analyzed cases of heterosexual intimate partner homicide that were closed between 1991 and 2009. Thirteen of these cases were intimate partner homicides (females killing males). Belknap, Larson, Abrams, Garcia, and Anderson-Block (2012) found that sexual jealousy was not included among the multiple sources—"newspaper articles, medical examiner records, police reports and court documents"—that were reviewed by Denver Metro Domestic Fatality Review Committee staff.

Johnson and Hotton (2003) investigated all homicides reported by police forces in Canada between 1991 and 2000. In a table describing characteristics of the sample, Johnson and Dawson (2011) report findings indicating that jealousy was the motive attributed to more than one-fifth (22.9%) of the male and female perpetrators by investigating police officers. Police attributions varied with gender, with jealous motivation being attributed to less than one-tenth of the females who killed male partners and more than one-quarter (26.4%) of the males who killed their female partners. When jealousy plus four other variables were entered into a logistic regression model, jealousy was found to be a statistically significant predictor of homicide by estranged male partners but not male partners in intact intimate partner relationships (partial odds ratio = 2.961). These findings indicated to the researchers that jealousy was gendered and that it is an important motive for femicide by estranged male partners. At the same time, the findings show that the motive of jealousy elicited by desertion was attributed to just over one-quarter of the men who killed their female partners. Moreover, no findings were reported indicating that females of reproductive ages were overrepresented among victims of jealousy-over-separation femicides.

Data from the same source (Canadian police officer attributions) but covering a longer period were analyzed by the authors of this book. We obtained a special run bivariate table (jealousy by femicide) from the Centre for Justice Statistics, Ottawa, for a 37-year period (1974–2012). During this period, 2,586 wives were murdered by their husbands and jealousy was the motive attributed by investigating police officers to the killers of 24% (n = 609) of the victims and not attributed to 76% of male perpetrators of femicide. The comparable figure for male perpetrators reported by Johnson and Hotton was 73.6%. The range of homicides motivated by jealousy varied from a low of 9% (7 of 76) in 1982 to a high of 33% (28 of 84) in 1983.

These findings raise two questions. First, how would MSP account for significant yearly variations in the number of men reported to experience such extreme jealousy over infidelity or separations initiated by their female partners that they kill them? Also, in any given year, why do only a small minority of men experience such extreme jealousy over separation or infidelity that they respond by killing female partners (Koziol-McLain et al., 2006, p. 19)?

Campbell, Webster, and Glass (2009) included the question "Is he violently and constantly jealous of you?" in the Revised 20 Item Danger Assessment (DA). This instrument was used to assess how effectively risk factors in the DA predicted intimate partner femicide in 310 cases compared with predicting the same outcome among 324 abused women residing in the same 11 U.S. cities. The DA was reported to have "accurately identified the vast majority of abused women who are at increased risk of femicide or attempted femicide as well as distinguish most of the IPV (intimate partner violence) cases that are at lowest risk of femicide or attempted femicide" (p. 669). Specifically, an impressive "90% of the cases were included in the area under the receiver operating characteristic (ROC) curve" (p. 653). No findings were reported indicating the strength of the association between "violent/constant jealousy" and intimate partner femicides associated with separation.

Based on the findings from a stepwise logistic regression, Snider, Webster, O'Sullivan, and Campbell (2009) included five items from the DA in a shortened version that included the question: "Is he violently and constantly jealous of you?" The shortened DA was used to predict "participants (in the sample) experiencing severe or potentially fatal assault during a nine-month follow-up period." They found that "violently and constantly jealous" did increase the odds of experiencing this outcome (OR 3.0, CI 95%, $p < 0.028$) and that 79 of the cases were included under the ROC curve (pp. 1212–1213). However, because a "yes" answer to *any three* questions was used to locate women in the high-risk category, we have no way of knowing how frequently "violently/constantly jealous" was included among the three questions. Moreover, the marital status of the female subjects located in the highest risk groups was not identified. Consequently, neither study provides strong support for the MSP explanation of the association between separation and femicide.

Finally, findings reported by Baker, Gregware, and Cassidy (1999), the European Parliament (2007), and Kandiyoti (1988) indicate that sexual jealousy/possessiveness cannot explain "family honor restoration" killings in traditional collectivistic patriarchal societies that are associated with the desertion and/or sexuality infidelity of wives/mothers because the killers tend not to be husbands but relatives—brothers, fathers—of the victims. Not infrequently, the killings are also motivated by retribution for damaging the marital prospects of her siblings—sons and daughters in the natal families of the victims.

Findings reviewed by Baker et al. (1999, p. 192) led them to the following conclusion: "In traditional honor killings … a husband's feelings of jealousy do not justify the murder of his wife" because (citing Kressel, 1981, p. 143) "the individual motivation of the (husband) is secondary;" … "the wife's family of origin bears the responsibility for (punishing/killing her) because her actions have brought shame on them and they are obligated to avenge the honor of their family" (Schneider, 1971). In short, traditional honor killings are collective projects in which the wife's male relatives do the killings; mothers and sisters are complicit in them and the local community supports them.

Our review of the research presented here yields three conclusions. First, MSP cannot explain traditional honor killings in collectivistic patriarchal societies. Second, the MSP hypothesis was not adequately tested because both motive (jealousy) and a "pervasive attitude" (proprietariness) were not measured, and specific design conditions for separation-associated femicides were not identified (Duntley & Buss, 2008).

Second, that femicide frequently follows shortly after separation may be interpreted as supporting the MSP hypothesis (Koziol-Mclain et al., 2006, p. 5), but findings reported by Ellis (2014) suggest an alternative explanation for the temporal association.

Third, when the motive of male sexual jealousy is used as an indicator of MSP, support for male sexual jealousy as the causal mechanism underlying the association between separation and femicide is not consistently strong. An alternative causal mechanism for which there is allegedly stronger supporting evidence has been identified by evolutionary theorists Buss and Duntley.

FEMICIDE ADAPTATION THEORY

According to evolutionary psychologists Buss and Duntley (2011), our ancestors were born to kill other human beings because they had to solve "adaptive problems for which murder was one effective solution" (p. 400). They ground their claim in adaptive logic. Homicide was an effective solution because in the specific recurring contexts in which homicide occurred, "the fitness benefits outweighed the fitness costs" (2011, p. 400). As a result, humans today "possess adaptations designed specifically for killing conspecifics (other human beings)" (Duntley & Buss, 2008, p. 43). All humans may possess these adaptations, but they do not kill other humans all the time—only sometimes. Moreover, compared with humans who use sublethal violence against other humans, relatively few humans use lethal violence against other human beings. The HAT formulated by Buss and Duntley (2205, 2008, 2011) explains "why sometimes" and "why very few."

Femicide adaptation theory (FAT) is the name we gave to the Duntley and Buss application of adaptive logic to the problem of explaining why intimate partner femicides are associated with female partner infidelity and desertion. The starting point of FAT is the evolved emotion of love. The evolution of love by selection inculcated in the brains of our ancestors' "psychological circuits" that motivated commitment to the long-term biparental care and control of their offspring. The survival of their genes was the reproductive payoff for ancestral moms and dads who were committed to each other and to investing significant resources in child rearing. Love, in short, solved the problem of commitment to a mate through good times and bad. Good times of mutual love, respect, caring, and sharing were a protective factor against "femicide mechanisms dormant in men." Bad times included times when these mechanisms were likely to be expressed in action, such as when "involved incentives to cheat" with men and women who were more attractive, healthier, less boring, and fitter than their regular mates.

Several benefits accrue to female partners who cheat with men who are usually younger, stronger, and fitter than their current male partners (Buss, 2005, pp. 78–83). These include producing children with better genes, that is, children with genes that increase their inclusive fitness. At the same time, cuckoldry is dangerous because "evolution works by differential reproduction … [and] selection can favor killing a mate who has been unfaithful … in certain circumstances" (p. 83).

In addition to female partner infidelity, desertion by female partners is one of the circumstances that most powerfully predicts "men's recurrent, persistent thoughts about killing their romantic partners" (p. 89). Evolved *femicide ideation* is selected for all men, but only a few of the men actually kill female partners who desert them. These are men who:

- personally catch their partners having sex with another man;
- are intoxicated during conflicts with their partners over their desertion or perceived intention to desert them;
- are between ages 20 and 49;
- are far younger than their female partners;
- have recently separated from their female partners; or
- who believe or know their female partners are deserting them for another man.

Having answered two interesting questions—why sometimes and why only a few men—Buss and Duntley proceed to demonstrate adaptation for intimate partner femicide by describing the specific circumstances (specific design features) under which dormant psychological mechanisms for intimate partner femicide are activated (Buss, 2005). These include:

- desertion or infidelity of female partners;
- absence of close kin of the wife who may retaliate;

- no biological children from the marriage;
- desertion or infidelity entails a significant decrease in status for the male partners who are dumped; and
- wives in reproductive age groups.

In sum, FAT theory proposes that "All men have evolved a psychology of mate killing that lies latent in their brains ... [and that] for many men the psychology never gets activated because they never face the relevant adaptive problems of infidelity or desertion and not in a way that triggers [femicidal] intent" (p. 98).

Unlike Daly and Wilson, who state that the killing of wives who desert their male partners is maladaptive—that is, it terminates their contribution to genetic posterity—FAT identifies circumstances under which femicides are adaptive—the benefits outweigh the burdens or evolutionary costs. In these recurring circumstances, femicide is not a by-product of other evolved psychological mechanisms (such as MSP) among humans. Instead, our human ancestors acquired specific adaptations for killing female partners who desert their male partners when killing them:

- restored honor and social standing lost by their desertion and thereby increased their ability to attract and marry younger virgins who will make a greater contribution to genetic posterity by producing more of his offspring;
- served to ensure the reproduction of their offspring by the wives they remarried because they would be deterred from deserting them; or
- no agnatic kin of the wives were around to retaliate by killing them and thereby terminating their contribution to genetic posterity (Buss, 2005, pp. 83–85).

Research

An evolved psychological mechanism (femicide and homicide ideation) for femicide and homicide requires the universal presence of these two types of lethal violence in human societies. Findings reported by Buss (2005, pp. 6–8, 25–34), anthropologists Fry and Soderberg (2013), and psychologist Pinker (2011, pp. 49–53) indicate that homicide and femicide were universally present and occurred relatively frequently in prehistorical human hunter-gatherer societies. Based on criteria used by other researchers in classifying/rating societies, they selected a sample of 21 Mobile Foraging Band Societies for study. They found that close to two-thirds ($n = 97$) of the 148 killings they recorded were cases in which homicide and femicide were used to settle interpersonal conflicts and that "[m]any of these conflicts involved two men competing over a particular woman sometimes the wife of one of them" and in 6% of the cases "husbands killed their wives" (pp. 271–272).

Buss hypothesized that femicide aimed at preventing desertion and infidelity that was adaptive, led him to believe that it resulted in the emergence of the evolved psychological mechanism of femicide ideation. Because it was adaptive for our human ancestors, femicide ideation is present but dormant in the brains of men today. As femicide ideation among our human ancestors could not be measured, Buss conducted laboratory experiments aimed at demonstrating the presence of homicide and femicide ideation "in the brains of men today." Durrant reviewed the evidence and concluded that it was not compelling because it did not demonstrate that femicide/homicide ideation only occurred when research subjects were asked to place themselves *in those specific circumstances* (emphasis added) predicted by FAT to reliably elicit it (2009, p. 377).

Durrant found "very little evidence" supporting the idea that hypothesized "psychological" adaptations for *homicide* possess the kinds of special design features that might indicate they have been selected for and more evidence supporting the hypothesis that the proposed psychological adaptations for *intimate partner femicide* after separation possess the kind of special design features that might indicate they were selected for (p. 377). Identification of specific design contexts that activate femicide after separation and those that activate nonlethal violence have the potential for making a positive contribution to the cumulative development of an evolutionary explanation of lethal and nonlethal male partner violence after separation. Realization of the potential depends upon the identification of an evidence-based specific design context for *both* lethal and nonlethal violence by FAT theorists.

PATRIARCHY THEORY

Dobash and Dobash (1979) define "the patriarchy" as a set of interrelated, differentiated, and hierarchically organized set of social institutions (societal structure) that define and maintain the subordination of women generally and wives in particular. Institutions are hierarchically organized, with men occupying top positions from which women are excluded. A gender ideology legitimating this arrangement accompanies it (p. 43). In the institution of the family, "physical violence against wives … is one of the most brutal and explicit expressions of patriarchal domination" (p. ix). Their theory of the patriarchy is a dual-focus one in the sense that it focuses simultaneously on husbands as perpetrators of wife battering and unhelpful community reactions to battering by agents of the criminal justice system, the medical profession, social workers, neighbors, friends, and relatives who are also influenced by the legacy of patriarchy.

Separations, battering, homicides—the legacy of patriarchal domination/control over wives—plus unhelpful third-party reactions are referred to in *Violence Against Women* (1979), but these concepts are not interrelated in a way that explains the empirical generalization linking separation with femicide. The deductive logical explanation of it that appears to be *implicit* in their theory of the patriarchy is that:

- battering eventually leads to permanent separations initiated by female partners partly on the basis of the increasing severity of the injuries inflicted and/or threats or violence against children and partly on the basis of advice ("leave him") given by otherwise unhelpful third parties;
- separation represents the ultimate challenge to male partner domination; and
- the ultimate expression of patriarchal domination to the ultimate challenge by a formerly subordinate wife is femicide.

Johnson and Dawson (2011) conclude that patriarchy as theorized by Dobash and Dobash (1979) and Walby (1990) "was central to early feminist theorizing" (p. 27). This conclusion is not warranted for two reasons. First, patriarchy remains at the heart of the contemporary "replacement" theories they refer to, such as "role theory," "feminist theory," and "feminist perspective," which have allegedly rendered redundant the patriarchy as an explanation of sublethal and lethal male partner violence against female partners (Hunnicutt, 2009, p. 553). Second, patriarchy is central to *contemporary* feminist theorizing on family honor killings (Welchan & Hossain, 2005). Contemporary feminist patriarchy theories of family honor killings advance earlier theorizing on patriarchy in a number of ways.

First, the concept of family honor is used to legitimate male (and female stepmother) domination of wives/mothers and daughters. Second, the strength of the association between patriarchal domination and its expression in the killings of women varies cross-culturally with the association between the patriarchy and women killing being strongest in societies with traditional, collectivistic, patriarchal cultures, and the acquisition of economic and other valued resources that flow from killing of women who demonstrate a lack of commitment to core value of family honor. In other words, material interests of men are also satisfied by killings perpetrated in the name of honor (Welchan & Hossain, 2005, p. 69).

Second, the patriarchy incorporates MSP (wives are property that are owned and can be exchanged by their husbands and also by agnatic kin in patrilineal societies) and Masculinities theory (hypermasculine husbands and fathers who rule their households are more likely to kill less masculine/more feminized sons who demonstrate a lack of commitment to the core value of family honor than hypermasculinized sons who demonstrate the same lack of commitment) (Marsiglio & Pleck, 2005).

Third, patriarchal domination that is expressed in family honor killings includes men (sons, brothers, uncles) and women (daughters, wives, mothers) as participants or perpetrators and as victims who may also be members of different class, ethnic, regional, religion, and lesbian, gay, bisexual, transgender, and queer groups.

Fourth, situational factors included in contemporary theories of patriarchy, such as the ties the family has with high-status third parties who support lesser types of punishment than killing (e.g., beaten, warned) help explain variations in the reactions of family members and agnatic kin to sons, daughters, mothers, and wives who demonstrate, or are suspected of demonstrating, a lack of commitment to the core family value of honor (Cooney, 2011).

Fifth, patriarchal domination that results in family honor killings is not merely condoned but actively supported by the local communities in which they occur (Welchan & Hossain, 2005).

Sixth, contemporary theorizing of patriarchy identifies the restoration of family honor as an explanation for the strong association between separation/divorces that bring dishonor to the family and family honor killings in societies with traditional, collectivistic, patriarchal cultures (European Parliament, 2007; Kulwicki, 2002).

Hunnicutt (2009) attempted to "stretch and reshape (the patriarchy) to bring it in line with contemporary intellectual developments … by broadening the scope of theorizing" (pp. 554 & 556). A broadened theory of patriarchy would include five key components (pp. 554–555), but none of them explains why separation is associated with femicide. However, an explanation does appear to be implicit in Hunnicutt's response to the following recurring criticism of patriarchy—"its failure to help us understand why only a few men use violence against women in societies characterized as patriarchal." The implicit explanation states that use of violence by male partners to establish or maintain dominance varies inversely with positions of dominance they hold in other, nonfamily institutions (p. 560). Male partners holding no position of dominance in any other institution are more likely than males who hold dominant positions in one or more other institutions to use violence "to reinforce ... the only position of domination available to them," that is, domination against wives who also do not hold positions of domination in any other institution. The resentment against superordinates in other institutions is compounded by resentment against wives who leave them with no position of dominance in the only institution in which they were dominant—their families. "Resentments are transformed into misogyny" (p. 560) and women who are hated for leaving their partners in this predicament are killed by them.

Research

In addition to historical evidence from European (mainly English) history, Dobash and Dobash (1979) reported findings from interviews with a nonrandom sample of 109 battered wives who were residents in shelters for battered women. They also reported "learning a great deal more about violence in the home" by perusing 34,000 police reports to discover and analyze all domestic violence incidents included in them. The number of domestic violence incidents they actually analyzed was not reported. Femicides (pp. 15–16) and separations (a pattern of leaving and returning) (p. 144) were reported, but no findings on the association between these two variables was reported. A few of the women in the sample—number not stated—left permanently. The process of leaving permanently and permanent separation may have increased the seriousness of injuries inflicted on the wives who left, but these findings were not reported by Dobash and Dobash. In short, they did not report any findings that could be used to test the implicit theory we derived from their theory of the patriarchy.

Qualitative (case file) data on the thoughts (cognitions) of 104 incarcerated men before and after the murder of their female intimate partners were analyzed by Dobash and Dobash using QSR/NVivo. One of the nodes identified by this qualitative software package was "possessiveness, jealousy, estrangement, and separation" (p. 14). These appear to be interrelated in the following way: Unilateral separations by wives instigate conflict and arouse fear, anger, and "heightened possessiveness and jealousy" that motivate men to kill their estranged intimate partners (2010, p. 14). Quantitative findings on the 104 incarcerated men in this subsample indicate that femicide was not motivated by jealousy-possessiveness for 72% ($n = 75$) of them (Dobash, Dobash, & Cavanagh, 2009). Moreover, neither study revealed how many of the 29 (28%) perpetrators of jealousy-possessiveness femicides were separated or in the process of separating at the time. These findings do not provide unequivocal support for jealousy-possessiveness as a causal mechanism underlying the association between separation and femicide. They do support the finding that conflict mediates the effect of separation on femicide (p. 212).

Like Wilson and Daly, Dobash and Dobash identify conflict as the context for femicide. Unlike Wilson and Daly, they identify a greater variety of sources of conflict between intimate partners that eventuate in femicide (Dobash et al., 2007). Following Wilson and Daly, jealousy-possessiveness and desertion are linked by Dobash and Dobash. In their more recent publications, findings supporting linkages among separation, jealousy-possessiveness, and femicide are interpreted as supporting a feminist perspective under which the patriarchy can be subsumed. Thus, a feminist analysis suggested to Dobash et al. (2009) that the incarcerated perpetrators of femicide they studied devalued women, objectified them, and treated them as property and that "the wider social (patriarchal) context" justified/legitimated the murder of their intimate partners (p. 217). However, the patriarchal attitudes of inmates who killed and did not kill their intimate partners were not measured. Moreover, evidence based on the meta-analysis of more than 70 studies indicated that between 1970 and 1995 attitudes had changed in the direction of becoming decreasingly patriarchal and increasingly feminist (Twenge, 1997). Specifically, "the attitudes of men in the 1990s were more feminist than those of the women in the 1970s" (Pinker, 2011, p. 404).

Sev'er (1997), a theorist who seeks the roots of male partner in the patriarchy (p. 571) and who hypothesizes that female-initiated separations "challenge the foundation of the male bastion: his power and control in the home" (pp. 571–572), investigated the association between separation and intimate partner femicide by analyzing data collected from "interviews with 11 divorced women and survivors of intimate violence and four femicides (by estranged husbands) reported in the media" (p. 566). She does not explicitly say how many women she interviewed or how many media reports were perused. The numbers reported here are based on our counts. Sev'er interprets the findings from the four media femicide reports as supporting the hypothesis that "recent or imminent" separations represent a challenge to patriarchal control and femicide is a response to this challenge (p. 581). Evidence based on "four media femicide reports" tends to be less persuasive than evidence based on the analysis of a larger randomly selected sample of cases.

Established in Massachusetts in 1977, EMERGE is the longest-running Batterer Intervention (Through Education) programs in the United States. During the 15 years he served as co-director of Emerge, Lundy Bancroft (2002) reports "accumulating a wealth of knowledge from the 2,000 or more cases I was involved in" (p. xvii). One of the things he learned was that abusive male partners are "jealous and possessive" and that their abuse was far more strongly associated with patriarchal attitudes than with emotional feelings of attachment. The inductive theory of male partner abuse he created was also grounded in the knowledge he acquired. The essentials of his inductive theory are described using the metaphor of a tree in which "the roots (of abuse) are in ownership, the trunk is entitlement, and the branches are control" (p. 75). Roots, trunk, and branches are threatened by unilateral female partner decisions to separate, and femicide is a reaction to the threat. Support for this hypothesis is undermined by the fact that Bancroft did not report findings revealing how many of the abusive male partners who attempted to kill their separating/separated female partners expressed extreme patriarchal attitudes compared with abusive male partners who did not kill or seriously injure female partners who were leaving or had left them.

After noting that abused women face a "particularly high risk of homicide or attempted homicide" after separation (p. 219), Bancroft reports an interesting finding about separation. The finding is that for an abusive male partner, "the relationship is over when [he] says it is over" and he decides "it is over" only when "he no longer wishes to be back with his female partner." Until that time comes, he still thinks he owns her and is therefore entitled to control her generally and specifically her relationships with other men. Femicide is a reaction against female partners who seriously challenge male partner ownership by clearly indicating that the separation is permanent (e.g., start formal separation or divorce proceedings or moving in with another man) regardless of his wishes, wants, or needs.

Family honor killings tend to occur most frequently in traditional, collectivistic, northern rural regions of India characterized by patrilocal residence and the presence of *khap panchayats* convened at the behest of family members. The actual killers who enforce compliance with family honor norms are usually agnates. The paradigmatic honor killing case is one in which "(angry) fathers and brothers kill their most beloved, their daughters and sisters (who were never allowed to be alone and/or uncovered in public)" (King, 2008). In the Indian states of Punjab, Haryana, Bihar, and Uttar Pradesh, angry husbands, brothers, and uncles also kill sons, wives, mothers, and fathers, and mothers kill their daughters (Bhargava et al., 2012). The killers are angry, in a rage, because marrying a member of the same subcaste (*gotra*), premarital sex, and especially extramarital sex are dishonorable deviations that require killing the deviants as a necessary and sufficient condition for the restoration of family honor (Civil Service India, 2012).

Separation and divorce are also included among the risk factors for family honor killings (Bhargava, Chand, Ranjan, & Pratyush, 2013). However, female-initiated separations and divorces are relatively rare in patrilineal societies because they entail:

- loss of a highly valued social (married) status;
- separation from their children, who belong to the fathers;
- the repayment of bride-wealth;
- placing a financial burden on members of their natal families who must support them;
- markedly reduced opportunities for remarriage because they are no longer virgins (Burch, 1983); and
- losing a valued anticipated position of dominance over younger female family members (new brides) flowing from the "patriarchal bargain" (Kandiyoti, 1987).

The patriarchal bargain refers to a bargain in which wives accept their subordinate position, reproduce and care for children, demonstrate fidelity and loyalty, perform unpaid household labor, and routinely prepare and serve food enjoyed by their husbands on time, in return for protection and financial support by their husbands and the anticipation of achieving a valued position of dominance over younger family members, including new brides, when they become mothers-in-law (Kandiyoti, 1998, pp. 282–284). Here, matriarchal rule in families coexists with patriarchal rule. The findings that follow indicate that silently enduring physical and sexual assaults by husbands should be included in the classic patriarchal bargain.

In some districts within classic patriarchal states in India, rates of intimate male partner violence vary greatly. For example, in the state of Uttar Pradesh, 36% of male partners in the district of Gonda admitted forcing their wives to have sex "at any time during their marriage." The comparable figure for the district of Kanpur Nagar is 14%. The percentage of male partners in the district of Banda who admitted hitting their wives was 45%. The comparable figure for Naintal was 18%. The percentage of male partners in Banda who reported hitting their wives "during the past year" was 33%. The comparable figure for male partners in the district of Naintal was 11%. The percentage of male partners in the district of Banda who agreed that a disobedient wife "should be beaten" was 50%. The comparable figure for male partners in the district of Naintal was 10% (Hoffman, Demo, & Edwards, 1994; World Health Organization, 2002). In all of these districts, including the districts with the highest rates of physical and sexual assault—Banda and Gonda—the patriarchal bargain would have made a significant contribution to preventing separations and divorces initiated by wives who were being physically and sexually assaulted by their husbands.

Banda and Gorda are districts in India. India has "the lowest divorce rates in the world [with] only 1 in 100 marriages ending in divorce" (Singh, 2012, p. 6). Consequently, the finding that separation is strongly and positively associated with femicide in modern patriarchal societies such as the United States and Canada may be generalizable to the classic patriarchies such as Pakistan and India only for separations/divorces that bring dishonor to families.

In sum, when patriarchal attitudes and/or jealousy/possessiveness are used as indicators, the findings reviewed here do not provide strong support for patriarchy as an explanation of the association between separation and femicide.

CONFLICT RESOLUTION THEORY

Conflict and conflict resolution were endemic in relationships between the intimate partners who were our human ancestors and in relationships between intimate partners in all contemporary societies (Black, 1998; Buss, 2005; Daly & Wilson, 1988; Fry & Soderberg, 2013; Shackelford, 2001; Straus, 1978; Straus & Gelles, 1990). Conflict and conflict resolution are conflated in this body of literature (Ellis & Anderson, 2005; Ellis, Sakinofsky, & Stuckless, 2012). Differentiating between the two phenomena is important because variations in the intensity of conflicts affect the choice of means used to resolve them.

The literature reviewed by Ellis et al. (2012) revealed two major competing definitions of conflict. In the blood-for-blood definition, conflict was objectively defined as "harmful interactions" such as fighting. In the "bad-blood" definition, conflict was subjectively defined as "mutual feelings of hostility." We find it more useful to ground contemporary conflict resolution theory in a definition that defines conflict as *a relationship characterized by mutual feelings of hostility* (bad blood) and conflict resolution as *attempts to resolve or settle conflicts* ("doing conflict" that could escalate to blood-for-blood) (Aubert, 1963; Ellis & Anderson, 2005; Ellis et al., 2012; Fine, 2001; Rogge & Bradbury, 1999; Simmel, 1955; Winstock, 2013).

This definition has greater utility for two reasons, First, the "harmful interactions" definitions of conflict conflates conflict with conflict resolution because harmful interactions such as abusive verbal arguments and fighting are frequently used in attempts to settle conflicts (Carnevale & Pruitt, 1992).

Second, mutual feelings of hostility and harmful interactions can vary independently. For example, mutual feelings of hostility are not reported by enforcers in professional hockey teams who fight each other (Ellis & Anderson, 2005). Another example: "blood-for-blood" (war between South and North Korea) can be differentiated from "bad blood" (hostile feelings between them before and after they signed a ceasefire agreement). Mutual feelings of hostility are frequently associated with harmful interactions and the greater the intensity of conflict ("blood is boiling"), the greater the likelihood that blood will be spilled. At the same time, mutual feelings of hostility may be present without being overtly expressed in harmful interactions.

Contemporary definitions that differentiate conflict from conflict resolution were anticipated by Hobbes more than 400 years ago. In *Leviathan* (1651), he defined conflict not in terms of "actual fighting" but "in the known disposition thereto" (Part 1, Chapter 13). In 1978, Murray Straus operationalized these two concepts in the instructions given to respondents before completing the CTS 1:

> No matter how well a couple gets along, there are times when they disagree on major decisions, get annoyed about something the other person does, or just have spats or fights because they are in a bad mood or tired or some other reason. They also use many different ways of trying to settle their differences. I'm going to read some of the things that you and your (husband/partner) might have done when you had a dispute and would like you to tell me for each one how often you did it last year.

The concepts of hostility and conflict were not included in these instructions because they may have decreased the response rate (pp. 3–4). Still, the instructions are noteworthy because they differentiate a conflated definition of conflict (disagree on major decisions/have spats or fights) from a clear definition of conflict resolution.

The conflict resolution explanation of the association between separation and femicide we shall describe is a dyadic proximate-situational theory in the sense that it focuses on interaction between intimate partners who are attempting to resolve conflicts associated with contested female partner-initiated decisions to separate. The circumstances surrounding attempts to settle or resolve separation-associated conflicts include the involvement of third parties such as lawyers, judges, and mediators when attempts to resolve the conflict by the parties themselves are not successful. The circumstances surrounding separation may also include a variety of other distal and proximal factors found to be associated with femicide.

The association between distal and proximal factors is acknowledged but, by definition, situational theory privileges the proximal over the distal. Thus, being intoxicated (proximal factor) when the femicide was perpetrated is privileged over distal factors such as "having a father with a drinking problem" or even "drinking prior to the [fatal] assault" because the association between this proximal factor and femicide is stronger than the association between these distal factors and femicide (Gondolf, 2002, p. 171; Roberts, 1996; Stout, 1993). Being an "alcoholic or problem drinker" was found to be a risk factor for femicide by Campbell et al. (2009), but as toxicology data on perpetrators (and victims) were not reported, we suspect that the proxy informants they interviewed were more likely to be aware of his/her alcoholism and problem drinking than the immediate circumstances surrounding the femicides they did not witness themselves.

Proximal factors central to conflict resolution theory include arguments as well as other means used by intimate partners to settle conflicts. In *Metaphors We Live By* (1980), Lakoff and Johnson describe how metaphors structure everyday interaction. The metaphor *argument is war* refers to a type of interaction that involves winning and losing, attacking and defending, giving and gaining ground (p. 4). As we stated previously (Chapter 1), the essence of a metaphor is "understanding and experiencing one kind of thing in terms of another." For Lakoff and Johnson (1980), the "one kind of thing" is arguments as a means of settling conflicts and the "other thing" is war as a method of settling conflicts (p. 5). These authors did not address the transition from verbal arguments to physical attacks. The description of an extreme transition is presented below.

Like most of the other men in his neighborhood, a young man named Cantanhede was carrying a knife for protection. During the soccer match he was refereeing, he gave one of the male players a yellow (warning) card for a violation of the soccer rules. The two of them got into an argument over the award of a yellow card. Cantanhede gave him a red (banished from the game) card for arguing. The argument escalated. Threats were exchanged. Cantanhede pulled out his knife and stabbed Abreu twice. He was rushed to hospital. Two of Abreu's friends who had been drinking ran onto the pitch headed toward Cantanhede. One of them hit him in the face with a bottle of wine. He was then run over with a motorcycle. Then they cut off his legs and his head, which was placed on a wooden fence. Abreu died in the hospital (Longman & Barnes, 2013).

Findings cited below indicate that arguments often escalate to the point where physical attacks are used to settle conflicts when arguments fail to do so. The most frequently cited source of information on escalated arguments that result in femicide are police officers who investigate them.

Most researchers using police reports as sources of data report findings indicating that attempts to settle conflicts by argument preceded the majority of femicides they investigated. The proportion of police reports identifying attempting to settle conflicts by argument as a precursor for killing an intimate female partner varies between 41% (Kowalski, 2005, p. 55), 52% (Wilson & Daly, 1994, pp. 5–6), and 63% (Silverman & Kennedy, 1993, p. 71). Sources of conflict tend not to be reported. Consequently, we do not know how frequently separation was the source of the arguments they reported. The accuracy of police attributions of motive have been questioned (e.g., Daly & Wilson, 1988; Wilson & Daly, 1992), but the statistics on arguments cited previously were not qualified by the researchers who published them.

Straus, Hamby, McCoy, and Sugarman (1996), Choice, Lamke, and Pittman (1995), and Kalmuss (1984) report findings indicating that the use of verbal aggression as a conflict resolution tactic increases the risk of the use of physical assault as a conflict resolution tactic. Straus et al. (1996) also report findings (Table 5) indicating that the use of these two conflict resolution tactics are highly correlated ($r = 0.67$, $p < 0.001$). As conflict resolution theory locates the use of sublethal and lethal violent conflict resolution tactics at different points on the same continuum, the use of physical assaults increases the risk of assaults resulting in serious injuries, which in turn increases the risk of the use of the ultimate struggle conflict resolution tactic of femicide (Carnevale & Pruitt, 1992; Crimmins, 1991; Daly & Wilson, 1988; Levi, 1981). Separation is one way of attempting to decrease the risk of first-time violence or further conflict resolution violence by male partners. For most female partners, separation decreases the risk of sublethal violence (Ellis & Stuckless, 2006). For a relatively few female partners, the intensity of conflict and consequently the risk of femicide increases as they move from a "continuing relationship" through "self-help" and "third-party intervention" phases of separation.

As we stated earlier, conflict is endemic in relationships between intimate partners. Compared with conflicts between other parties (e.g., friends, workmates strangers), the intensity of recurring conflicts between intimate partners is higher because they:

- are strongly attached to each other emotionally;
- have intimate knowledge of their respective vulnerabilities and strengths;
- have become skilled in using this knowledge to hurt each other;
- cannot use "masks and formulas" available to parties involved in nonintimate relationships; and
- find it far more difficult to end conflicts by ending the relationship (Goode, 1971, p. 632).

During the "self-help" phase of separation, the parties attempt to settle conflicts associated with separating themselves while they are still living together. Goode's research led him to conclude that the intensity of conflict is higher in this separation phase than in continuing relationships because conflict over the female partner's unilateral decision to separate that "finally appears in the war of words is so sharp, the feeling of betrayal and loss … of an intimate partner perceived as unique and not replaceable … is so great, that redress must be physical and destructive" (Goode, 1971, p. 632; Goussinsky & Yassir-Borochowitz, 2012).

In the second "third-party involved" separation phase, the parties are living in separate residences and are participating or about to participate in formal separation proceedings. The intensity of conflict tends to reach its apogee in this phase for at least two reasons.

First, in the separating phase when the parties are still living together, there may be some uncertainty on the part of one or both parties as to whether the current separation is permanent, especially if she has left and returned on one or more previous occasions. In the second separated "third-party involved" phase, uncertainty is replaced by certainty, especially when the partner who has left initiates formal separation proceedings. Separation is associated with significant emotional arousal generally and hostility in particular in male partners who see themselves as being "dumped forever" by their female partners (Arendell, 1995, chapter 4; Buss, 2005, p. 96; Coser, 1956; Simmel, 1955).

Second, the failure of intimate partners to settle separation-associated conflicts themselves tends to escalate the intensity of conflict for at least two reasons First, female partners may decide to separate or apply for a divorce, and male partners may increase the use of serious injury-producing assaults aimed at preventing the use of these options. Not infrequently, conflict over separating and divorcing is the context in which escalating male and female partner violence results in the death of female partners.

Second, family court property and financial (alimony) decisions that are financially favorable to female partners may increase male partner reliance on serious injury resulting in death because a formerly potent power/control resource (economic dependence of the female partner) has been eliminated (Gauthier & Bankstron, 2004, p. 103).

After separation and divorce, male and female partners/parents who cannot achieve the outcomes they wanted by negotiating a "settlement package" themselves through negotiation usually participate in formal separation and divorce proceedings.

Most couples attempt to settle conflicts associated with separation (financial support, primary care and control of children, access to children, and property division) by participating in adversarial proceedings. A minority (10–20%) participate in collaborative proceedings (Braver & O'Connell, 1998). Collaborative proceedings include mediation and representation by lawyers who practice collaborative law. Mediators do not make decisions on outcomes or impose solutions on the parties. Instead, they facilitate communication and negotiations between the separating parties who jointly make decisions on outcomes that usually are or tend to be positive sum (win–win).

Collaborative lawyers use nonadversarial negotiation tactics, emphasize joint problem solving, and obtain in writing a commitment from the parties they represent not to attempt to get what they want by threatening to engage in litigation/go to court. If they do, their lawyers, by prior agreement, will no longer represent them (Tesler, 2008).

Adversarial proceedings are those in which the parties and the lawyers who represent them conceive of outcomes as zero-sum (win–lose), perceive each other as enemies or adversaries, and use struggle win–lose tactics appropriate for this perception.

Choice of proceedings (adversarial or collaborative) is fateful because victims and perpetrators of all three types of sublethal and lethal domestic violence tend to be concentrated among those who participate in proceedings that escalate rather than deescalate conflict. Participation in adversarial proceedings increases the intensity of conflict for one or more of the following reasons:

- participants use adversarial proceedings to harass, threaten, and abuse each other (Arendell, 1995; Braver & O'Connell, 1998; Canadian Panel on Violence Against Women, 1993; Durham Response to Woman Abuse, 2007, pp. 15–18; Kurz, 1995; Pruett & Jackson, 1999);
- outcomes (minutes of settlement, court orders, and judgments) are perceived to be unfair by one or both parties for a number of reasons: one partner could not afford to pay for a lawyer and so represented himself/herself; both parties were represented by a lawyer but one of them had the financial resources to pay a more experienced and effective family lawyer whereas the other party was represented by duty counsel or represented himself/herself; judges are perceived to be biased against them (Arendell, 1995; Braver & O'Connell, 1998; Durham Response to Wife Abuse, 2007);
- submission of affidavits that include exaggeration, embarrassing, and hurtful false allegations (Ellis, 1994);
- transaction costs (psychological—stress, uncertainty, anxiety, frustration—and financial) are high, sometimes very high (Ellis & Stuckless, 1996; Sander & Goldberg, 1994); and
- when children are involved, parenting and financial support arrangements imposed by judges are perceived to be zero-sum and morally outrageous by fathers who view them as the outcome of collusion between judges and mothers.

Participation in divorce mediation decreases the intensity of conflict and consequently the risk of fatal and nonfatal domestic violence for one or more of the following reasons (Ellis & Anderson, 2005; Emery, 2012; Emery, Lauman-Billings, Waldron, Sbarra, & Dillon, 2001; Emery, Matthews, & Kitzmann, 1991).

- Participation is governed by collaborative norms;
- the parties themselves jointly determine the terms of memoranda of understanding that may be subsequently included in minutes of settlement;
- outcomes of mediation on many or most issues are more likely to be positive-sum than zero-sum;
- mediators facilitate constructive communications, neutralize or reframe destructive communications, and make continued participation in mediation contingent upon compliance with ground rules against the use of aversive, conflict-escalating tactics such as verbal abuse and threats;
- mediated agreements are likely to be perceived as fair when mediators derive power-balancing interventions from an interpersonal process theory of power

emphasizing the differential possession of potent power resources as well as differences in the willingness and ability of the parties to use their resources effectively (Ellis & Anderson, 2005; Gulliver, 1979, pp. 186–208);
- use of a gender-neutral, empirically validated (field tested) domestic violence instrument specifically designed to assess *and* manage the risk of violence during and following participation in separation and divorce proceedings; and
- affidavits that escalate conflict are not part of the mediation process.

DYNAMICS OF CONFLICT RESOLUTION

In a publication entitled *Marital Conflict and Violence in Evolutionary Perspective*, Wilson and Daly (1989) formulated a theory of human (interpersonal) conflict that links conflicts instigated by the desertion (or infidelity) of female partners still young enough to bear children with the use of violence by male partners who do not control/possess alternative, less costly nonviolent means (e.g., negotiation) of settling such conflicts. The conflict resolution dynamic that sometimes results in femicide is described by Wilson and Daly (1989) in the following terms: "Coercive use of sublethal violence [by male partners] is a potentially costly way of getting others to pursue [their] preferred agendas. Instead of making [their female partners] *wish* to comply, violence inspires them to defy [male partner] perpetrators when the opportunity arises. Severe assaults can lead to severe self defense measures … and retribution by others. It follows that violence is often the recourse of desperate people lacking the capacity to dispense positive incentives that would inspire more 'voluntary' compliance with their [male partner's] wishes" (p. 57).

The use of sublethal violence to settle conflicts increases the likelihood of the use of homicide as a conflict resolution tactic for two reasons. First, severe assaults by male partners tend to instigate equally severe self-defensive or retaliatory assaults by female partners that, in turn, instigate even more serious assaults by their male partners. Second, the use of violence to settle conflicts by male partners tends to increase the likelihood their female partners will leave them. The imminent or planned departure of female partners tends to increase the intensity of conflicts between the leavers and the left. As the intensity of conflicts over desertion increases, so does the likelihood of femicide.

After 35 years of study, Dobash and Dobash reached two conclusions that are central to a conflict resolution explanation of intimate partner femicide. First, conflict is endemic in relationships characterized by the violence. Second, "intimate partner relationships that are highly conflicted (high-intensity conflicts) are at risk … of murder." Third, possessiveness-jealousy is only one of a number of sources of conflict (Dobash et al., 2007, p. 344).

These researchers also made a significant contribution toward the cumulative development of a conflict theoretic explanation of separation-associated femicide by describing the dynamic underlying the use of femicide as a means of settling conflicts associated with separating.

The dynamics they describe were based upon information obtained from incarcerated perpetrators of femicide. The specific circumstances in which separation-associated femicides occurred are described in the following terms: Initially, perpetrators attempted to settle conflicts associated with the female partner's unilateral decision to separate by using tactics (promising, cajoling, and threatening) aimed at persuading them to remain in the relationship. When it became clear to the eventual perpetrators that these tactics would not produce the kind of settlement they wanted—for the partner to remain in the relationship—they killed them. For the perpetrators, the "project" had changed from settling conflicts by getting her to stay to settling conflicts by getting rid of her permanently (2007, p. 83).

A similar dynamic is described by Stack (1997) in the following terms: She leaves or communicates her intention to leave him. He can't live without her and feels helpless to persuade her to stay/return through discussion, negotiation, threats, promises, and assaulting her. The conflict over her decision to separate escalates to the point where he settles the conflict by killing her.

The vast majority of males involved in conflicts over the female partner's unilateral decision to separate do not settle them by killing their partners. Treating the dyad (male and female partner) as the unit of analysis, Winstock and Eisikovits (2007, pp. 292–293) describe the dynamic ending in femicide for the very few male partners who settle the separation-associated conflict by committing femicide in the following terms:

- she communicates her decision to end recurring conflict and his use of violence to settle them by separating;
- he strongly opposes her decision and attempts to persuade her to stay by providing reasons why she should stay (e.g., he will change, treat her with more respect, the children want them to stay together, he will never abuse her again, will find a job and stick to it, will stop drinking so much);
- she confirms her determination to separate;
- his attempt to "be nice" is not working but he still exercises self-control of the conflict resolution tactics he uses;
- she is adamant about leaving with the children;
- his feelings of hostility increase because in addition to the fact of her leaving is added his manifest inability to control her using nonviolent means; and
- the mutual use of violent means escalates from verbal exchanges, to arguments, to threats (of physical violence, obtaining sole custody of the children, taking him/her for all he/she has got), to the use of mutual violence inflicting less serious injuries to lethal violence.

In a later publication, Winstock (2013) states that escalation is "the heart of partner conflict dynamics" and he identifies two major mechanisms of conflict escalation. The first is the cost–benefit (C–B) ratio and the second is the sensitivity to harm (S–H) ratio. Applied to the settlement of conflicts over separation, the C–B ratio states violence inflicting increasingly serious injuries and resulting in death will be used if the female partner refuses adamantly to comply with his demands for her to stay *and* the value to him of her staying with him is greater than the punishment inflicted upon him by killing her. The S–H ratio states that physically and emotionally harmful tit-for-tat exchanges tend to escalate because intimate partners are more sensitive to the injuries done to them than the injuries they inflict on their partners. Because of this "sensitivity gap," each partner inflicts increasingly serious injuries on his/her partner to the point of causing the death of one of them (p. 130).

A DOMESTIC CONTEXT-SPECIFIC THEORY OF CONFLICT RESOLUTION

The set of interrelated conflict theoretic propositions that helps explain the association between separation and femicide is described in the following sections. The first five propositions are supported by theory and research referred to earlier in this chapter. Findings supporting the sixth proposition will be cited in the appropriate place for them.

Propositions

- Conflict is endemic in social relationships generally and between intimate partners in particular;
- the greater the emotional attachment between intimate partners, the greater the intensity of conflict between them when separation is initiated by one and opposed by the other;
- the more recent the separation, the greater the intensity of conflict;
- the greater the intensity of conflict, the greater the risk of lethal male partner violence;
- participation in adversarial proceedings increases the intensity of conflict;
- therefore, participation in adversarial proceedings by recently separated intimate partners increases the risk of femicide and femicide–suicide.

Intensity of conflict, recency of separation, and risk of suicide are presented graphically in Figure 5.1.

Research

Proposition 1: Conflict and conflict resolution are endemic in prehistoric and contemporary intimate partner relationships. Among prehistoric human ancestor societies, theory and research supporting this proposition are provided by Buss (2005), Coser (1956), Duntley and Buss (2008), Daly and Wilson (1988, 1995), Fry and Soderberg (2013), Pinker (2011), and Shackleford (2000). Evidence supporting this proposition in historical and contemporary societies is provided Coser (1956), Elias (1939/2000), Pinker (2011), Simmel (1955), Straus (1978), and Straus and Gelles (1990).

Proposition 2: The greater the emotional attachment between intimate partners, the greater the intensity of conflict between them when separation is initiated by one party and

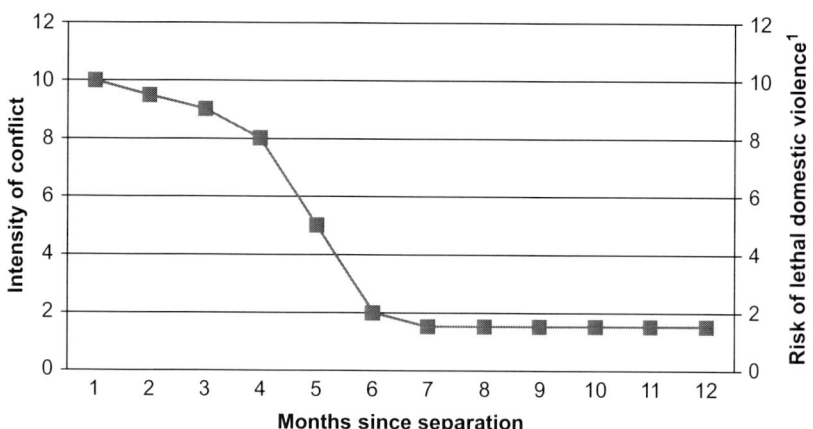

12 = Highest
1 = Lowest
[1]Femicide, femicide–suicide

FIGURE 5.1 Femicide and femicide–suicide risk, intensity of conflict, and months since separation.

opposed by the other. Theory and research supporting this proposition are provided by Adler (1999), Black (1998), Gillespie, Hearn, and Silverman (1998), Henry and Short (1954), Simmel (1955), and Stack (1987).

Proposition 3: The more recent the separation, the greater the intensity of conflict. Evidence supporting this proposition is presented in the chapter on separation (Chapter 1). Reasons for an escalation in the intensity of conflict during and shortly after separating permanently are presented in the "phases of separation" segment (pp. 125–126) in this chapter.

Proposition 4: The greater the intensity of conflict, the greater the risk of male partner violence. Evidence of a strong positive linear relationship between the intensity of conflict and the use of increasingly injurious conflict resolution tactics is reported by Black (2004), Flynn and Graham (2010), Gillespie et al. (1998), Huer and Penrod (1986), and Simmel (1955).

Proposition 5: Participation in adversarial separation proceedings increases and participation in collaborative proceedings decreases the intensity of conflict. Evidence providing support for this proposition is presented on pages 78–84 of this chapter.

Proposition 6: Therefore, participation in adversarial proceedings by recently separated intimate partners will increase and participation in collaborative proceedings will decrease the risk of femicide and femicide–suicide. Evidence supporting this proposition follows.

Participation in formal separation and divorce proceedings is a relatively recent phenomenon. Historical evidence indicates that during the Middle Ages, as late as 1530, "England was neither a separating nor a divorcing society [and] death was almost the sole agent for dissolving a marriage" (Stone, 1992, p. 2). Most of the deaths were natural but some were femicides because the options of separation and divorce were not available for most people. Consequently, the association between separation and femicide was very much weaker than the association between marriage and femicide. On top of major societal changes such as industrialization and urbanization associated with capitalism, femicides and homicides involving husbands and wives as perpetrators and victims threatened the institution of traditional marriage. Clearly a "safety-valve" was needed to protect husbands and wives and maintain the institution of marriage. The safety value took the form of providing husbands and wives with the options of separation and divorce (Gillis, 1996, p. 1277).

By the end of the nineteenth century, divorce on the basis of a limited number of specific grounds was legal in France. Nonviolent means of ending marriages—separation and divorce on demand—were now available to French couples whose use of them markedly increased the rate of separation. The effect of the increased rate of separation on "deadly domestic quarrels" that were recorded between 1852 and 1910 was investigated by Gillis (1996).

Longitudinal aggregate data (annual rates of separation and divorce and homicide) collected from official French sources (e.g., *Annuaire statistique de la France*) motives identified in coroner reports were analyzed by Gillis using a multivariate statistical method of analysis appropriate for analyzing time series data. The following two findings are noteworthy:

- the rate of participation in adversarial separation and divorce proceedings was a significant predictor of adultery-motivated...domestic homicides by males (p. 1296); and
- the rate of participation in adversarial separation and divorce proceedings is positively associated with "spontaneous femicides and homicides" and negatively associated with "premeditated domestic homicides" (and femicides) (p. 1273).

This finding elicited from Gillis the suggestion that "abandoned spouses can become homicidal" when female partners unilaterally initiated contested separations or divorces and participated in adversarial proceedings.

During the 1960s and 1970s, an increasing number of U.S. states with mutual consent divorce regimes (32 by 1978) adopted "divorce regimes" that permitted divorce without the consent of the other party. Dee (2003) investigated how unilateral divorce laws influenced spousal homicides. To this end, he collected information on spousal homicides and femicides included in FBI's Supplementary Homicide Reports for the years 1968–1978 and how "marital property was treated in divorce settlements" in different states with the same unilateral divorce regime (pp. 167–169).

In common-law states, marital property or assets were distributed in a way that favored husbands. In community-property states, marital property was distributed in a way that favored wives. The major finding reported by Dee was that spousal homicides (murders of husbands by wives) increased by more than 20% in the four common-law states with easy access to divorce proceedings and marital property distribution that favored husbands (p. 163). The mechanism underlying this increase in these states was, we hypothesized, an increase in mutual feelings of hostility associated with participation in adversarial proceedings plus increased hostility toward husbands caused by the impoverishment of wives. Dee found no unilateral divorce regime states with marital property distribution that favored wives, but findings reported by Arendell (1995, pp. 111–120) indicate that the same mechanism underlies spousal femicides by male partners who see themselves as being emasculated, impoverished, and/or stripped of their rights by decisions made by family court judges adjudicating adversarial proceedings.

Gauthier and Bankstron (2004) collected data on 157 spousal and 140 dating homicides recorded between 1984 and 1990 in U.S. cities with 10,000 or more residents. Findings they reported did not support their hypothesis that easier access to divorce would be associated with a higher spousal sex ratio of killings favoring male partners. They also found no support for the hypothesis that property resolutions by judges favoring female partners "provoked the use of [lethal] self-help measures" by male partners and for sex differences in the spousal sex ratio of killings (pp. 11–112). Given the low "high levels of public assistance" distributed to the individuals included in their sample, the value of the property available to be distributed may be mainly responsible for the lack of support for their property division hypothesis. Lack of support for their access to divorce hypothesis may be mainly because individuals who were receiving public assistance are less likely to actually participate in costly formal divorce proceedings in both husband-biased and -unbiased property division cities.

In some jurisdictions, divorce applicants and respondents are required to submit affidavits as an early step in the proceedings. Because of inflammatory content such as blaming, accusing, demeaning, and demonizing, affidavits significantly increase the intensity of conflict. Ellis (1994) found that affidavits accounted for more of the variation in postprocessing male partner violence against female ex-partners than the other two statistically significant predictors of this outcome—physical abuse during the six months preceding separation proceedings and level of education (p. 65). Perhaps perpetrators of homicides in the Dee study and the divorced fathers expressing femicidal ideation in the Arendell study were also concentrated in jurisdictions that required the submission of affidavits.

Couples we would expect to exhibit higher rates of violence resulting in injuries resulting in femicide and homicide—high-conflict, angry, young low-income couples—were randomly assigned to a collaborative proceeding (mediation for an average of 5 hours) and adversarial custody settlement proceedings by Emery (2012, 1991). Of the 71 families originally assigned to collaborative and adversarial groups, 27 mothers and 25 fathers in the mediation group and 25 of the mothers and 23 of the fathers in the adversarial group hearings before a judge remained during the 12-year follow-up period. Four of the findings are noteworthy.

First, residential parents (parents whose homes were the primary residence of the children) gave better "grades" to nonresidential parents in all 10 areas of parenting that were measured. Second, the process of decision-making improved significantly. Indicators of "improved significantly" included working collaboratively as coparents, respect for the voice of the other party, and adopting a longer run perspective. Third, fathers in the mediation group were more satisfied with the process and outcomes of mediation than fathers in the litigation group, and the difference was statistically significant. Fourth, levels of conflict reported by couples in the mediation group were lower, even though *opportunities* for conflict were far greater in the mediation group because couples in this reported significantly greater parental involvement and contact with each other and their children than parents in the adversarial group. For couples who participated in mediation, these findings are entirely inconsistent with use of violence to settle conflicts and no violence was reported.

In a quasi-field experimental study group, comparison in a real-life setting but no random assignment of subjects to treatments published in 1984, Pearson and Thoennes reported findings similar to those reported by Emery et al. (2001). Compared with couples in the litigation group, couples participating in divorce mediation reported more positive shorter- and longer-term effects such as "improving the relationship" and "lower re-litigation rates" that would tend to decrease the likelihood of intimate partner violence.

Some of the findings reported here describe the effects of "law in the books" (unilateral divorce laws); others describe "law in action" (participation in separation and divorce proceedings). Because between 85% and 95% of separations and divorces are negotiated by lawyers, it seems fair and proper to conclude that in the majority of states most separations and divorces are settled by negotiations between family lawyers (Braver & O'Connell, 1998; Ellis, 1994). Family lawyers can be located on a continuum with collaborative lawyers who decrease the intensity of conflict at one end and highly adversarial lawyers who increase it at the other end.

In a survey conducted by Hedeem and Salem (2006), adversarial lawyers represented a fairly large proportion of the 219 family lawyers included in the family law practitioner sample they selected (p. 603). Schneider and Mills (2006) analyzed data from their survey, and this was one of their major findings: "Compared with civil, criminal, commercial, corporate, property and other lawyers, family lawyers had the highest percentage of unethically adversarial lawyers" (2006, p. 617). Ethical adversarial and unethically adversarial lawyers accounted for almost 40% of the family lawyers in the sample. The corresponding figure for all lawyers is 33%. If the potential for sublethal and lethal violence is greater in destroyed relationships than in continuing collaborative relationships, then lawyers in this sample may be unintentionally increasing the risk of both types of male partner violence by "engaging in … behavior that destroys … relationship[s]" (p. 618).

The specific context for relationship-destroying negotiations is an adversarial system that, not infrequently, produces fateful zero-sum or negative-sum outcomes for couples caught up in its heavy machinery. In this context, "uncertainty about the decisions made by judges in any particular case motivates family lawyers to prepare and process all cases as if they were going to court" (ver Steeg, 2003, p. 231). You may recall a finding we reported earlier—going to family court was "highly common amongst most homicide-suicide perpetrators" (Logan et al., 2002, pp. 1060–1062).

SUMMARY

A summary of the causal mechanisms explaining the empirical generalizations that are derived from or implicit in the theories described in this chapter is presented in Table 5.1.

Table 5.1 Theories and Causal Mechanisms for the Association between Separation and Intimate Partner Femicide

Theory	Causal Mechanisms
Evolutionary psychological	Jealousy-ownership
Patriarchy	Challenging male partner domination
	Restore family honor
Conflict resolution	Intensity of conflict

COMMENT

Daly and Wilson's evolutionary psychological explanation of the empirical generalization linking separation with femicide is a significant intellectual achievement. Their insistence upon the integration of aggregate (structural and cultural) variables with individual level variables in theories of femicide and homicide will, in our estimation, greatly improve their explanatory power. They are also to be commended for challenging sociologists offering structural and cultural explanations of homicide and femicide to demonstrate the direction of causation or influence. Thus, when sociologists such as Block (2000) and Gauthier and Bankstron (2004) report findings indicating that cultural (and material) differences may help explain why intimate partner homicide rates among African-Americans are equal or asymmetric favoring females, Daly and Wilson (1988) suggest that the rates may have influenced the emergence of cultural support/legitimation of homicide by intimate female partners in the first place (p. 290).

The Daly and Wilson theory elicits the following comments. First, they define evolutionary psychology as "the attempt to understand (cognitions underlying MSP) and normal social motives (sexual jealousy) as products of evolution by natural selection" (p. ix). The key or core outcome of natural selection is diversity of traits. Traits that promote reproductive success or "fitness" survive. Life and death are obvious necessary and sufficient conditions for reproductive success because "death terminates one's capacity to promote one's fitness; if inclinations have been shaped by natural selection, life should always be preferred to death ... life is valued because of its historical contribution to fitness, and not as an end in itself" (p. 5). The contribution made to genetic posterity by females in reproductive ages ends when they are killed by their male partners. Therefore, pathological personality traits, depression, or mental illness may have to be called upon to explain why a few males—perhaps those located at the extremely strong end of the continuum of MSP and motivation to dominate female intimate partners—engage in conduct that, from a natural selection perspective, is maladaptive. That is to say, the "utility" of demonstrating domination by killing female (reproductive) partners results in the failure of reproductive success.

Second, Daly and Wilson refer to the presence of cross-cultural (universal?) social and legal norms and values supportive of MSP (1992, pp. 85–86). They also include a cultural factor "pervasive attitude" in their definition of MSP. Norms, values, and attitudes are cultural variables. At the same time, they criticize sociologists who formulate cultural explanations of variations in homicide rates across time and space. Specifically, they criticize them for ignoring individual level variables such as competitiveness and risk-proneness that actually explain the association between culture and homicide. This specific criticism is part of a more general critique of structural and cultural explanations for their "failure to incorporate a specific account of the ways in which (structure and culture) influence individual actors and interpersonal interactions" (p. 288). The findings on differences in homicide and femicide rates for Chicago, Canada, and New South Wales they report (Table 3.4) provide them with an opportunity to provide a natural selection thinking account of the "specific ways in which (culture) influences individual actors and interpersonal interactions," but they do not seize it.

Third, in the evolutionary psychological theory formulated by Wilson and Daly, femicides associated with desertion are motivated exclusively by sexual jealousy flowing from a violation of MSP rights. In patrilineal societies (or locations within them) in which wives are the reproductive property of both their agnatic kin and their husbands, desertions that bring dishonor to both families—she leaves her husband to live with another man who is a member of an ineligible caste—are followed by femicides that are motivated primarily by the restoration of honor (see previous discussion in this chapter). These findings raise questions about the alleged universality of an MSP explanation for the association between separation and femicide.

Fourth, the findings presented here indicate that the motive of sexual jealousy is reported for varying proportions of males who kill their female partners. This suggests that factors in addition to or interacting with sexual jealousy are at work. For example, if conflict mediates the impact of jealousy on femicide (Chimbos, 1976; Dobash et al., 2007), then differences in the conflict resolution tactics (nonviolent/violent/extremely violent) used by intimate partners to settle conflicts could help account for more of the variation in femicide. Alternatively or additionally, other significant sources of conflict, such as conflicts over stepchildren, may be present in some cases but not others (Miner, Shackleford, Block, Starratt, & Weekes-Shackleford, 2012). Furthermore, the degree to which partners are intoxicated or guns are present in homes may vary. Small sample sizes and/or the lack of information on other probable explanatory factors when large samples are being investigated (e.g., Block & Christakos, 1995; Stack, 1987) make it difficult to control them to assess the independent effect of sexual jealousy on femicide.

Fifth, a more general problem that may have to be addressed by researchers interested in testing the MSP hypothesis has to do with the operationalization/measurement of MSP. As it is defined by Wilson and Daly (1992), MSP refers to "a more encompassing mind-set, referring not just to one's own feelings of entitlement, ... but to proprietary entitlements in [wives] as identical to entitlements in land, chattels and other economic resources" (p. 85). This definition requires that both ownership (proprietary entitlements) and jealousy aroused by perceived violations of ownership of reproductive capacity be measured because female-initiated separations can violate the proprietary entitlement norm without arousing jealousy. For example, as in patrilineal societies in which wives are owned by their agnatic kin and her husband and his kin, her killers can include her own father, brother, or uncle. These perpetrators are not motivated by jealousy but by the fact that the women they own through marriage or birth brought dishonor to both families. In individualistic societies such as the United Sates, individual male partners can vary in the degree to which proprietary entitlements in their nonhuman chattels are perceived as identical with or similar to the ownership of their wives and also in the intensity of feelings of jealousy (simmering vs. rage) aroused by their separations.

Finally, Daly and Wilson do not exclude the application of MSP theory to femicide (1988, pp. 92–93). At the same time, they do not identify specific design features that differentiate lethal from nonlethal male partner violence instigated by infidelity or desertion. Applied in collectivistic, patriarchal, patrilineal societies such as India or Pakistan, special design contexts for femicide may be different from the specific design contexts for throwing acid in the face of women who reject offers of ownership (marriage) by men or elope with lovers (Asian Human Rights Commission, 2010; International Herald Tribune, 2012; Roy, 2011). Applied in an individualistic society such as the United States, the specific design context for nonlethal acts of male partner violence after separation could be differentiated from a specific design context for relatively rare femicides after separation.

The conflict resolution theory formulated by Wilson and Daly (1992) and Daly and Wilson (1988) makes a positive contribution to the cumulative development of a conflict resolution theory of femicide by (1) defining homicide as a means of resolving conflicts; (2) describing femicide as a means of resolving conflicts that is most likely to be used by male partners who cannot change or prevent the desertion their partners using alternative resources available to them; and (3) making male partner control/female partner resistance central to the dynamics of brinkmanship in conflicts that result in spousal homicides.

The claim that threats to MSP is the only or the most important source of conflict between intimate partners and that male partner control is exercised only or mainly with the objective of eliminating/reducing threats to proprietariness has been questioned by Dobash et al. (2007) and Dobash, Dobash, Cavanagh, and Lewis (2000). They acknowledge MSP as one among a number of sources of conflict-instigated lethal male partner violence (p. 329). Consequently, they suggest that lethal domestic violence risk assessment instruments should include items not only measuring male partner possessiveness but also items measuring other sources of conflict (2007, p. 329; Dobash et al., 2000, pp. 24–30).

If Dobash et al. (2007) are correct when they conclude that "the study of lethal violence has concentrated almost solely on conflicts related to jealousy and possessiveness" (p. 6), the time may be ripe for viewing jealousy-possessiveness as only one of a number of sources of conflict that a relatively small number of male partners attempt to settle by killing their female partners.

The evolutionary psychological theory of Buss suffers from its failure to provide evidence of femicide ideation as the mechanism underlying the killing of females who desert their male partners. Additionally, the design features differentiating nonlethal from lethal male partner violence against females who desert them were not specified.

The review of patriarchy theory and research elicits a number of comments. The first three focus on theory.

First, theories of the patriarchy tend to derive the patriarchal family from the culture and institutional structure of the patriarchal society (Bograd, 1988; Pence and Paymar, 1973) or the patriarchal structure of society from the patriarchal family (Dobash & Dobash, 1979). A third persuasive alternative is suggested by family sociologist Jessie Bernard (1972). Her starting point is "the patriarchal conception of marriage" in which the husband's domination of wives "rested on the unchallenged superiority of males" and support from "the institutional machinery of society." Yet, the study of families over many years led her to the following conclusion:

> … the actual day-to-day relationships between husbands have been determined by men and women themselves. All that the institutional machinery could do was confer authority; it could not create personal power for such power cannot be conferred and women can generate it as well as men. Thus, keeping women in their place has been a universal problem, in spite of the fact that almost without exception, institutional patterns give men positions of superiority over them.
>
> p. 13

The relative autonomy of husbands and wives from the institution of the family in the classic patriarchy of England during the Middle Ages—consider the Wife of Bath in Chaucer's *Canterbury Tales* (1375–1400)—and in modern patriarchies such as the United States creates space for gender-egalitarian, male-dominant, and female-dominant families in twenty-first-century America (Coleman & Straus, 1986). One hypothesis suggested by findings reported by Coleman and Straus is that female partners in male-dominant families who regard their domination by male partners as illegitimate and who initiate separations are most likely to be killed by dominating male partners who interpret them as a challenge to their domination.

Second, male power, control, and domination figure prominently in the patriarchal explanation of the association between separation and femicide we derived from the patriarchy theory created by Dobash and Dobash (1979). These concepts are also central to interpersonal theories of power. Yet, they do not appear to inform patriarchal theorizing on *how* these variables could mediate the impact of separation on femicide.

For Foucault (1982), there is nothing more to power than its exercise. In Thibaut and Kelley's (1959) social psychological analysis of interpersonal power, male partners are dominant when they exercise "fate control." Male partners achieve fate control when they determine outcomes for female partners by varying the use of rewarding or punishing resources they possess or control regardless of how their female partners use the resources they possess or control. Male partners are exercising "behavior control" when, by varying their use of the rewarding or punishing resources they possess or control, they make it worthwhile or desirable for female partners to do/not do something they might otherwise have done/not done or selected outcomes they might otherwise have chosen or not chosen. The critical or essential difference between fate and behavior control is that in the latter, the choices of female and male partners vary as a function of the *interaction* of their choices, whereas in fate control the outcomes of female partners are fully determined by the choices of their male partners. When female partners initiate and follow through on permanent separations regardless of male partner threats, promises to change, and/or offers of significant rewards for not leaving, they are exercising fate control over their male partners. The *transition* from exercising fate control to being the recipient of fate control may instigate emotional arousal to the point where femicide ideation and femicide follow separation.

Third, together with other feminists, Shelley Gavigan (2013) seeks to change extant family law that she conceives of as patriarchal. Changes in family law that permit one spouse to divorce the other without his/her consent (unilateral divorce) were introduced in many U.S. states during the 1960s and 1970s and are extant today. If these specific laws are patriarchal, they should consistently favor applicant and respondent husbands. Consequently, they should decrease their motivation to murder ex-wives who, in collusion with the state, used divorce proceedings to ruin them financially, take their children from them, and violate their rights (Arendell, 1995).

In a study described earlier, Dee (1991) found that unilateral divorce laws in patriarchal states were associated with a statistically significant increase of between 21% and 23% in murdered *husbands* (emphasis added) (p. 173). Clearly, this finding does not support a patriarchal explanation of the association between separation and femicide. Instead, it suggests that extreme anger instigated by impoverishment after participation in divorce proceedings explains this association.

Findings reported for classic patriarchies in the northern Indian state of Uttar Pradesh do support a patriarchal explanation for the association between separation/divorce and femicide. Specifically, they indicate that male partner and father domination of female family members legitimated by collectivistic, patriarchal values and attitudes prevents or markedly *reduces* femicides after separations and divorces by preventing them and *increases* femicides following separations and divorces that bring dishonor to families.

Findings reported here support a patriarchal explanation of the association between separation and femicide only if family patriarchy is operationalized as male partner domination, patriarchal attitudes, and a legitimating/justifying ideology. However, the co-presence of these three indicators was measured in only one (Dobash & Dobash, 1979) of the studies we reviewed. The findings described here can be interpreted as supporting a contemporary theory of the patriarchal family only if single measures such as "male partner entitlement" or "possessiveness-jealousy" or "highly controlling male partner" are regarded as valid indicators of family patriarchy in the contemporary United States. Not infrequently, when explanatory concepts such as MSP or the patriarchy are used to interpret findings, these concepts are either not measured or measured inappropriately (e.g., Yllo & Straus, 1984). For a discussion of this widespread problem, see Sampson (1989).

In sum, the findings presented here suggest that the empirical generalization (female-initiated separations are positively associated with femicide) that obtains in modern patriarchal societies such as the United States and Canada is generalizable to the classic patriarchies such as Pakistan and India only for separations/divorces that bring dishonor to families.

The conflict theoretic explanation of the finding that separated female partners are more likely than co-resident intimate partners to participate in adversarial separation and divorce proceedings may be challenged by a social selection hypothesis which states that separated couples in Wilson and Daly sample constitute a "relatively violent subset of all couples … with a history of discord" (Wilson & Daly, 1994, p. 8). If separate-residence couples are concentrated among those who are most likely to choose to participate in adversarial separation proceedings, then selection may be "incidental" to femicide after separation via their effect on choice of proceedings. However, qualitative data from the cases investigated by Wilson and Daly indicated that the association between separation and femicide was "more than incidental" (p. 8). Moreover, findings indicating that separated couples with a history of violence (violent subset couples) were overrepresented among those choosing to participate in adversarial proceedings were not reported. This evidence undermines but does not eliminate a selection explanation.

A selection explanation can be eliminated by implementing a field experimental study design with random assignment of thousands of separating couples to collaborative and adversarial proceedings and following them for a number of years. Such a study is neither ethical nor feasible.

Findings reported by researchers using different nonfield experimental study designs do not support a selection explanation. For example, Mahoney (1991) and Kelly and Johnson (2008) report findings indicating that some femicides associated with separation involved male perpetrators who had not previously used violence against female partners. These couples do not constitute a violent subset of separating couples.

Wardle's (1994) analysis of a random sample of stories in Salt Lake City and Provo newspapers about femicides and homicides involving intimate partners and family lawyers as victims was interpreted by her as illustrating "the violence that afflicts the (unilateral, no-fault adversarial) legal system … constructed to 'resolve' domestic relations disputes" (p. 741). The intensity of conflict between perpetrators and victims was probably high, but qualitative findings reported by Mnookin (2010) indicate that adversarial family lawyers involved in negotiations aimed at settling conflicts associated with separating tend to increase the intensity of conflict between separating parties regardless of the intensity of conflict between them. A paradigmatic case is described here.

> Hostility between lawyers [for Brenda and Thomas] bordered on demonization [of the other lawyer's client] and could lead to all-out legal warfare ... worse yet, their lawyers seemed to be egging them on [and] ... exchanged venomous letters without managing to resolve the most urgent and basic issues of this early phase [of negotiations].
>
> p. 213

The lawyers described in this case are not individuals with the personalities of warriors with an extreme commitment to the value of winning, but individuals with a variety of personalities and value orientations engaged in protecting the legal rights of clients in the context of an adversarial system.

Finally, it is important to note that the positive effects of settling conflicts using collaborative means are as robust as the negative effects of using violence to settle conflicts (Cummings & Davies, 1994; Fine, 2001, pp. 372–373; Odoms, 2001; Rogge & Bradbury, 1999).

DISCUSSION QUESTIONS

1. Evaluate this statement: MSP is the causal mechanism underlying the association between separation and intimate partner femicide. Do you agree or disagree? Give reasons for your answer.

2. Evaluate this statement: Homicide ideation is the causal mechanism underlying the association between separation and intimate partner femicide. Do you agree or disagree? Give reasons for your answer.

3. Evaluate this statement: Intensity of conflict is the causal mechanism underlying the association between separation and intimate partner femicide. Do you agree or disagree? Give reasons for your answer.

4. Evaluate this statement: Family honor is the causal mechanism underlying the association between separation and intimate partner femicide in traditional, collectivistic "classic patriarchies." Do you agree or disagree? Give reasons for your answer.

Separation and Intimate Partner Femicide–Suicide

CHAPTER 6

LEARNING OBJECTIVES

Readers who have achieved the objectives set for this chapter will be able to:

- Derive causal mechanisms underlying the association between separation and intimate partner femicide–suicide from the theories described in this chapter
- Demonstrate the ability to assess support for causal mechanisms implicit in theories of intimate partner femicide on the basis of findings that tested the theories, as reported in this chapter
- Compare and critically evaluate causal mechanisms derived from different theories of femicide–suicide

EVOLUTIONARY PSYCHOLOGICAL THEORY

According to Daly and Wilson (1988, p. 205), nonlethal coercive control—motivated violence against intimate female partners suspected of having or known to have violated norms of fidelity and loyalty is adaptive (Wilson & Daly, 1992, p. 93). Lethal violence that is expressed as femicide–suicide, or familicide when children are also killed, is located on the same continuum as nonlethal coercive control violence but is placed at the extreme, rarely expressed end of this continuum—the tip of the iceberg (Wilson & Daly, 1992, p. 93). Femicide–suicides, especially those involving the killing of children, are maladaptive with respect to fitness maximization. However, adaptation has more than one level. In addition to the direct or level of fitness, maximization adaptation involves the indirect or by-product psychological level of male sexual proprietariness (MSP).

Unlike femicide, which is a one-edged sword, femicide–suicide is a two-edged sword. When "desperate husbands, filled with rage and despair" use these swords against women (and sometimes their children) who are separating from them, they are demonstrating their willingness and ability to "call the shots and exert their authority" (1988, p. 215) even though they "have lapsed into futile spite, acting out their vestigial agendas of dominance to no useful end" (p. 219). For the very few deserted husbands who perpetrate femicide–suicides, losing a wife (and children) by killing them is "no more disastrous than losing them by desertion" (p. 215). The causal mechanism underlying the association between separation and femicide–suicide is desperation and rage motivated by the challenge to male dominance entailed by separation.

Research

Cooper and Eaves (1996) selected a sample of 124 deaths among 148 victims classified as "family homicides" by investigating police officer reports in British Columbia. Of the 124 perpetrators, 18% (n = 23) committed suicide after the homicide. Information on perpetrators, victims, and circumstances was collected from multiple sources—coroners, police, and forensic and community mental health files. Two variables were described as being of "primary importance": the relationships between perpetrators and victim and the "main precipitating condition." Nine main precipitating conditions were identified. Separation was found to be the leading precipitating condition, followed by mental illness, accounting for 31% and 14%, respectively, of 123 cases. Data were analyzed using cross-tabulations.

Findings reported by Cooper and Eaves indicated that 44% (n = 22) of 50 femicides were followed by the suicide or attempted suicide of the perpetrator (p. 104). In 18 of these cases, the female partner had separated and was involved with another man (n = 7) or was in the process of separating because of the perpetrator's repeated violence (n = 11). The authors found that "these perpetrators were more likely than not to commit suicide or seriously attempt to do so after femicide" (p. 106). In fact, more than two-thirds of these perpetrators (13 of 18) committed femicide–suicide. They also found that of the seven batterers whose chronic violence escalated to the point of intimate partner femicide, separation was a precipitating condition for only one of them.

Notwithstanding this finding, the authors conclude that their findings support "male proprietariness as an explanatory concept" because of the "extreme proprietary behavior" exhibited by the men who perpetrated separation-instigated femicide–suicides and familicides. Because the secondary data they analyzed did not include information on variables that could be used as measures of MSP (e.g., jealousy, possessiveness entitlement, proprietary attitudes), Cooper and Eaves appear to have found support for "male proprietariness as an explanatory concept" solely on the basis of the finding that the femicide–suicides they studied followed a separation.

Polk (1994) collected data on 380 homicides that were recorded in the files of the office of the coroner for the State of Victoria between 1985 and 1989. Information from multiple sources (police investigations, prosecutor briefs, forensic pathology reports, coroner's inquests, and trials) was included in the files. Case histories were completed for each homicide in the file, and Polk conducted "a detailed (qualitative) thematic analysis" of them. Using "victim–offender relationships" as a criterion, he classified 58 (15%) of them as intimate partner femicides and 15 (4%) as femicide–suicides (p. 23). Polk found that these femicides were an outcome of the joint effects of male partner control and extreme depression (p. 44). Control was evident in decisions made by male perpetrators to destroy themselves but only after they had decided to destroy their female partners (p. 44).

As neither desertion (separation/divorce/elopement) nor any indicators of MSP (ownership/entitlement/jealousy/possessiveness) were identified by Polk as precursor themes, we are left to conclude that the findings he reports offer only weak support for Daly and Wilson's (1988) MSP explanation of femicide–suicide. It becomes a little stronger if we find it reasonable for extremely depressed male perpetrators, some in their sixties and seventies, to "act out their vestigial agendas of domination" by killing themselves after killing their female partners.

Polk informs readers that his analysis of case histories of femicide–suicide was not done "blind." Instead, his coding of cases and analysis of them to discover themes were informed by Daly and Wilson's (1988) evolutionary psychological theory of femicide (1994, p. 22). In the study conducted by Ellis, Sakinofsky, and Stuckless (2012), analysis of the responses to the final open-ended question ("*Is there anything else you would like to say?*") included in the interview schedule administered to 36 federal penitentiary inmates serving time for femicide and femicide–suicide in Canadian penitentiaries was done blind. That is, the answers were coded and analyzed without the use of theoretical filters. Instead, we used computer-assisted data analysis software NVivo 9.2 (Ellis et al., 2012) to produce modes and themes. The following six main modes (themes) were identified:

1. Regret
2. Love
3. Alcohol and/or other drug use
4. Relationships with significant others
5. Mental illness/depression
6. Spur of the moment

Dobash and Dobash (2010) collected qualitative data from the case files of 104 inmates incarcerated in Great Britain who were convicted of murdering their female partners. NVivo analysis of the data identified the following eight themes:

1. Denial of the murder
2. History of nonlethal violence against a current or former partner
3. Authority and control
4. Possessiveness, jealousy, estrangement, and separation
5. Denying responsibility/blaming the victim
6. Lack of empathy and remorse
7. Resistance to engaging in the process of change

None of the modes revealed by the NVivo analysis of the Canadian penitentiary inmate data is an indicator of MSP. The NVivo analysis of British prison data reveals three nodes (items 2, 3, and 4) that are indicators of MSP, and Polk's qualitative analysis of Australian case histories revealed that one indicator of MSP (male partner control) was positively associated with femicide–suicide. Two kinds of "filtering" may help account for differences between the Polk and Dobash and Dobash studies, on the one hand, and the Ellis et al. study, on the other hand.

First, with confidentiality assured, the voices and words of incarcerated men in Canadian penitentiaries were communicated directly to trained research assistants conducting a York University research project supervised by Ellis and colleagues. In both the Polk and Dobash and Dobash studies, the voices of incarcerated men were filtered by criminal justice system professionals who produced the case histories. Second, no filter other than one used by the prison inmates themselves produced the modes identified in the Canadian study. The thematic analyses in the British and Australian studies were filtered (that is, informed by) theory.

Between 1974 and 1990, 551 intimate partner femicides were recorded in Ontario, Canada. Thirty-nine percent (n = 220) of the 551 femicides were femicides followed by suicides or attempted suicides that resulted in the deaths of 767 individuals, including 62 children. Femicide–suicide is, by definition, a crime/noncrime committed exclusives by males. No case of homicide–suicide was reported by Crawford and Gartner (1992). The male perpetrator's "anger or rage over the actual or impending estrangement from his partner" was found to be the "predominant motive" in 29% (n = 160) of the cases in which a motive could be reliably established or inferred (p. 44).

This study was not actually designed to test Wilson and Daly's MSP theory, but the theory was used to interpret the findings on femicide, including femicide followed by suicide "indicating [the] male's preoccupation with proprietary control and sexual ownership of their female partners" (p. 28). Women's stories, newspaper accounts, and qualitative data from official sources were used to support an MSP explanation, but the relative importance or weight of themes of "proprietary control" and "sexual ownership" compared with alternative themes such as nonviolent partners who kill in the "the heat of passion," "revenge," "intoxication," "fear of abandonment," "extreme dependency," and/or "depression" was not assessed using two or more coders or through the use of computer-based software such as NVivo.

Findings reported by a number of researchers indicate that pathologically possessive/amorous jealous male perpetrators of femicide–suicide may also be depressed and/or extremely dependent emotionally on their female partners (Bourget, Gagne, & Moamai, 2000; Dutton & Kerry, 1999; Liem, 2010; Liem, Hengeveld, & Koenrdraat, 2009; Liem, Postulart, & Nieuwbeerta, 2009; Liem & Roberts, 2009; Liem, Roberts, Hengeveld & associates, 2009; Marzuk, Tardiff, & Hirsch, 1992; Palermo, 1984; West, 1966).

Perusal of this body of literature reveals differences in the dynamic underlying the association between separation and femicide–suicide. For Marzuk et al. (1992), actual or suspected female partner infidelity instigates "morbid amorous jealousy" in some abusive male partners who, in a fit of rage, perpetrate femicide–suicide when their female partners leave or threaten to leave them. Here, the domestic context is a "chaotic, abusive relationship" in which separation is the "triggering event" for femicide–suicide. The association between separation and femicide–suicide is not explained by a dynamic that links morbid jealousy with separation and separation with femicide–suicide.

For other male partners described by Marzuk et al. (1992), perceived/actual infidelity arouses "morbid amorous jealousy" that motivates femicide–suicide in the absence of any indication that their female partners intend to separate from them. This dynamic cannot explain the association between separation and femicide–suicide because separation is not part of it.

For Liem (2010) and Dutton and Kerry (1999), extremely emotionally dependent depressed male partners tend to perceive female-initiated separations as utter abandonment and respond to "a life no longer worth living" by taking their own life after killing their partners. Infidelity, perceived or actual, is not part of the dynamic resulting in femicide–suicide. In the dynamic described here, perceived abandonment is the mechanism that explains the empirical generalization.

SOCIOLOGICAL SOCIAL CONTROL THEORY

Sociological social control theory differs from Daly and Wilson's (1992) natural selection informed MSP/coercive control theory by grounding male partner control in social factors such as childhood gender role socialization and situational, structural, and cultural factors. In Chapter 5, we described the difference between fate and behavior control. Both of these forms of control are not necessarily zero-sum (win–lose). In the domestic context, a male or female intimate partner can also exercise behavior or fate control in ways that yield positive-sum outcomes (win–win). Sociologist Donald Black (1988) conceives of a type of male partner control that he refers to as "penal control." Penal control differs from behavior and fate control on two grounds. First, it is exclusively punitive. Second, it is exercised by males against female partners and against themselves. Third, it is a way of controlling and being controlled by the "crime" of separation initiated by female partners.

In Black's sociological theory of control applied to the domestic context, male partners believe they are "executing" their female partners when they kill them for committing the egregious "crime" of ruining their lives by separating from them. In executing their female partners, men are simultaneously violating norms proscribing physical violence that they internalized during childhood socialization and committing the ultimate violent crime against a person to whom they are strongly attached emotionally. Consequently, they execute themselves as punishment. In this theory, "just deserts" appears to be the mechanism underlying the association between separation and femicide–suicide.

Research

Between 1989 and 2001, 42 cases of homicide–suicide were recorded in New Orleans. These cases were studied by Harper and Voight (2007). Information about them was obtained from multiple sources: newspaper articles, interviews with police officers who investigated the cases, and friends and relatives of victims and perpetrators. Data were analyzed qualitatively and quantitatively using NVivo. Information on "social structural and social psychological factors" was used to create a *sociological autopsy* on each case.

They found that 71% ($n = 30$) of the 42 homicide–suicides in their sample involved intimate partners as perpetrators and victims. All but one of the perpetrators (29 of 30) were male. In all but one of the 30 cases, the relationship between perpetrators and victims was "violent and chaotic," and in 27 of 30 cases, homicides involved "a current or former wife or intimate partner" as victims.

Harper and Voight state that Black's "penal (crime and punishment) style" (of) control is especially relevant to their homicide–suicide explanation, but findings supporting this statement are not reported. NVivo findings did indicate that male dominance was a "common theme" among homicide–suicide cases, but they did not identify crime and punishment as a common theme (node) or even a subtheme. Findings linking male dominance with homicide–suicide have been reported by a number of researchers (e.g., Daly & Wilson, 1988; Silverman & Mukerjee, 1987), but male partner dominance expressed via penal control differentiates Black from these researchers. Template analysis (NVivo) did not identify "dominance or control along the lines suggested by Black" as a common theme. Moreover, while Black referred to homicide–suicide as an outcome of penal control being exercised against female partners who separated or were suspected of wanting to separate, Harper and Voight interpret their findings as indicating that homicide–suicide is an outcome of loss of control associated with female partner–initiated separations (p. 304). In short, Harper and Voight did not collect data that would enable them to adequately test Black's theory.

ATTRIBUTION THEORY

Psychologist Fritz Heider (1958) is generally credited with creating the attribution theory that many psychologists (e.g., Kelley, 1967) have built on or modified. Heider's theory can be economically described in terms of an assumption, a theory, and a motive. The assumption is that human beings have an inherent need to understand the causes of human behavior. The theory is that the causes of behavior may be located in persons, situations, or both. The motive is that human beings are motivated to simplify a complex world and make an unpredictable world more predictable.

Sociological attribution theory developed independently of psychological attribution theory. Unnithan and associates (1994) made an important contribution to sociological attribution theory by modifying and adding to the frustration–aggression explanation formulated by Henry and Short (1954). In the theory of Unnithan and associates, business cycle fluctuations are hypothesized to be a direct cause of frustration, but the reaction to frustration is mediated by culture.

In collectivistic cultures, the interests of individual members of a group are subordinate to the interests of the group (Oyserman, Coon, & Kemmelmeier, 2002). Where collectivistic value orientations are predominant, individuals tend to attribute blame to others (external causes) for the harms they experience and they react with other-directed violent acts such as homicide. In cultures where individualistic value orientations are predominant, individuals tend to attribute blame to themselves (internal causes) for success and failure. The experience of failure induces guilt and lowers self-esteem. Guilt and low self-esteem are hypothesized to be positively associated with suicide. The conditions under which both attributions—external and internal causes—may be associated with femicide (other harm)–suicide (self-harm) is not a salient feature of the stream theory of Unnithan and associates.

Stack (1997) builds on the attribution theory of Unnithan and associates by hypothesizing that "the combination of rage and depression in the ambivalent offender may be compared to a blend of other-blame and self-blame in Unnithan and associates" (1994, p. 440). In Stack's attribution theory of femicide–suicide, the two attribution styles identified by Stack are "extreme self-blame/depression" and "extreme other-blame/anger." The first attribution is associated with suicide and the second with homicide. In the case of femicide–suicide, these two attribution styles are blended as follows: The male perpetrator is in a rage because of the extreme frustration he experiences when the intimate partner whom he loves is leaving or has left him. At the same time, the perpetrator, who is ambivalent about the relationship in the first place, experiences extreme depression and blames himself for it (p. 440).

Research

Perusal of the Chicago Police Department's homicide files for the years 1965–1990 revealed to Stack (1997) that 265 of the homicide–suicides did not involve suicide pacts; 16,245 homicides were included in these files during this 25-year period. A large sample such as this should yield stable findings on the effects of attribution styles on homicides compared with homicides followed by suicides. Multivariate logistic regression was used by Stack for analyzing the effects of attribution styles on a dichotomous dependent variable (homicide–suicide = 1; and homicide = 0) controlling six demographic factors that may also differentiate one outcome from the other.

A number of interesting findings on the effects of victim and offender characteristics and level of positive attachment between them on the odds of suicide following homicide are reported by Stack. However, none of the variables included in his attribution theory are actually measured at the individual level or at the aggregate (structural) level. In the absence of individual-level (or structural/proxy) measures of the variables he interrelated in his attribution theory, he uses findings from qualitative studies to support the following tentative conclusion: "perhaps homicide–suicide can be thought of as containing both attribution styles discussed by Unnithan and associates" (Stack, 1997, p.449).

Stack's attribution theory of femicide–suicide was also tested in another city in a different country (Utrecht, the Netherlands), by Liem (2010). Liem collected individual-level data because her objective was to test Stack's theory by investigating "the dynamics underlying ... homicide–parasuicide, homicide and parasuicide" (p. 2). To this end, she collected data on 10 cases in each of these groups—matched on marital and parental status, employment, and mental disorder—from two different sources (psychiatric observation hospital files and medical center files on serious parasuicide (attempted suicide) cases requiring medical care). The data were analyzed qualitatively with a view toward identifying "recurrent themes" in the information provided by individuals in each of the three groups. The attribution of internal and external blame by the perpetrators for each of the three outcomes was measured using "analytic coding" (p. 250).

Findings reported by Liem indicate that two of the 10 homicide–parasuicide perpetrators in the homicide group attributed blame to the intimate partner from whom they were estranged and two of the 10 individuals in the suicide group attributed blame to themselves for attempting suicide after killing their child(ren). Seven of 10 in the homicide–parasuicide group were found to be extremely dependent on their female partners and attributed blame to their "intolerable situation." For them, homicide–parasuicide represented a "total solution" to a situation involving estranged female intimate partners (p. 256).

Liem (2010) set out to test Stack's attribution theory of separation-instigated femicide–suicide, but in the discussion that followed the presentation of her findings, she did not relate them to his theory. One of Stack's unstated assumptions was that humans are "cognitive misers" who prefer the least-taxing, dichotomous (external/internal) cognitive explanation for their own conduct and the conduct of others (Semin, 1980). Liem's findings challenge this assumption. The attributions made by the humans she studied were more complex in the sense that attributing blame to external factors involved differentiating situational from cultural factors and both of these from other humans who they may perceive as blameworthy.

Differences in the dependent variable—homicide–suicide for Stack and homicide–parasuicide for Liem—are probably not significant because Liem assures us that the parasuicide instances included in her sample were genuine attempts at suicide, that is, attempts that would have been successful were it not for the interventions of others or some extraneous reason. Of greater concern to us is Liem's interpretation of her own findings. Specifically, she appears to link attributions of external and internal blame with "primarily homicidal" and "primarily suicidal" homicide–parasuicides, respectively, on the basis of attributions made by two of 10 individuals in each of these groups.

Finally, Liem's qualitative analysis does explicitly identify attributions as a dominant mode or theme in perpetrator explanations for their conduct. Criteria used to classify attributions but not frustration, dependency, or depression as dominant themes need to be explicitly stated. This will inspire greater confidence in the generality of the underlying dynamics she describes in her six case studies and the discussion of her findings.

MASCULINITY THEORY

> Harry Emde, a 59-year-old German carpenter, shot and killed his wife of 12 years, Emma, and his 5-year-old daughter, Hilda. Emde then slashed the "blood vessels" on his wrists and on his forehead and hanged himself from the hinge at the top of the kitchen door in his home ... Emma [had] recently "applied" for a divorce.
> **Adler, 1999, p. 3**

Age, gender, social class and ethnicity, and separation/divorce are associated with femicide–suicide in the case of Harry and Emma. One or more of these variables are also associated with 256 other cases of femicide–suicide investigated by Adler (1999). Adler's theory of estrangement-associated femicide–suicide takes the form of specifying public social humiliation as the underlying causal factor accounting for the association between separation (threatened or completed) and femicide. Public humiliation flowed from the evident loss of control by male heads of the households over wives who initiated separation proceedings and the negative impact of these proceedings on their valued identity as "respectable family men" (pp. 13–14). For the disproportionately high number of German perpetrators of femicide–suicide in Chicago studied by Adler, femicide–suicide was a solution to the problem of public humiliation in a context in which status as a man who controls his household and wife and his reputation as a respectable family man who heads a harmonious household were highly valued.

Research

Adler (1999) studied 257 cases of femicide–suicide that occurred in Chicago during a period (1875–1910) when "the interaction of structural (economic) and cultural forces produced an explosion of homicide" by causing "[o]verlapping shifts in gender roles and class ideologies [that] profoundly disrupted social relations for [German immigrants]" who in earlier and later historical periods might have committed homicide or suicide instead of intimate partner femicide–suicide. Between 1875 and 1910, 69% of German immigrant husbands who perpetrated intimate partner femicide committed suicide afterward. The comparable figure for non-German husbands who murdered their wives was 42%. Almost all German husbands who killed their children (92%) committed suicide. The comparable figure for non-German husbands who did the same thing is 56%.

One reason for the overrepresentation of German immigrant husbands among those perpetrating intimate partner femicide–suicide in Chicago was the fact that Germany, the country from which they emigrated, had one of the highest rates of suicide in Europe (p. 8). These findings indicate that Adler implicitly defines femicide–suicides as "extended suicides." Additional support for this definition comes from Taylor, who found "social failure" and "social disgrace" to be "two types of problems particularly associated with suicide" (1982, p. 114).

In addition to qualitative demographic (aggregate) data, individual-level qualitative data were collected from suicide notes and media descriptions of the circumstances surrounding femicide–suicides provided by relatives and neighbors. Analysis of the qualitative data yielded information on public humiliation as a causal factor underlying the association between separation and femicide–suicides and on factors associated with femicide–suicide by residents of Chicago in general. Feelings frequently associated with suicide, such as desperation, hopelessness, and despair (Goussinsky & Yassour-Borochowitz, 2012), were also found to be associated with femicide–suicide. The sources of these feelings varied with gender. Among wives, health problems were most frequently mentioned. Among men, the most frequently mentioned factor was public humiliation following economic failure for husbands whose status as a man was contingent on his ability to improve the socioeconomic status of his family.

Finally, Adler reports findings indicating that a "strong emotional attachment" between the perpetrator and the victim was strongly and positively associated with femicide–suicide. Specifically, he found approximately 2% of the victims of homicide–suicides to be a stranger, co-worker, or neighbor (odds ratio = 0.8). The corresponding figure for spouses and lovers combined was 49% (odds ratio = 5.25, or 7 times higher).

ATTACHMENT/FRUSTRATION-AGGRESSION THEORY

The attachment theory described in this section is referred to as an integrated theory because it integrates Durkheim's sociological integration (social ties to others) theory of suicide (1897) with Dollard and associates' (1939) psychological frustration-aggression theory. The rates of suicide are higher for men and women who are not involved with each other as "married couples," but being involved with each other as a married couple increases the risk of frustration-instigated femicides and, under specified conditions, femicide–suicide.

In his book *The Making of the Modern Family* (1975), historian Edward Shorter reports that "most couples in traditional (European) societies were characterized by a lack of affection." Marriages were arranged with considerations other than mutual love of the parties for each other in mind (pp. 138–139). The emergence of individual choice of marriage partners on the basis of romantic love in the late eighteenth and nineteenth centuries and the subsequent emergence of the nuclear family as a "state of mind" in which family members "enjoy a privileged emotional climate they must protect from outside intrusion" (p. 205) significantly increased the intensity of emotional attachment between husbands and wives. This was the historical context in which Henry and Short (1954) formulated the hypothesis that homicide–suicide varies with the degree of positive attachment between perpetrators and victims (p. 127).

In their landmark study *Suicide and Homicide*, sociologists Henry and Short (1954) theorized homicide and suicide during a historical period (1950s) when positive attachment between husbands and wives reached its apogee because they were now "the primary source of nurturance and love" for each other. They did not theorize homicide–suicide nor did they collect their own data on this type of lethal violence, but their analysis of 66 homicides and 34 homicide–suicides that occurred in England and Wales suggested that the former could be differentiated from the latter "in terms of the degree to which the act of murder destroys a primary source of nurturance and love" (p. 117). Both femicide and femicide–suicide destroy the source of frustration—wives who stop the flow of nurturance and love by initiating separations and divorces—but perpetrators of femicide–suicide are differentiated from the perpetrators of femicide on two grounds. First, perpetrator and victim were more "positively attached" to each other. Second, stronger prohibitions against expressing aggression outwardly were inculcated in perpetrators during childhood socialization" (pp. 117, 126–127). The femicide–suicide dynamic is described in these terms:

> Homicide destroys the source of frustration in the external world. The internalization consequent to the loss of nurturance re-establishes the source of frustration

within the self ... the self (is blamed) and becomes the legitimate target for aggression.

p. 117

For Henry and Short, divorce is "an act of aggression ... against the spouse that ... stops the flow of nurturance" (p. 116). Stopping the flow of nurturance and love is a major source of frustration for the deserted spouse. Because the Henry and Short theory is grounded in Dollard and associates' (1939) frustration-aggression theory, one would expect separation-instigated frustration to be followed by aggression, including homicide.

Building on Henry and Short's analysis, Stack (1997) formulated an attachment theory in which separation-instigated homicide–suicide stems from two sources: (1) "a frustrated intimate relationship" that ends in separation and/or divorce and (2) "a blend of self and other blame in one's attribution style" (p. 435). Here, a narrowly conceived attribution style (recurrent blaming of self or other) has been substituted for "strength of internalized norms proscribing external aggression" as an underlying causal mechanism for femicide–suicides following separation and divorce.

According to Wolfgang (1958), guilt is also identified as a causal mechanism for suicides that follow homicides in general and homicides involving the perpetrator's own children in particular, because they were responsible for bringing them into the world and for their subsequent care and control. Core concepts in Stack's attachment theory derived from both Henry and Short and from Wolfgang are positive attachment, frustration, homicide, blended self/other blame, responsibility/guilt, and suicide.

Research

Adler's masculinity theory is supported by his analysis of aggregate- and individual-level data. His structural explanation of the association between separation and homicide–suicide is supported by findings regarding individuals that identified humiliation as the causal mechanism. This is a rare and worthy achievement. At the same time, his study elicits two critical comments. First, his analysis of data on individual perpetrators of homicide–suicide suffers from the failure to indicate how many individual cases were analyzed and how they were analyzed. The systematic analysis of individual case data using computer-assisted qualitative analysis software (e.g., NUDIST or earlier versions of NVivo) would have identified not only humiliation but also other possible themes and the relationships among them.

Second, his findings on homicide–suicides perpetrated by German immigrants residing in Chicago at the turn of the nineteenth century may not be generalizable to German immigrants residing to Chicago during earlier and later historical periods or to German immigrants residing in other U.S. cities during the same historical period.

Between 1965 and 1990, 6,245 homicides and 267 homicide–suicides were recorded in the murder files kept by the Chicago Police Department. Stack's (1997) homicide–suicide sample included 265 cases because two suicide-pact cases were excluded. Degree of positive attachment was measured by relationship of the victim to the perpetrator, with "own child" ranked first (highest degree of positive attachment with the parent perpetrator), followed by "spouse," "ex-lover" (includes ex-spouse and ex–common law wife and husband), "boy-girl friend," and "friend." Stack found a statistically significant association ($p < 0.05$) between level of attachment and risk of homicide followed by suicide for individuals in each of the five victim groups. The odds ratio he reported was highest (12.68) for perpetrators who killed (ex-lovers), but they were ranked third with respect to their level of positive attachment to their victims. Spouses are ranked second highest with respect to their level of positive attachment to the perpetrator, but homicides in which spouses are victims increase the odds of suicide eight times (p. 447). In short, the odds of suicide by perpetrators who killed ex-lovers are 1.6 times greater than the odds of the same outcome by perpetrators who killed their current spouse.

One way of interpreting this finding is to assume that the level of positive attachment is actually higher among perpetrators and ex-lovers than it is among perpetrators and spouses. Stack's interpretation—"for persons very dependent on the old bond, this loss of their love object can be unbearable" (p. 448)—suggests that this assumption may be reasonable. Stack's explanation of homicide is the intensification of jealousy associated with becoming an ex or being one (p. 448). His explanation of suicide is guilt for killing a former source of nurturance and love. Stack's interpretation and explanation suggest that emotional dependency, jealousy, and guilt mediate the impact of separation on homicide followed by suicide.

PERSONALITY THEORY

Of the nine diagnostic criteria for *Borderline Personality Disorder* (BPD) identified in the *Diagnostic and Statistical Manual of Mental Disorders*, 4th Edition (DSM-IV), *Personality Disorders* (*301.83*, "frantic efforts to avoid real or imagined abandonment") is the first criterion on the list. In the fifth edition (DSM-5, 2013), fear of abandonment is replaced by *Separation Insecurity* (American Psychological Association, 2013). *Separation Insecurity* is indicated by "fears of rejection and/or separation from significant others, associated with fears of excessive dependency and complete loss of autonomy." This pathological personality trait is subsumed under the first of three domains, the domain of *Negative Affectivity*. Three other pathological personality traits are subsumed under the same domain: *Emotional Lability* (emotions that are easily aroused, intense, and out of proportion to events such as unwilling separation), *Anxiousness* (panic and fears of falling apart often in reaction to interpersonal stresses associated with the perceived future negative effects of stressful events such as separation), *Depressivity* (frequent persistent feelings of hopelessness, inferior self-worth, and thoughts of suicide and suicidal behavior), and *Separation Insecurity*.

The second domain is *Disinhibition*, which is characterized by two pathological personality traits: *Impulsivity* (acting on the spur of the moment in response to stimuli without consideration of consequences and a sense of urgency and self-harming behavior under emotional distress) and *Risk-taking* (engaging in dangerous, risky, and potentially self-damaging activities and denial of the reality of personal danger).

The third domain is *Antagonism*, which is characterized by *Hostility* (persistent or frequent angry feelings; anger in response to minor slights and insults).

These seven pathological personality traits are "essential features" of BPD. The other essential feature is "impairments in personality (self and interpersonal) functioning." *Identity* (impoverished, unstable associated with excessive self-criticism and chronic feelings of emptiness) and *Self-direction* (instability in goals, values, aspirations) are impairments in self-functioning and in *Empathy* (inability to recognize the feelings and needs of others associated with hypersensitivity) and *Intimacy* (intense, unstable, conflicted close relationships marked by distrust, neediness, and anxious preoccupation with real or imagined abandonment; close relationships often viewed in extremes of idealization and devaluation and alternating between involvement and withdrawal). A diagnosis of BPD is contingent on the presence of both essential features *and* impairments in personality functioning and pathological trait expression:

- Relatively stable across time and consistent across situations
- Deviant for the individual's developmental stage or sociocultural environment
- Not exclusively caused by the direct physiological effects of alcohol or other drug abuse or brain injury

BPD is a clinical category. One of the problems with this category is that relatively few individuals meet the criteria for a diagnosis of BPD, and those who do not meet the criteria (possess the stipulated number of traits in DSM-IV) are excluded. Gunderson (1984) created a new clinical category, *Borderline Personality Organization* (BPO or BP), which would include a larger number of persons demonstrating fewer or less intense BPD traits or characteristics. Dutton hypothesized that "characteristics of BP identified by Gunderson—intense unstable interpersonal relationships … intense anger and impulsivity … intolerance of being alone, abandonment anxiety … and extreme personality shifts from love to hostile rage … increase the chance of violence in intimate relationships" (p. 213).

"Extreme shifts from love to rage" are two phases of the five phases in the "cycle of violence" revealed by the battered women interviewed by Walker (1979). More specifically, the interview data she collected and analyzed revealed a cyclical pattern of male partner violence in which a *Loving* phase was followed by a *Tension Building* phase that was followed by a *Battering* phase, followed by a *Justification* phase, followed by an *Appeasement* phase, followed again by a *Loving* phase. In the *Appeasement* phase, the battered woman did whatever she had to do to appease her batterer. Dutton (2006) was interested in the "inner workings" of batterers who behaved as if they were two different men—loving during one phase and battering a loved one in another. Based on his observation of the similarity between the inner workings of Walker's male "cycle of violence" batterers and the same characteristic in BPO males, he theorized a connection between BPO and male partner violence (p. 212).

In an earlier publication, Dutton and Browning (1988) described the dynamic specific to BPO/partner relationships that end with violence in the following terms: the female partner's actual or suspected decision to end the relationship instigates conflict and high emotional arousal, which is interpreted as anger by an impulsive male BPO partner with poor verbal conflict-resolution skills (p. 173). In this account, conflict-resolution skills used by a male BPO partner in his attempts to settle conflicts over female partner–initiated separations mediate the impact of her perceived abandonment on his violence. Roberts and Noller (1998) identified dysfunctional communication patterns as the causal mechanism that explains the association between "fear of abandonment" (a DSM-IV pathological personality trait) and conflict-instigated (*couple*) violence (p. 323). Roberts and Noller linked fear of abandonment with the increases in the intensity of conflict and the use of violent conflict resolution tactics in conflicts over actual or perceived abandonment (p. 324).

Research

A sample (type unspecified) of 90 men convicted of spousal homicide (intimate partner femicide) incarcerated in federal penitentiaries located in Ontario, Canada, was selected by two psychologists interested in investigating the modus operandi of these men and their personality disorders (Dutton & Browning, 1988). Data were collected from two sources: prisoner interviews and institutional records. Personality disorder was identified at intake using the Millon Clinical Multiaxial Inventory-II (MCMI-II; Millon, 1987). Evidence of a personality disorder was indicated by scores exceeding 85 on specified severe syndrome scales. Dutton and Kerry (1999) note that "the scales on this test measure constructs closely resemble those in DSM-IV." Information in institutional records were coded to reveal "evidence of estrangement," "a recorded history of previous violence," and 11 modus operandi variables such as whether the homicide was planned or spontaneous and the type of weapons used (pp. 290–291). Findings were reported using percentage differences and a significance test (*t*-test).

Findings reported by Dutton and Kerry indicate that one-third of the 90 inmates in their sample perpetrated femicide-attempted suicide; two-thirds (60) of the femicides were estrangement associated, and of these, 90% of them had experienced prior separations.

One of their major findings was that perpetrators who murder their female intimate partners "are almost invariably personality disordered" (p. 294) with "overcontrolled" personality disorders being overrepresented among perpetrators. Inmates with passive-aggressive and dependent personality disorders (overcontrolled men) were more likely to commit "abandonment femicide–suicides," to kill reactively, and to perpetrate femicide–suicides "during a failed reconciliation, or when a woman first announced her intentions to leave" (p. 294). The constructs measured by using DSM-5, which "closely resemble" those measured by the MCMI-II, are *Separation Insecurity* (excessive dependency) and *Hostility* (angry feelings) that is not expressed in action.

Another major finding was that 87% (78 of 90) of the perpetrators of femicides and femicide–suicides were "sudden murderers" (p. 296) whose lethal actions were not premeditated but were sudden, rage-motivated, "reactive, unplanned events" (p. 292). Pent-up rage was indicated by "over-killing" victims. Similar findings were reported by (Campbell, 1992; Crawford & Gartner, 1992, pp. 45–46; Goetting, 1995, p. 26). The DSM-5 construct of *Impulsivity* is measured by indicators such as "acting on the spur of the moment in response to immediate stimuli." Close to 90% of the femicides and femicide–suicides they investigated were "abandonment-precipitated rage killings" (p. 297). The origins of such killings ("early development, including … attachment problems") and their motivational basis (after viewing a video showing a wife "abandoning" her husband, men convicted of wife assault responded with more anger and anxiety than did nonviolent married men) were suggested by Dutton and Browning (1988).

The objective of a study in the Netherlands conducted by Liem and Roberts (2009) was "to assess the differences among male intimate partners who did and did not commit a self-destructive act following the homicide" (p. 339). To this end, they examined the institution (clinical) records of 297 male intimate partner perpetrators of homicide and 44 male partners who perpetrated homicide–suicide who were incarcerated in a forensic psychiatric institution because they had committed crimes "thought to be related to a mental disorder" (p. 343). During their seven-week period of incarceration, they were subjected to court-ordered multidisciplinary (including psychological and psychiatric) assessments. All of the 341 men in their sample were not convicted at the time of the assessments, but all of them were convicted in court subsequently. Chi-square tests and one-way analyses of variance were used to find out if differences between the two groups—homicide and homicide–suicide—were statistically significant.

Two findings are noteworthy. First, men in the homicide and homicide–suicide groups were similar to each other. This is indicated by the fact that non–statistically significant differences between them were found for 21 of the 26 differentiating variables included in their analysis (p. 346). This finding led Liem and Roberts to conclude that the men in the homicide–suicide group "had more in common with suicide victims than with homicide-perpetrators" (p. 349).

Second, they found a statistically significant difference between the two groups for "symbiosis," "suicidal threats," and "depressive disorder" ($p < 0.05$). A higher proportion of men in the homicide–suicide group were diagnosed with the disorder and communicated suicide threats. A significantly higher proportion of the men in this group (34% vs 7%) were also involved in an asymmetric symbiotic relationship in which the victim had become part of the extremely dependent perpetrator who kills his female partner when his fear of abandonment fails to persuade her to stay with him (p. 348). The three differentiating factors identified by Liem and Roberts are similar to indicators of DSM-5 constructs of *Intimacy* (anxious preoccupation with real or imagined abandonment), *Separation Anxiety* (excessive dependency), and *Depressivity* (frequent feelings of hopelessness). Here, it may be relevant to note that Holtzworth-Munroe and Stuart's (1994) dysphoric/borderline batterers who are diagnosed with BPD are hypothesized to be "pathologically dependent" on their female intimate partners.

The lifestyle of male partners diagnosed with a BPD is characterized by pathological personality traits (impulsive, risk-taking, self-harming) that are associated with types of comorbidities such as "alcohol and drug abuse" that are excluded from a diagnosis of BPD (Boles and Miotto, 2003). Because being intoxicated or "high" is strongly associated with the perpetration of femicide–suicide, BPD will do a much better job of explaining the association between separation and femicide–suicide when the effects of comorbidity associated with being "loaded" or "high" are added to the effects of BPD than when they are excluded. BPD and comorbidity may also have independent effects on reactive nonlethal and lethal violence, but the joint additive effects are stronger.

Roberts and Noller (1998) recruited a nonrandom sample of 181 couples from local counseling and community centers and first-year university psychology students who had been living together for at least 12 months and who were likely to have experienced "violence and marital problems" (p. 328). Of the 181 couples who returned completed questionnaires, 49% (89) were returned by psychology student couples and the remainder by community couples. Questionnaires completed by all couples included questions on conflict resolution (Conflict Resolution Tactics Scales), attachment, and communication patterns. Questionnaire data were analyzed using descriptive statistics (means and standard deviations) and bivariate correlations and hierarchical multiple regression.

Three findings they reported are worth noting. First, compared with couples in nonviolent relationships, couples in violent relationships are not as securely attached to each other and are more likely to engage in conflict-escalating dysfunctional patterns of communication in attempting to settle conflicts between them (p. 332). Second, the functionality/dysfunctionality of communication patterns varies with the security of attachment, with low security/high fear of abandonment couples being far more likely to engage in dysfunctional, conflict-escalating communication patterns of communication. Third, dysfunctional conflict-escalating communication patterns mediate the effects of insecure attachment/fear of abandonment on couple violence (p. 336). Cross-cultural findings pointing to the significance of couple conflict/conflict resolution as the final interaction context for femicide–suicides have been reported by a number of researchers including Godbole and Kudke (India) (2007) and Carach and Grabosky (Australia) (1998).

CONFLICT RESOLUTION THEORY

"If I can't have you, no one can" (Campbell, 1992, p. 99) is one of the most widely cited quotes in the literature on femicide. This quote was attributed to a jealous (spiteful?) husband who demonstrated his power and control over his wife by killing her. Far less frequently cited is a quote attributed to William Arf, who committed femicide–suicide: "If we can't live in peace, we might as well die together" (Adler, 1999, p. 14). The conflict resolution segment that follows provides a context for this quotation and a conflict resolution explanation for femicide–suicide in Chicago.

In their frequently cited multicity U.S. study of femicide–suicide and femicide, Koziol McLain and associates (2006) found two risk factors—suicide threats and "ever married to the perpetrator"—to be unique to femicide–suicide (p. 3). In their final logistic regression model (Model 7), "having a new partner," " prior threats to use a weapon," and "using a gun" significantly increased the risk (adjusted odds) of femicide–suicide (p. 17). Conflict resolution theorists define suicide threats, threats to use a weapon, and use of a gun as conflict resolution tactics and female partner-initiated separation/divorce as the source of the conflict that was settled by femicide–suicide. All these variables may be in play, but conflict resolution theorists would probably add extreme emotional dependency of the male on the female partner and link this variable with extremely high-intensity conflicts over outcomes (final separation/divorce) that mean he and she (and occasionally children) will never live together again. If they cannot live together, they can be together by dying together. This theory suggests that the quest for togetherness is the causal mechanism underlying the association between separation and femicide–suicide.

Research

In 2008, 17 states submitted information on violent deaths to the National Violent Death Reporting System (NVDRS) (2008). Between 2003 and 2005, information on 420 homicide–suicides, 20,188 suicides, and 5,932 single-perpetrator homicides were submitted to NVDRS. Data on these cases were quantitatively analyzed by Logan and associates (2008). Three major findings involving conflict/conflict resolution were reported. First, "intimate partner conflict was the most common preceding life event factor among 208 perpetrators of intimate partner only homicide–suicides (62%) and intimate partner plus other homicide–suicides (58%)" (p. 1060). The corresponding percentage for perpetrators of both filicide-suicide and extra-familial homicide–suicides was 36%. Compared with males who died by suicide, perpetrators of intimate partner femicide–suicide were over two times more likely to have a history of intimate partner conflicts (56% vs. 26%)" (p. 1062).

Second, of the 208 perpetrators of homicide–suicide with a history of intimate partner conflicts, 92% ($n = 161$) used a gun in the incident, and 39% of the 161 perpetrators who used a gun (39%, $n = 75$) "were believed to have retaliated in response to a divorce request or break-up" (p. 1060).

Third, almost one-fifth (18%) the 191 perpetrators who used a gun in the intimate partner homicide–suicide incident participated or were participating in family court proceedings at the time of the incident. Participation in adversarial separation and divorce proceedings tends to escalate the intensity of conflict (Ellis, 2013).

Barber and associates (2008) analyzed NVDRS data on 74 homicide–suicides, 18 homicide-attempted suicides, and 3,167 suicides recorded in four states and three counties. The data were analyzed quantitatively (cross-tabulations). Two findings are noteworthy. First, jealousy or arguments preceded most separation-instigated intimate partner homicide–suicides. Second, 90% of 61 homicide–suicide incidents involved intimate partner conflict or "the killing of a sexual rival" (p. 291). This finding was not clearly presented so we may have misinterpreted it.

Findings reported by the Violence Policy Center (2008) indicate that arguments between intimate partners are frequently settled by femicide–suicide. The conflict described below illustrates the process of escalation:

> Shane Brad, a 39-year-old man with a history of domestic violence, shot and killed his 9-months' pregnant wife, Una, before turning the gun on himself. The year before, Una Brady had filed for a temporary restraining order requiring her husband to refrain from harassing or abusing her. Una's two teen-aged daughters who witnessed the incident told the police that after the couple engaged in an argument, Shane shot his wife in the face and chest and then shot himself in the head.
>
> **Violence Policy Center, 2006**

We do not know the cause of the argument between Shane and Una, but we may reasonably infer that they were separated because of the restraining order. Arguments are not the only but are the most common precursor (63%) of the 1865 murder-suicides involving intimate partners that occurred in 1987.

Morton and associates (1998) studied 99 intimate partner femicide–suicides reported in North Carolina between 1988 and 1992. They found that "evidence of conflict" was present in almost one-third (31%) of the cases, with "conflict prior to the conflict" being present in 26% of the cases where the couples were separated and 36% of the cases of couples who were not separated (p. 96).

A summary of the causal mechanisms explaining the empirical generalizations that are derived from or implicit in the theories described in this chapter are presented in Table 6.1.

Table 6.1 Theories and Causal Mechanisms for the Association between Separation and Intimate Partner Femicide–Suicide

Theory	Causal Mechanisms
Evolutionary psychological	Challenging male partner ownership
Sociological social control	Crime and just punishment
Attribution	Other blame/self-blame
Masculinity	Shame/humiliation
Attachment	Frustration and other/self-blame
Borderline personality disorder	Depression/extreme dependency/abandonment
Conflict resolution	Extreme dependency/intensity of conflict

COMMENT

Henry and Short's (1954) theory of the effects of the business cycle on homicide and suicide is grounded in the theory of frustration and aggression formulated by Dollard and associates (1939), and "strength of the relational system" is identified as the focal explanatory variable for homicide or suicide (pp. 13–19). With specific reference to the relationship between married couples, Henry and Short conceive of husbands and wives as sources of both nurturance/love and frustration (p. 116). Divorce, as we indicated earlier, is defined as an act of aggression and a source of frustration. Stack's attachment theory was designed to test a hypothesis formulated by Henry and Short, and his theory is also grounded, at least in part, in frustration-aggression theory. This is evident in his conception of homicide–suicide as "stemming from a frustrated intimate relationship" (p. 435).

As it was originally formulated by Dollard and associates (1939), the frustration-aggression hypothesis was bold in the sense that the association between frustration and aggression was hypothesized to be invariable—frustration is always a cause of aggression and aggression is always a consequence of frustration. This hypothesis was central to the frustration-aggression theory used by Henry and Short in their research linking the business cycle with homicide and suicide and in their relatively brief analysis of homicide–suicide.

Frustration-aggression theory has been subjected to sustained criticism, modification, and reformulation by a number of theorists and researchers (Berkowitz, 1989, p. 59). In 1941, Neil Miller, one of the authors of the original frustration-aggression theory, wrote an article in which he concluded that "frustration can sometimes lead to aggression, and aggression can be caused by things other than frustration" (1941, p. 338). Berkowitz (1989) reformulated the frustration-aggression hypothesis by demonstrating that the effect of frustration on aggression is mediated by other factors. Bandura (1989) concluded that frustration only creates a subjective state of emotional arousal and learning through imitation and reinforcement influenced how individuals respond to this subjective state. Thus, the unilateral decision to divorce made by wives may cause frustration among husbands who are left, but their responses to this source of frustration vary. In 1989, Berkowitz observed, "Most psychologists still think of the frustration-aggression hypothesis as almost entirely as it was first spelled out (in 1939) by Dollard and associates" (p. 59).

Stack's attachment theory does not appear to be informed by the literature on the frustration-aggression hypothesis published prior to the year (1987) his article was published. If, as he suggests, jealousy, guilt, and attribution style mediate the effect of frustration/separation on homicide–suicide, then the association between homicide-suicide and a "frustrated intimate relationship" is not invariant but is present only under certain conditions. These could be included in a revised version of attachment theory that compares the strength of the association between separations (unilateral contested and jointly decided) and homicide–suicide where the victim is the perpetrator's wife, common-law partner, ex-lover, or girl/boyfriend.

Structural explanations of the association between separation rates and homicide–suicide rates that identify "proxy variables" as explanatory mechanisms are valid sociological explanations. Proxy variables are substitutes for real variables that are only revealed by collecting data from individuals. Real variables provide more valid information about "individual-level causal processes" that underlie structural explanations than do proxy variables (Sampson, 1989, p. 4). Stack used "guilt" as a proxy variable to explain the association between homicides and suicides that follow them. Adler collected data on individual perpetrators of homicide followed by suicide. They did not express guilt or remorse (1999, p. 11). In other words, guilt was not found to be a real variable that explained Adler's structural explanation of homicide–suicide in Chicago. Stack also used attribution style as a proxy variable. Data we collected from incarcerated perpetrators of femicide-attempted suicide and individuals participating in separation/divorce proceedings revealed more than two attributions of responsibility or blame for these outcomes—self, other, both, and neither (Ellis, 1994; Ellis et al., 2012). Stack's proxy variable includes only two attribution styles—self and other. Stack did not really test his attribution theory of homicide–suicide, and Liem's findings do not support his theory.

Stack's research also elicited three positive comments. First, he was among the first sociologists to test the Henry and Short hypothesis that homicide–suicide varied with the degree of positive attachment between perpetrators and victims. Second, he reported findings supporting it, and he went beyond it by reporting findings indicating that the odds of suicide following a homicide were highest for perpetrators with a high degree of positive attachment to their separated victim or were previously involved in a relationship with a high degree of mutual positive attachment. Third, he made an explicit attempt to identify mechanisms that explained his structural explanation of homicides followed by suicides.

Gillespie, Hearn, and Silverman (1998) created an attachment theory in which the "focal explanatory variable" was Henry and Short's "strength of the bond between the offender and his victim" (1939, p. 53). The hypothesis they derived from Henry and Short's theory was that homicide–suicide will vary positively with the intimacy of the relationship between the perpetrator and the victim. Unfortunately, the effects of ending intimate relationships that vary in intimacy through separation or divorce on homicide–suicides were not theorized. This is one reason why their attachment theory cannot account for the association between separation and femicide–suicide.

Another reason may be their failure to also ground their adult attachment theory in Bowlby's (1977) attachment theory. Psychoanalyst Bowlby defines "attachment theory" as a way of conceptualizing the propensity of human beings to make strong affectional bonds to particular others and of explaining the many forms of emotional distress and personality disturbance ... to which unwilling separation and loss give rise (1977, p. 201). This theory links the reactions of "anxiously attached" (fear of abandonment) infants to unwilling separation from a primary or preferred person (usually the mother) with the reactions of "anxiously attached" (fear of abandonment) adults to separation from wives and lovers (anxiety, self-blame, despair, intense anger) that we hypothesize would increase the likelihood of femicide–suicide. Anxiously attached children who experience threats of abandonment, physical abuse, and other forms of emotional abuse are experiencing events that make a significant contribution to the emergence of an adult personality disorder associated with homicide and suicide (Dutton, 2006, p. 222).

Our review of personality theory and research elicits four comments. First, the following seven variables should be interrelated in explanations of the association between separation and femicide–suicide that include BPD. The time-ordered variables are:

- Childhood experiences of actual or threatened separation and abuse
- BPD as an adult
- Chaotic, conflict-filled intimate partner relationship characterized by dysfunctional communication
- Unwilling separation instigated by BPD
- High-intensity conflict over separation motivated by fear of abandonment
- One or both partners intoxicated during the final conflict
- Use of femicide–suicide to end the conflict

Second, the most valid source of information on the motives, thoughts, feelings, and immediate circumstances surrounding femicide–suicides are perpetrators (femicide-attempted suicides), but we found it difficult and time-consuming to actually interview men who survived genuine attempts to kill themselves after killing their female intimate partners, even when they were all located in one place (penitentiary) (Ellis et al., 2012). As a result, researchers tend to collect and analyze "secondary data" on perpetrators of femicide–suicide from institutional files and records.

Collecting data on perpetrators from institutional records or files located in police headquarters, penitentiaries, and forensic assessment centers frequently, if not invariably, subordinates the collection of data for testing theory to the administrative, political, and policy objectives of bureaucratic institutions. This is evident in the data collected by Dutton and Kerry (we interviewed inmates in the same penitentiaries) and Liem and Roberts. In both of these studies, comorbidity (e.g., alcohol and/or other drug abuse) was not included as a variable, presumably because the information was not included in the institutional records from which they collected their data. As a result, they could not investigate the independent, interactive, and additive effects of comorbidity on femicide and femicide–suicide.

Third, a more robust explanation of the association between separation and femicide is, in our view, more likely to be provided by a "dyadic" (couples) approach in which BPD, comorbid, and situational factors (e.g., presence of own children) are integrated than by an approach that focuses exclusively on the personality traits of individuals (Roberts & Noller, 1998; Winstock, 2013).

Fourth, although BPD is a diagnostic category, it is important to remember that the pathological personality traits identified in DSM-5 are extreme manifestations of traits that are manifested, albeit to different degrees, by many, if not most, individuals. In other words, most of us can be located on a severity of traits continuum with pathological at one end and normal at the other.

Many researchers have reported findings indicating that depression is significantly associated with suicide and with femicide–suicides that are primarily suicides (Ellis et al., 2012). Daly and Wilson (1988) do not invoke mental illness or depression to explain why a relatively few individuals engage in futile, spiteful behavior that is maladaptive. Neither "mental illness" nor "depression" is in the index of their book. In cases where depression is found to be strongly associated with femicide–suicide, it is trumped by the "proprietary attitude" of depressed perpetrators (p. 216). Cooper and Eaves interpret their findings as supporting Wilson and Daly's MSP theory of femicide–suicide. However, they do not discuss the implications for this theory of findings indicating that mental illness followed separation as the second main precipitating condition for femicide–suicide (p. 102). Moreover, it is difficult to interpret their findings as supporting MSP theory when indicators of MSP such as "proprietary attitudes" and "extreme jealousy" were not included among the main precipitating conditions identified by Cooper and Eaves because information on these variables was not included in coroner files.

Conflict resolution theory is not fully supported by the findings cited in support of it because individual-level data on variables that constitute the heart of it—dependency, intensity of conflict, strength of motivation for togetherness—were not collected and analyzed. Indeed, apart from Adler, none of the theory-testing research studies we reviewed here reported findings identifying causal mechanisms underlying the association between separation and femicide–suicide based on the analysis of both structural and individual-level data.

DISCUSSION QUESTIONS

1. Evaluate this statement: Male sexual proprietariness is the causal mechanism underlying the association between separation and intimate partner femicide–suicide.
   Do you agree or disagree? Give reasons for your answer.

2. Identify, compare, and critically evaluate the causal mechanisms underlying the association between separation and femicide–suicide derived from attribution and masculinity theory.

3. Evaluate this statement: Extreme separation anxiety is the causal mechanism that explains the association between separation and femicide–suicide. Do you agree or disagree? Give reasons for your answer.

4. Identify, compare, and critically evaluate the causal mechanisms explaining the association between separation and femicide–suicide from Daly and Wilson's evolutionary psychological theory and conflict resolution theory.

Separation and Suicide

CHAPTER 7

LEARNING OBJECTIVES

Readers who have achieved the learning objectives set for this chapter will be able to:

- Derive causal mechanisms explaining the association between separation and suicide from the theories described in this chapter
- Assess the strength of any theory from which a causal mechanism is derived by analyzing findings that test it
- Assess the degree to which theories from which causal mechanisms are derived have developed cumulatively over time
- Demonstrate an understanding of problems associated with deriving valid causal mechanisms from theories by using official statistics to measure suicide rates

SOCIAL INTEGRATION–REGULATION THEORY

Described as "the dominant influence on the sociological study of suicide" by Danigelis and Pope (1979), Emile Durkheim published his landmark sociological study in 1875. In his sociological theory, the causes of variations in rates of four different types of suicides—egoistic, altruistic, anomic, fatalistic—were located in "states of the various social environments in which they occur." In society and its constituent social environments or institutions (family, religious, political, military society) "social/moral forces drive individuals to their deaths, each one believing that he/she is obeying only him/herself" (Taylor, 1982, p. 21). The social environment we shall focus on in this chapter is "domestic society." Domestic society includes two different types of societies or associations. One is the *conjugal* group that unites members of the same generation (husbands/wives), and the other is the *family* group that unites members of different generations (parents and children). Durkheim states that "These two societies have not the same origin nor the same nature and consequently ... the same effects" on egoistic suicide (p. 185).

Durkheim's structural theory of suicide in domestic society is a social integration–regulation theory because it is designed to explain both egoistic (integration) and anomic (regulation) suicide. Egoistic suicide is defined as a suicide that "results from (caused by) lack of integration of the individual into society" or its constituent institutions. Low integration is associated with "excessive individualism." Excessively individualistic individuals "are not included in many things that happen in society (and its institutions), they feel unattached, helpless, useless" (p. 14). The family and egoistic suicides are linked in this proposition: Egoistic suicide varies with the degree of integration of the individual into society and into families of which they are members (p. 209). This proposition is supported by findings indicating that separated persons who are less well integrated into society have higher suicide rates than married persons who are more highly integrated (p. 171).

Among married persons, egoistic suicide rates vary with the *density* of the family. Density is a structural variable that varies across conjugal groups and family groups with one, two, three, four, or more children. The greater the number of group members, the greater the density of the domestic group and the lower the rate of suicide. That is to say, the "coefficient of protection" from suicide is greater for members of larger than for smaller families and greater for smaller families than for couples. Conversely, the risk of suicide is greatest for unwillingly separated persons who were members of large (high-density) families because of the forced transition from a group with collectivistic values that regulates individual behavior for the good of the family as unit, to a marital status (single/separated) group that invites or permits excessive individualism or does little to regulate or control it.

The causal mechanism underlying the association between separation and egoistic suicide is the low social integration of separated persons into society. Feelings of loneliness, isolation, and helplessness associated with excessive individualism/low integration are likely to be greater for separated individuals who were once members of a collectivistic/high-integration group and then experienced an unwilling transition into an individualistic/low-integration group than for single/never married individuals. Consequently, suicide rates should be higher for members of the transition group who do not remarry than for members of the nontransition group.

Anomie is usually a temporary condition in which norms no longer effectively regulate behavior because they are not appropriate for changed or changing conditions or outcomes. In the context of domestic society, anomie is a condition "which afflicts widows and widowers as well as those who have experienced separation and divorce" (1897, Book 2, Chapter 3). Separated and divorced individuals—especially husbands—are inflicted with anomie because the transition to this status from the status of married has weakened the regulation they experienced as married persons. Anomic suicide, then, varies inversely with marital regulation, with unmarried persons being less effectively regulated than married persons. Unmarried persons include both single/never married and separated/divorced individuals. Anomic suicide rates are higher for divorced than for single persons because marital conflict usually precedes divorce and conflict decreases marital regulation. Participation in adversarial divorce proceedings prolongs and escalates the intensity of conflict and the experience of social deregulation or anomie. From this account, it follows that regulation is the causal mechanism underlying the association between separation and anomic domestic suicide.

As did Durkheim, Henry and Short (1954) viewed suicide as "a function of the weakening of social controls over behavior" (p. 74). Following Max Weber (1947), they conceived of social control as inherent in social interaction because behavior is invariably regulated by parties who want the relationship to continue. Under this condition, regulation involves taking into account the wants and expectations of the other party as well as anticipating the reactions of the other party prior to initiating action (p. 74). Social relationships are differentiated into "social" and "cathectic" relationships. Unlike social relationships, cathectic relationships involve emotional investment in other persons. The greater the number of cathectic relationships with other persons, the greater the strength of the individual's relational system. The greater the strength of an individual's relational system, the greater the degree to which his/her behavior is regulated or controlled by others and, consequently, the lower the risk of suicide.

From this set of assumptions Henry and Short derived the hypothesis that the probability of suicide varies inversely with the strength of the relational system of the individual and they postulate that married persons have lower suicide rates than single persons *because* their relational system is stronger than the relational system of separated persons (pp. 74–75). Strength of relational system is the causal mechanism underlying the association between separation and suicide.

Single persons include two marital status categories—widowed and divorced—that are similar to each other with respect to the possible/probable presence of children. Strength of external restraint cannot explain differences in suicide rates between these two "weak external restraint" marital status categories, which are also similar to each other in that members of both were married and had lost a partner. However, the way in which their partners were lost is different. Unlike divorce, which is a "deliberate and motivated act" that Henry and Short assume to be both an aggressive act and a source of frustration against the perpetrator's "primary source of nurturance and love," the natural or accidental death of a partner occurs "independently of the wishes of the surviving partner" or his/her frustration-instigated aggressive actions. The absence of strong external restraint among the divorced and widowed—they do not have to conform on an everyday basis to the demands and expectations of other family members—undermines the legitimation of aggression against spouses who frustrated them by intentionally "ending the flow of nurturance and love" through divorce. The dynamic that results in the "denial of legitimacy" to aggression directed against the spouse and increases the likelihood of suicide is described in the following terms:

> Aggression against the marital partner destroys the marriage and with it a primary source of nurturance and love. The resulting inhibition of aggression and internalization of the attitudes of the source of frustration serve to deny legitimacy to the outward expression of aggression consequent to future frustration (by divorce) and the result is an increased tendency to express aggression inwardly against the self.
>
> p. 116

Gold (1958) attempted to "build upon and amplify a portion of Henry and Short's theoretical structure" by offering a social–psychological explanation of the same outcome (choice between suicide and homicide) investigated by Henry and Short. Gold's theory took the form of identifying social class differences in child socialization as the variable that mediated the effect of a structural factor (business cycle) on the direction of aggression (inner versus outer directed). Henry and Short reported findings based on seven comparisons to support their theory. The seventh comparison was between married and unmarried individuals. Gold did not identify childhood socialization as a variable that also mediates the effect of separation on suicide because he was only interested in offering an explanation of that portion of Henry and Short's theory accounting for the choice between homicide and suicide. Bowlby's (1977) attachment theory and findings linking child abuse with borderline personality disorder (BPD) (Dutton, 2006) strongly suggest that threats of parental abandonment and child abuse also mediate the effect of a structural factor (married/separated) on suicide. Mediation would have the effect of rank ordering rates of suicide within and between married and separated persons, with the highest rates of suicide being found among a relatively small number of separated adults who experienced the most serious and frequent abandonment threats and abuse as children.

Regulation or restraint can be external (ties to/expectations and reactions of others) and internal (conformity with internalized values and norms). For Henry and Short, strength of relational system referred to external control or restraint. Maris (1969) builds upon Henry and Short's theory in two ways: First, he subsumes both sources of restraint under the concept of external constraint. Second, he attempts to explain why individuals in societal contexts, such as those described by Henry and Short, engage in "self-destructive behaviors" or follow suicidal careers. In the context of domestic society, external constraint would be the causal mechanism underlying the association between separation and suicide.

Like Durkheim, structural sociologist Taylor (1982) believes that the sociological (structural/social realist) study of suicide involves the "discovery of underlying mechanisms that caused the relations between observable phenomena" (p. 195). Unlike Durkheim and the plethora of sociologists who represent the "sociological tradition" characterized by the use of rates as variables, Taylor concludes and gives reasons for concluding (Chapter 3) that "suicide rates are a most inappropriate source of data for studying suicidal actions" and that "*suicidal actions will not be satisfactorily explained without reference to the actor's intentions and the micro-social context of his actions*" (p. 194). Compared with sociologists such as Maris (1969), who advocated "putting Durkheim to bed," and Danigelis and Pope (1979), who state that the cumulative theoretical development of theory "can be achieved only by focusing on the leading theory—Durkheim" (p. 1081), Taylor builds upon and radically reorients Durkheim's theory of suicide.

Reorientation has two dimensions: Dimension 1 takes the form of conceiving of suicidal actions or performances as an outcome of "the *combination* of detachment from others *and* uncertainty about one's existence or certainty that one's life is over" (p. 178). Dimension 2 is the differentiation between "inner-directed" and "other-directed" suicides. Inner-directed (ecotopic) suicides are an outcome of "a strong or extreme sense of *detachment* from others." Individuals who are "immune to or psychologically protected from" communications addressed to them by others (thoughts, feelings, pleas, wishes, advice, warnings) are most likely to commit ecotopic (inner-directed) suicides. Other-directed (symphysis) suicides are an outcome of a strong or extreme sense of attachment to others. Taylor describes these individuals as symphysic because they have "no real existence independent of others' favorable validation of them" (p. 178). Unlike inner-directed suicides, which are an outcome of *monologues*, other-directed suicides are an outcome of *dialogues* with a significant other or others.

To this point, the effects of attachment were differentiated from the effects of detachment and ectopic (inner-directed) suicides, as monologues were differentiated from symphysic suicides as dialogues. In the penultimate part of his theory, Taylor differentiates between "two *focal points of the actor's meaning*." These are "communications *about* suicide and communications *through* suicide." The latter are characteristic of symphysic (other-directed) suicide (p. 180). Other-directed suicides of doubt are defined as doubt about whether the significant other cares whether he lives or dies. These suicides are Janus-faced because they "combine the wish to die with the wish for change in others and an improvement in the situation: they are both acts of despair and of hope" (p. 180).

The situation, or microsocial context, in which appeals "other-directed" suicides are most likely to occur are described in the following terms:

> The situations in which appeals suicides are most likely to occur are characterized by direct warnings, pleas, threats and dire prognostications. If the unbearable doubt and attachment to the other continue … the individual cannot certainly kill himself because then he would never find out, but neither can he not kill himself, for other means of validation have failed. He therefore gambles with death with some hope that he might live and yet be responded to as if he had died.
>
> p. 180

In sum, appeals suicides are described as "communications through suicide … produced by the individual's uncertainty about the other and his complete attachment to the other" (p. 185).

Research

Durkheim (1897) collected official statistics on marital status, suicide, presence of children, age, and sex from France and Oldenberg in Germany between 1873 and 1891. The data were analyzed using cross tabulations. In some tables, age and sex were used as independent variables, and in others they were used as control variables. Findings were interpreted using "coefficients of preservation and aggravation." The coefficient of preservation is defined as "the number showing how many times less frequent is in one group than another" (p. 177). When the coefficient of preservation decreases below one, it becomes a coefficient of aggravation. Two major findings are noteworthy: First, compared with unmarried persons, married persons of both sexes age 20 years and older experience a coefficient of preservation that varies with age reaching a maximum of 3.20 between the ages of 25 and 30 for men and women in France (Table 20, p. 177). In France, the coefficient of preservation of married persons also changes with sex, with the coefficient for married men averaging 2.73 compared with 1.56 (43% less) for women.

Second, family density was found to be strongly associated with immunity from suicide. Findings reported by Durkheim indicate that husbands with children experience a coefficient of preservation significantly higher than the coefficient for unmarried men (2.9) and higher than the coefficient for husbands without children (1.5) (p. 197).

Almost 100 years after the publication of *Suicide*, Danigelis and Pope (1979) tested Durkheim's theory of integration–regulation suicide in domestic society (the family) by analyzing three sources of data: the French and Oldenberg data presented by Durkheim in three tables; suicide rates by marital status, sex, and age published by the World Health Organization (WHO) for 10 Western European countries plus Australia and New Zealand; and official French statistics on suicide rates cross-classified by sex, age, and marital status for nine census years between 1886 and 1931. Data were analyzed using a "standardized suicide difference coefficient" that avoids the problem of a disproportionate contribution to averages made by very large coefficients of preservation. Data were also analyzed using N-Way analysis of variance in order to go "beyond Durkheim" by demonstrating the main and interaction effects of the variables he investigated. Analysis of the three data sets yielded three major findings, which are described below.

First, Durkheim's data support the hypothesis that married persons are more integrated than divorced persons. Consequently, suicide rates for divorced persons are higher than suicide rates for more integrated married persons. Findings based on the analysis of WHO data indicate that marital status (married versus divorced) explains 25.4% of the variation in suicide. Here, a significant amount of variation was explained by a single variable, and the findings support the integration portion of the Durkheim's integration–regulation theory of egoistic domestic suicide. Actually, to the degree that integration is associated with more effective regulation than low or no integration, this finding supports both portions of his theory.

Second, French data support the hypothesis that family density is strongly associated with suicide rates. Specifically, comparisons of standardized suicide difference coefficients reveal that married or widowed persons with children are significantly less likely to commit suicide than married, widowed, or divorced persons without children. Within the category of divorced persons, those with children should also be less likely to commit suicide than those without children. These findings led the authors to conclude that marital integration, as measured by the presence of children, "is associated with important variation in social suicide rates" (p. 1099).

Third, Durkheim's "chronic anomie" theory of domestic suicide predicts that suicide rates for divorced persons would be higher than the rates for single persons because the process of divorcing usually increases feelings of mutual hostility (conflict) between estranged spouses and (we would add) not infrequently, the outcome of divorce is frequently chosen by one of the spouses against the wishes of the other. As individual-level data on conflict-instigated anomie were not available to either Durkheim or Danigelis and Pope, the hypothesis that this mechanism mediates the effect of divorce on suicide was not tested.

Divorced and married persons live in households that vary in their composition (family density). Following Durkheim, Danigelis and Pope investigated the contribution made to suicide rates by one indicator of "family density"—presence/absence of children. Findings reported by both Durkheim and Danigelis and Pope that, among both married and divorced persons, the presence of children made a significant contribution toward protecting them from suicide. The protection was significant but not equal. Married persons with children experienced greater protection than divorced persons with children. This finding strongly suggests that marriage and the presence of children are causal mechanisms underlying the association between divorce and suicide.

In addition to presence of children and a married partner who is a source of nurturance, love, and support, family density can also be measured by the presence of other family members such as relatives. Moreover, the effects of family density may vary with location in different marital status categories. Finally, the unwilling or willing transition from one marital status to another that varies in family density may markedly increase or decrease the risk of suicide, depending upon the degree of deregulation, isolation, and loss of social support entailed by the transition.

Beyond the presence/absence of children, official statistics on the density (structure) of the households in which members of different marital status categories live were not available to Durkheim or Danigelis and Pope. They were available to Denny (2010).

The health status of the population of the United States is assessed annually by a cross-sectional National Health Interview Survey of 40,000 households conducted by the National Center for Health Statistics. Between 75,000 and 100,000 individuals residing in these households were interviewed. The response rate to requests for interviews (90%) was very high. Different sources of data were linked to create a linked household and prospective mortality file (NHIS-LMF) on individuals age 18 and over. Consequently, Denney obtained information on 825,462 adults who were interviewed between 1986 and 1996, which was linked with 1,116 suicides recorded between 1986 and 2002.

The data collected by Denney permitted him to measure the size of the household (density) and the following household living (composition) arrangements:

- single, living alone;
- married with no children;
- married with children;
- unmarried, living with other relatives;
- unmarried with children; or
- living with unrelated adults.

Single, living alone is used as a reference type in multivariate statistical analyses involving household living arrangements as an independent variable. The size of the sample and the use of multivariate statistical analyses of the data enabled Denney to examine the effects of household living arrangements and density on suicide while controlling a number of predictors (covariates: age, sex, race/ethnicity, and education) of suicide. The following four major findings were reported by him:

First, as household size increases, the risk of suicide decreases. Specifically, Denney found that the risk of suicide decreased by 6% each time another person was added to the household (p. 16). This finding indicates that household density is strongly and inversely associated with the risk of suicide.

Second, after including sociodemographic control variables in the analysis, Denney found that compared with adults single/living alone:

- married/living with no children families reduced the risk of suicide by 34%;
- married/living with children families decreased it by 51%;
- unmarried/living with other relatives (not including children) families decreased it by 24%;
- unmarried/living with children families decreased it by 16%; and
- unrelated adults living in the same household slightly increased the risk of suicide.

Third, after health covariates were included as control variables, he found that compared with single adults/living alone, married persons without children experienced a 33% decreased risk, and married persons with children experienced a 48% decrease in the risk of suicide risk. The greater protection from suicide experienced by living in a family with children is indicated by the finding that the difference in the risk of suicide is statistically significant ($t = 62.5$, $p. 01$).

Fourth, after including a number of individual-level control variables in the analysis, individuals living in unmarried families with other adult relatives and those living in unmarried families with children experienced a 29% and 22% decrease in the risk of suicide. Compared with unmarried individuals living in both of these households, being married with children is associated with a significantly greater decrease in the risk of suicide ($t = 30.0$, $p < 0.01$).

Taken together, the findings presented in Table 7.1 provide an empirical basis for the following rank-ordering of household living arrangements according to the contribution they make toward decreasing the risk of suicide (see Table 7.1):

Table 7.1 Household living arrangement decrease in risk of suicide

Married with children	48%
Married with no children	33%
Unmarried with other relatives	29%
Unmarried families with children	22%
Unmarried adults*	

*"Slight increase" indicated by coefficients of 1.02 and 1.11 in Models 2 and 3, respectively (Denney, 2010, p.15).

Findings reported by Denney are important for a number of reasons. First, they make a cumulative contribution to Durkheim's integration–regulation theory of suicide by measuring family density as a variable rather than a category and then linking variations in family density with suicide. Second, he demonstrated that family density is more strongly associated with suicide when both the quantity and the quality (married partner, children, other relatives, other adults of the relationships among copresent family members, married partner, children, other relatives, unmarried adults) are taken into account. Conflict associated with the more frequent presence of stepchildren among cohabiting/common law couples (unmarried families with children) may explain why the risk of suicide is higher for them than it is for unmarried persons living with relatives (Daly & Wilson, 1991, 1998).

Third and most importantly for our purposes, Denney's findings support the following hypothesis: The transition from "married with children" to "living alone because of an imposed divorce" entails a greater loss of social and emotional support and a more intense experience of isolation and deregulation (anomie) than the transition from any other family living arrangement. The combined effect of these three variables may well account for the association between separation/divorce and suicide.

The analysis of all three sets of data led Danigelis and Pope to conclude that Durkheim's integration–regulation theory is supported by findings indicating that "the main effects of marital status (and sex) account for approximately 50% of the variation in suicide rates in the WHO data and between 66% and 75% of the variation in the French over time data" (p. 1100). Further support for this theory is provided by findings reported by Denney.

Support for Durkheim's theory-derived predictions about the protective effects of suicide have been supported by a number of researchers in addition to the ones cited here (e.g., Gove, 1972; Lester, 1987). Since 2000, one of the most frequently cited of them is Kposowa (2004). After controlling on a number of variables found to be associated with suicide (e.g., income, race/ethnicity, age, education), he found that:

- men were almost five times more likely to commit suicide than women;
- "divorced/separated" persons were over twice as likely to commit suicide than married persons (RR = 2.08, 95% CI 1.58–2.72);
- divorced/separated men were almost 2.5 times more likely to commit suicide than married men (RR = 2.38, 95% CI 1.77–3.20); and
- no statistically significant differences in the risk of suicide were found for women in different marital status categories.

The implementation of a prospective (nine-year) study design, selection of a large sample ($n = 545$ suicides), and the use of multivariate statistical procedures that enabled him to simultaneously control other probable sources of suicide risk (e.g., age) lend credibility to the findings reported by Kposowa. His attempt to explain the significant association between separation/divorce and suicide among men takes the form of citing explanations formulated by others. Included among them is Durkheim's integration–regulation (anomic) theory of suicide (p. 259).

Durkheim's theory has been supported by suicide rate findings based on the comparison between family members living in households that varied in their size (density), the presence of others and the kinds of others who were present (children, relatives, other adults), and between members of a variety of marital status categories (married/unmarried, married/divorced, married/single, divorced/widowed). "Separated" as a distinct marital status category was not included in any of the studies reviewed here. Consequently, differences in suicide rates based on comparisons with "separated" as one of the marital status categories are not reported in any of them. Contributions toward closing this gap were made by Cantor and Slator (1995) and Wyder, Ward, and De Leo (2009).

Cantor and Slater conducted a cross-sectional study designed to test the following phase-of-disruption hypothesis: "the acute disruption of attachments by separation [are] associated with a different suicide rate compared with the longer phase of divorce" (1995, p. 91). Their sample was composed of 1,375 individual residents of Queensland, Australia, whose deaths between 1990 and 1992 were recorded as suicides. In addition to reporting findings supporting Durkheim's integration–regulation theory (marriage was a protective factor for both husbands and wives), they found that separated men were more than six times more likely to commit suicide than divorced men. We suspect that separated men living alone who contested separations initiated by partners, and who had little or no contact with their children, were overrepresented among those who killed themselves. The involvement of men in interpersonal conflicts with their estranged partners during the process of separating was identified as the reason for the difference in the relative risk of suicide by separated and divorced men (p. 101). These findings suggest that conflict escalation is the mechanism underlying the association between separation and suicide by separated men.

Queensland was also the site of a study conducted by Wyder et al. (2009). The Queensland Suicide Register records include information on all ($n = 6062$) suicide cases recorded between 1994 and 2004 forwarded to them by coroners and police officers who investigated the cases and police officers who administered psychological autopsy forms to proxies of suicide victims. Multivariate statistical analyses (linear regression) of the data produced these major findings:

- Compared with divorced men in the highest relative risk category (ages 15–24), separated men in the same risk category and same age group were more than four times more likely to have been included as a suicide case in the Queensland Suicide Register.
- Compared with the marital statuses of married, divorced, single, and widowed, the relative risk of suicide was four times greater for both separated men and women.

The authors of this study included themselves among a number of other researchers who reported findings supporting Durkheim's theory of integration (e.g., Hassan, 1995; Torre et al., 1999; Stack, 2000).

In the study conducted by Cantor and Slater, suicide was found to vary by phase of marital breakdown, with the risk of suicide being significantly higher in the few months following separation (proximal phase) than in the three or more years (average) following divorce (distal phase). Using three electronic databases (MEDLINE, PSYCHLIT, and SCOPUS), Ide, Wyder, Kolves, and De Leo (2010) reviewed the 52 articles on suicide published between 1966 and 2008, with a view to discovering if similar findings had been reported by other researchers. One of their major findings was that the relative risk of suicide associated with separation and divorce was *separately* assessed in only two studies (p. 1701). Cantor and Slator's (1995) was one of them. The other study was conducted in Turin, Italy, by Torre et al. (1999).

They reported findings indicating that the risk of suicide among separated males and females was five and six times higher, respectively, than the suicide rate for divorced men and women. It should be noted that the context for this study was a Catholic country in which sin-free indefinite separations were more frequently initiated than sinful divorces. The effects of membership in one of four phase categories identified by Ide et al.—acute (recent) separation, long-term separation (divorce), early divorce, and late divorce—were not investigated in any of the studies they reviewed.

BORDERLINE PERSONALITY THEORY

The pathological personality traits subsumed under the domain of *Negative Affectivity* (fears of rejection and/or separation from significant others, excessive dependency on them, emotions that are easily aroused fears of falling apart in reaction to interpersonal stresses, frequent and persistent feelings of depression and hopelessness, thoughts of suicide and suicidal behavior) and *Disinhibition* (impulsivity and risk taking) suggest that BPD would be strongly associated with separation-instigated suicides. Findings reported by Fryer, Frances, Sullivan, Hurt, and Clarkin (1988) indicate that the association between (BPD) and "extended suicides" (femicide–suicides) is likely to be especially strong when comorbidity includes depression and impulsivity and risk taking, include using violence to settle conflicts, suicide attempts, and abusing alcohol and/or other drugs.

In a thoughtful and provocative article published in 1980, Baechler described different types of suicides "with each one having its own mechanism" (p. 78). The type of suicide most likely to be associated with separation by individuals with BPD/comorbid symptoms would appear to be "appeal suicides."

Taylor (1982) conceives of appeals suicides—attempts to communicate through suicide—as suicide performances resulting from *dialogues* rather than *monologues*. Persons who "have no 'real' existence independent of the other's (presence)" engage in suicidal performances which "are part of a dialogue with (the partner who unilaterally initiated the separation)." In the context of a unilaterally initiated separation and asymmetric emotional dependence on the partner initiating the separation, attempts to communicate through suicide are characterized by ambivalence (despair and hope)—"the wish to die combined with the wish for change in others and improvement in the situation" (p. 180). Our reading of Taylor suggests that individuals with BPD/comorbid symptoms are likely to be overrepresented among separating/separated intimate partners who, as a last communicative performance, commit appeals suicides.

Research

In the Dialectical Behavioral Model for BPD, Linehan (1993) identifies six behavioral patterns for BPD. Included among them are "recurrent suicidal behavior, gestures or threats or self-mutilating behavior," "inappropriate, intense anger or difficulty in controlling anger (e.g., frequent displays of temper, constant anger, recurring physical fights)," and "affective instability due to a marked reactivity of mood (e.g., intense episodic dysphoria/depression or anxiety)," "severe difficulty in regulating negative emotions," and "impulsivity in areas that are self-damaging" (e.g., alcoholism and substance abuse). Taken together, these patterns have been found to increase the risk of suicide directly and indirectly (Frances, Fryer, & Clarkin, 1986; Stone, Hurt, & Stone, 1987). In practice, these behavior patterns and other symptoms of BPD identified in the DSM-IV Axis II definition cannot be taken together because they are not always copresent. In some cases, individuals may meet five of the nine criteria needed for a diagnosis of BPD, and five of the six behavioral patterns, but not the criterion/pattern "intense episodic dysphoria."

In an attempt to identify precipitants and risk factors for the severity of suicide attempts specific to BPD and major depression disorder (BPD/MDD) and major depression disorder without BPD (MDD), Brodsky and associates (2006) selected a sample of 80 subjects (43 BPD/MDD and 37 MDD) who had made at least one suicide attempt ("a deliberate self-injurious act performed with at least some intent to die"). The results of a logistic regression analysis revealed that compared with MDD-only suicide attempters, BPD/MDD suicide attempters had a greater number of suicide attempts (OR = 1.56, 95% CI 1.02-2.36, $p < 0.04$) and higher levels of lifetime aggression, hostility, and impulsivity (OR = 1.18, 95% CI 1.00-1.40, $p < 0.06$).

In the DSM-V, depression is a pathological personality trait of BPD that is subsumed under the domain of *Negative Affectivity*. Based on their analysis of a large number of cases ($n = 9276$) that probably included a disproportionate number of BPD individuals, the Centers for Disease Control and Prevention (2011) reported findings indicating that almost three-quarters (74.6%) of those who committed suicide were depressed at the time. The direct and indirect effects of depression on suicide and attempted suicide have been documented by researchers using different study designs, samples, measurements, and methods of analysis (e.g., Blair-West, Cantor, Mellsop, & Everson-Annan, 1999; Bernal et al., 2007; Diserud et al., 2003; 2005; Harris & Barraclough, 1997; Hegerl, Rummel-Klugeand, Varnik, Arensman, & Koburger, 2013; Isacsson & Rich, 2003; Lecomte & Fornes, 1998; Liem & Roberts, 2009; Malone, Ocquendo, Haas, Ellis, & Mannand, 2000; Mortensen, Agerbo, Erikson, Qin, & Westergaard-Neilsonand, 2000; Mosiciki, 1997; Oquendo et al., 2007; Qin, Agerbo, Westergaard-Neilson, Eriksson, & Mortensenand, 2000; Skogman, Alsen, & Ojehagen, 2004). The evidence presented by these researchers suggests that the conclusion reached by Marzuk, Tardiff, and Hirsch (1992) based on their review of the literature—"depression was the most convincing, unifying diagnosis common to all types of murder- suicide" (p. 3182)—may also apply to BPD-associated suicide.

Other researchers report findings indicating that great weight should also be given to the BPD criterion of "impulsivity/aggression" as a risk factor for suicide because of its strong association with one of the most reliable predictors of suicide: number of prior suicide attempts (Brodsky, Malone, Ellis, & Mann, 1997; Conner, Duberstein, Conwell, Seidlitz, & Caine, 2001; Hawton, Houston, Haw, Townsend, & Harris, 2003; Leon, Friedman, Sweeney, Brown, & Mann, 1990; Linehan, 2012; Sansome, Gaither, & Songer, 2002; Soloff, Lynch, Kelly, & Mann, 2000).

McGirr, Paris, Lesage, Renaud, and Turecki (2007) reported findings indicating that the copresence of impulsivity-aggression and substance abuse more reliably differentiated BPD individuals who committed suicide from those who did not than impulsivity-aggression alone. This finding emerged from a case–control study of 120 BPD individuals—50 control subjects and 70 who died by suicide between 2001 and 2005. Proxy interviews—interviews with relatives and others with more than superficial knowledge about the individuals who committed suicide—were used to collect the data on those who died.

CONFLICT RESOLUTION THEORY

The pathological personality traits subsumed under the domains of *Negative Affectivity, Disinhibition,* and *Antagonism* (DSM-5) strongly suggest that BPD individuals are hard to get along with. As a result, relationships with their intimate partners are likely to be chaotic and conflict-ridden. Frequent conflict increases the likelihood of separation, and conflicts associated with separations initiated by one partner are likely to escalate the intensity of conflict. Increases in the intensity of conflict are associated with the use of sublethal and lethal means of settling conflicts. Suicide is one way in which high-intensity, separation-instigated conflicts may be settled. Conflict resolution theory identifies the escalation of conflict as the variable underlying the association between unwilling separation and suicide.

Research

Tallinn, the capital city of Estonia in Eastern Europe, was the site of a study of suicide undertaken by Kolves, Varnik, Schneider, Fritze, and Allik (2006). In 1999, 159 suicides were recorded in Tallinn. Information on these suicides was collected by two trained psychiatrists who conducted face-to-face interviews with spouses, parents, children, friends, and relatives of 156 of the 159 individuals who committed suicide. The average lapsed time between the suicide and the interview was five months. The researchers were interested in comparing the death-by-suicide group ($n = 156$) with a group of 156 control subjects selected (by random digit dialing) from the general population. As gender, age, and ethnicity were known to be risk factors for suicide, the control subjects matched the sex, gender, and ethnicity of the suicide group of subjects. Information on control subjects was collected by means of face-to-face interviews conducted by doctors (GPs) who were trained to conduct them. Statistical analyses of the data yielded information on the relative risk of suicide (odds ratios), the significance of differences in odds ratio between the two groups, and the independent effects of recent "life events" such as separation, mental and physical illness, unemployment, and conflict on suicide.

Findings reported by Kolves et al. indicated that one or more of the 11 life events they included as predictor variables were experienced by 126 (81%) individuals. A comparison of life events experienced during the preceding three months by individuals in the suicide and control groups revealed that weighted odds ratios for family conflict and separation were significantly higher for the suicide group (OR 26.0, CI 95%,6,8-220.4, p<0.001, and OR 22.0, CI 95% 53.6-908.0, p<0.001, respectively). This compares with weighted ORs ranging between 0.1 and 4.0 for the remaining eight life events (no data on loss of job). Logistic regression (conditional) analysis yielded findings indicating that family conflict during the preceding 3 months made a significant independent contribution toward suicide (OR 25.2, CI 95% 6.0-105.5, p<0.0001). High levels of separation-instigated interpersonal conflict were also found to make a significant independent contribution to the 1,375 suicides investigated by Cantor and Slator (1995).

Researchers such as Crimmins (1991) and Levi (1981) conceive of homicide and suicide as "violent resolutions to conflicts" (Crimmins, p. 103). Findings reported by the Centers for Disease Control and Prevention (2012) indicate that "intimate partner conflict" preceded 20% of the 10,982 suicides and 28% of the 10,982 homicides that occurred in the United States during 2003–2004 (pp. 2–3). Kowalski (2005) found the "escalation of an argument" to be the motive most frequently attributed to husbands who kill their wives (41%) by investigating police officers in Canada (p. 55). Mercy and Saltzman (1989) found that "arguments . . . preceded 67% of spouse homicides" recorded in FBI Supplementary Homicide reports, 1976–1985 (p. 376). In Australia, the corresponding figure was 56% (Davies & Mouzos, 2007).

As we indicated earlier, verbal arguments tend to escalate to the use of physical force, if and when words do not settle conflicts by producing outcomes desired by one or both of the parties. The repeated use of violent conflict resolution tactics by male partners, especially tactics that result in increasingly serious injuries, has been defined by Ogle and Jacobs (2002) as "battering," and battering was defined as a "homicidal process" often resulting in the death of the battered partner. Findings reported by other researchers indicate the battering may also be a "suicidal process" for battered women without children who (1) end the battering by separating, (2) do not or cannot separate safely, or (3) are unable or unwilling to kill their batterers in self-defense (Browne, 1987; Kowalski, 2005; Mercy & Saltzman, 1989).

During a period of eight months, 118 battered wives sought emergency care in a hospital in Sweden. This sample of women was studied by Bergman and Brismar (1991). They found that 70% (n = 82) of them had attempted suicide. When they compared the women in their selected sample with an unselected sample of women who were being treated for attempted suicide in the same hospital, they found that women in their battered woman sample were eight times more likely to attempt suicide than the women in the unselected sample.

The medical records of women attending the emergency service of a hospital in Connecticut were investigated by Stark and Flitcraft (1996). Compared with women who were not battered, battered women were 2.5 times more likely to attempt suicide on more than one occasion. Moreover, almost 37% of the battered women attended the emergency service for treatment of an injury caused by the suicide attempt *on the same day* they had visited the hospital for treatment of an injury caused by male partner violence. The temporal proximity that characterizes femicide–suicide also seems to characterize serious male partner violence and attempted suicide. Golding's (1999) meta-analysis of 40 studies revealed a positive association between battering and elevated rates of suicide attempts. Similar findings are reported by Afifi et al. (2009), McFarlane, Campbell, and Watson (2002), Seedat, Stein, and Forde (2005), and Simon, Anderson, Thompson, Crosby, and Sacks (2002).

Bergman and Brismar (1991) studied the medical records of 118 battered women whose suicide attempts resulted in injuries serious enough to require hospitalization. These records were studied for a period of 10 years prior to the suicide attempt and six years after it took place. They found that conflict-resolution attempts preceded the suicide attempt in one-third of the cases.

In the Brodsky et al. study (2006), referred to in the preceding section, precipitants of the first suicide attempt made by BPD/MDD and MDD subjects were found to be different. Specifically, the former were more likely to attempt suicide "when faced with interpersonal conflict or disappointment" in conjugal and other relationships, whereas suicide attempts by the latter were more likely to be precipitated by job- and health-related experiences (p. 318). This finding supports the hypothesis that the relationship between BPD/MDD and the severity of suicide attempts is mediated by the situational/proximal factor of interpersonal conflict.

Leone (2011) investigated the association between two types of male partner violence—intimate terrorism and situational couple (conflict-instigated) violence and suicidal behavior among 258 low-income African-American women who had experienced one or other (or both) types of violence and 111 who had not. When suicidal behavior was regressed on five risk factors for this outcome at the same time, only posttraumatic stress disorder (PTSD) was found to be a statistically significant predictor of suicidal behavior (OR = 1.15, 95% CI = 1.04–1.28) and women who experienced conflict-instigated violence also experienced "significantly more PTSD symptoms" (p. 2585). These symptoms mediate the impact of conflict-instigated violence on suicidal behavior. The reader may recall that in the Tallinn study (Kolves et al., 2006), recent interpersonal conflict and separation were found to be statistically significant predictors of suicide.

SUMMARY

A summary of the causal mechanisms explaining the empirical generalizations that are derived from or implicit in the theories is described in Table 7.2

Table 7.2 Theories and Causal Mechanisms for the Association between Separation and Intimate Partner Suicide

Theory	Causal Mechanisms
Integration–regulation	Extreme individualism/ineffective regulation
Relational system	Frustration/legitimacy of lethal aggression
Microsocial	Extreme attachment/detachment from others
Borderline personality disorder	Depression/despair/hope
Conflict resolution	Dependency/depression/abandonment/intensity of conflict

COMMENT

Durkheim's sociological integration–regulation theory of suicide is a classic, paradigmatic example of a creative structural theory that was tested using data, methods of measurement, and quantitative analysis that met and may have even exceeded extant standards, but which do not meet standards set by contemporary sociologists such as Pope (1976), who attempted to test his theory. Of more interest to us is the contribution made by some researchers to the cumulative of Durkheim's theory and the identification of causal mechanisms (living arrangements and the quality of the relationship between individuals who are living together) underlying the association between separation and suicide.

Another comment elicited by the theory and research reviewed here is the degree to which Durkheim's integration–regulation of suicide in domestic society has influenced sociological theory and research on suicide by members in different marital status categories during the past 130 years. Most of the studies reviewed here do not reveal progress toward the cumulative development of an integration–regulation theory of suicide in domestic society that would specify more precisely the conditions (e.g., phase of separation or separation versus divorce) under which integration and/or regulation may more fully account for the association between separation and suicide. One step in this direction is for theorists who claim to be going "beyond Durkheim" to assume, as Durkheim did, that egoism and anomie are "merely two different aspects of a (single) social state" that causes both types of suicides (1951, pp. 288 & 382) (Danigelis & Pope, 1979, p. 1082; Taylor, 1982).

Danigelis and Pope conducted a sociological study that was explicitly designed, not to contribute to the cumulative development of Durkheim's theory but to assess "its empirical validity" by collecting better quality (more reliable/valid) French and WHO official suicide statistics and analyzing the data using multivariate statistical procedures. Their findings support Durkheim's theory of integration–regulation and consequently, the identification of integration and regulation as factors underlying the association between divorce and suicide. They do not support the association between separation and suicide because data on this marital status was not available to them. Given the problems associated with collecting official statistics on separation referred to earlier (Chapter 2), separation and divorce are routinely conflated in contemporary sociological and epidemiological studies on marital status and suicide (e.g., Kposowa, 2000; Kposowa, Singh, & Breault, 1994).

The use of the conflated marital status—"divorced–separated"—as a risk factor is a significant limitation for two reasons. First, the effects of separation cannot be separated from those of divorce. If separation poses a far greater risk, then the use of "divorced–separated" as a risk factor will underestimate the risk of suicide. Second, if the early post-separation phase is the period of greatest risk, then the use of separated–divorced as a risk factor will divert attention from the period of greatest risk because divorces are initiated much later than separations.

Like Kposowa, Denney (2010) contributed to continuity in conflation because he did not differentiate "single/living alone" from "separated/living alone" or even include separated as a distinct marital status category. However, he went "beyond Durkheim" and most other sociologists studying suicide by reporting findings indicating the effects on suicide of the presence of others in domestic society that include, but are not limited to, conjugal and family, varies with the quality of the relationship with others (unmarried lovers, strangers, friends, relatives) who contribute to its density.

Sociologists such as Danigelis and Pope, who claim continuity with Durkheim by focusing on his integration–regulation theory of suicide in domestic society (p. 1081) and using quantitative methods of analysis, tend to derive their conclusions from findings based on the analysis of the association between marital status rates and suicide rates controlling rates of other variables known to be associated with suicide. The use of suicide rates to measure suicide—especially rates of suicide produced by people living in different countries—has been criticized on the grounds of their validity and/or reliability (Douglas, 1969; Ettlinger & Flordah, 1955; Taylor, 1982, pp. 43–64; Timmermans, 2005). Danigelis and Pope used WHO suicide data from different countries. Danigelis and Pope stated two reasons for using rate data. First, "there are no alternatives to official statistics." Second, "they have been found (by other researchers) to be reliable enough to be used in attempts to assess explanations of variations in suicide rates" (p. 1084). Neither reason addresses the validity problem identified by Douglas and Taylor. Collecting and analyzing individual-level data on the meanings of and motives for suicide does address it. Unfortunately, we could not find studies reporting findings on appeals suicides that simultaneously supported Taylor's creative theoretical analysis and validated findings based on the analysis of aggregate (rate) data.

Validation could also take the form of creating a theory that integrated sociological and psychological explanations of suicide. Henry and Short's attempt to integrate them suffers from the conception of restraint exclusively in external or physical terms—restraint located in the wishes, expectations, reactions of others—instead of external and internal restraint—shared, internalized values and norms that constitute Durkheim's collective conscience. The exclusion of internal restraint not only undermines their attempts to integrate the two levels of explanation but also "precludes examination of social psychological variables," which may explain the association of between separation and suicide (Taylor, 1982, p. 28). Moreover, the explanatory power of the psychological (frustration–aggression) theory of aggression they integrate with external restraint theory suffers from findings indicating that frustration is not strongly associated with aggression, or that frustration is more reliably associated with aggression under a specified set of conditions that were not specified by Henry and Short (Buss & Duntley, 2011). Consequently, the case for including strength of external relational system and frustration among factors that mediate or moderate the effects of separation and divorce on homicide and suicide is creative but weakened by its partial grounding in frustration–aggression theory.

DISCUSSION QUESTIONS

1. Evaluate this statement: The causal mechanisms derived from Durkheim's social integration–regulation theory of suicide adequately explain the association between separation and suicide. Do you agree or disagree? Give reasons for your answer.

2. Compare and critically evaluate causal mechanisms derived from the theory of Henry and Short and Borderline Personality Disorder theory.

3. Evaluate this statement: The causal mechanism derived from conflict resolution theory adequately explains the association between separation and suicide. Do you agree or disagree? Give reasons for your answer.

4. Which of the causal mechanisms derived from the theories described in this chapter best explains the association between separation and suicide? Give reasons for your answer.

CHAPTER 8

Preventing Intimate Partner Homicide and Femicide

LEARNING OBJECTIVES

Readers of this chapter who have achieved the objectives set for it will be able to:

- Identify essential features of each of the three models of preventing lethal male partner violence against female partners
- Describe the use made of domestic violence risk assessment instruments in each of the models of prevention
- Assess the effectiveness of risk assessment instruments designed to predict the risk of femicide, femicide–suicide, and serious injuries inflicted on female partners
- Demonstrate awareness of the contribution made by women's shelters to preventing fatal and serious violence against current and former residents

COMMUNITY/LAW ENFORCEMENT INTERVENTIONS

The review/evaluation that follows focuses on three recent innovative programs or models aimed at preventing femicide and femicide–suicide that are national in scope: the Domestic Abuse, Stalking, and Harassment (DASH) Risk Identification and Assessment and Management model; the Maryland Lethality Assessment Program (LAP); and the Domestic Violence High Risk Team (DVHRT) model. Given the terminological confusion evident in definitions of assessment, prediction, and prevention stated in different publications and even in the same publication (see Chapters 1, 3, and 5 in *Assessing Dangerousness*, edited by Campbell (1995)), we shall start by defining what we mean by prevention, assessment, and prediction.

Preventing homicide involving adult intimate partners as perpetrators and victims means stopping it from happening. Assessing intimate partner homicide using quantified lethality assessment instruments refers to estimating the risk of homicide by individuals located in ranked risk categories. Predicting homicide refers to forecasting homicide based on the location of individuals in risk categories.

Assessing the risk of homicide is viewed by Campbell (1995) and organizations, such as the Maryland Network Against Domestic Violence and the Jeanne Geiger Crisis Center in Newburyport, Massachusetts, as the first step toward preventing it.

Predicting homicide accurately is extremely difficult because homicide is a complex phenomenon with a very low base rate. For example, the rate of sublethal violent offenses reported by victims is 24.6 per 1,000 persons, compared with an official homicide rate of 5.6 per 100,000 persons (Rand & Catalino, 2007). Based on his analysis of the Kansas City study (pp. 231–236) data suggesting that prior domestic calls served as "early warning signs for homicide," Sherman (1992) concluded that "predicting homicide from chronic domestic disturbance calls (to the police) would be wrong 997 times out of 1,000" (pp. 235–236). Findings from the field experimental study of arrest effects conducted in Milwaukee indicate that between April 7, 1987, and February 8, 1989, "Homicide was no more likely to occur ... between the roughly 13,000 people with prior domestic violence records than among the 585,000 people with no prior domestic violence records" (Sherman, 1992, p. 235; Sherman & Berk, 1984).

Individuals who use violence against their partners more frequently and/or injure them more seriously are likely to be overrepresented among those with police records for domestic violence, yet they were no more likely to kill their partners than those with no record or a much shorter one. The oft-cited hypothesis stating that "the frequency and seriousness of domestic violence escalates up to the point where murder occurs" (e.g., Campbell, 1995; Walby & Myhill, 2001) is not supported by this finding (p. 231). More generally, the findings he reviewed led Sherman to conclude that domestic homicide is unpredictable when prediction is grounded in a police record for frequent or even chronic/serious violence (p. 232).

Sherman does not qualify his conclusion, but we are going to do so by stating that it is applicable only to predictions made on the basis of one factor—official police records on prior domestic violence. Predictions of intimate partner homicide and femicide, based on the use of multiple factors, researchers found to be strongly associated with these lethal outcomes and may make them more accurate. For some practitioners, more reliable prediction means more effective prevention.

The primary objective of Maryland's LAP is to "prevent domestic homicides, serious injury, and re-assault." Prevention is conceived as a two-pronged process. First, assessors (police officers and field practitioners) are trained to use a shortened (11-item) version of Campbell's Danger Assessment (2004) to identify abused women whose male partners are most likely to escalate the seriousness of injuries they inflict to the point of seriously injuring or killing them. Police assessors encourage potential homicide/serious injury victims to telephone a local 24-hour hotline. Hotline counselors discuss the case with callers, contact the police officer who referred the caller, and jointly discuss an individualized safety plan that includes the options using "shelter, counseling, advocacy, and support services of domestic violence programs" (Maryland Network Against Domestic Violence, 2004, p. 1). Collaboration and coordination among service providers as well as following up cases with home and telephone calls increases the effectiveness of their interventions.

Findings included in *The Maryland Lethality Assessment Report, 2006*, (September 1, 2010) indicate that 22,428 Danger Assessment Lethality Screens were administered to abused female partners by staff at 88 domestic violence agencies. The use of a standardized scoring protocol identified 54% ($n = 12,069$) of their abusive male partners as "high danger." Fifty-nine percent ($n = 7,090$) of women with "high danger" male partners called and spoke to a hotline counselor. Less than one-third (30%, or 2,072) of those who conversed with a hotline counselor subsequently used any of the domestic violence program options that were presented to them. Victims with "high danger" male partners who decided not to call and speak to a hotline counselor (41% or 4,979 of 12,069) were encouraged to contact a local domestic violence agency and were provided with safety-promoting information by the investigating police officers. The information imparted by first responding police officers included the identification of risk factors for homicide "so she could be on the lookout for them" and referrals to other safety and wellness promoting agencies.

The LAP Maryland Model of First Responders has been operating since 2004, but it has not yet been independently evaluated, so no findings on the prevention of homicide and serious injury to abused female partners have been published by the agency (Maryland Network Against Domestic Violence) responsible for administering it. Consequently, we do not know whether or not the degree to which the Maryland LAP achieves its primary objective of "preventing domestic homicides, serious injury, and re-assault." An evaluation of an LAP replication is being conducted in Oklahoma and plans have been made to publish its findings.

In our view, the evaluation should include the following two outcomes. The first one is the identification of factors associated with a low (30%) rate of using domestic violence protection services by women with "high danger" male partners. Second, rates of serious injury or homicide among female partners who did and did not speak to a hotline counselor and/or who used and did not use domestic violence program options should be compared and published.

In 2005, one year after the formation of the LAP Maryland model, DVHRTs were created in Newburyport, Massachusetts, by Dunne and associates of the Jeanne Geiger Crisis Center. The creators of high-risk teams (HRTs) believe that Campbell's domestic homicide risk assessment instrument—Danger Assessment—does reliably predict domestic homicide by male partners and that they could use it to "predict which domestic-abuse cases were most likely to end in homicide" (Snyder, 2013, p. 37). According to Rosenfeld (2012), a "central tenet" of the DVHRT Model is the belief that Campbell's Danger Assessment makes "DV homicide ... so predictable as to be preventable" (p. 33). To embed Danger Assessment in the DVHRT Model is to say it is a model that includes both prediction grounded in risk assessment *and* referral to HRTs for preventive action. In other words, the effect of prediction on prevention varies with the availability of HRTs in the location in which the Danger Assessment was made.

HRTs organized by the Jeanne Geiger Center in Newburyport, Massachusetts, include representatives from the prosecutor's office, police, probation, parole, batterer's intervention programs, the local hospital, victim advocacy groups, and other service providers (excluding shelters). Members of the HRT provide a collaborative, coordinated response to cases in which the Danger Assessment completed by abused female partners yields a score locating the abusive male partner in the highest (extreme/serious danger) risk categories and/or the abuser's conduct (e.g., violating a court protection order) locates the abuser in the same high-risk categories based on the intuition and experience of members of the HRT. Referrals to the HRT are made by a crisis center or by local police departments in more than 25 locations in Massachusetts where HRTs are operating (Jeanne Geiger Crisis Center, 2012).

Following an arrest, high-risk accused male partners, including those with no prior police record of using physical violence against their partners, are required to attend a "dangerousness hearing." If the evidence presented at this hearing indicates that an accused presents a significant threat of serious or lethal violence against his female partner, he will be sentenced to "preventive detention" until his trial. The dangerousness hearing and preventive detention are viewed as "two of the most effective tools available to the HRT" (Snyder, 2013, p. 38).

Beyond arrest and preventive detention—especially during the three- or four-month period following the female partner's decision to separate—the process of protecting abused female partners from their potential killers continues with "offender accountability." Of the 106 high-risk cases referred to the Greater Newburyport DVHRT, 73 (74%) were prosecuted in criminal court. Of the 73 prosecuted in court, 59% experienced preventive detention and 35% were released on bail. The remaining 6% were released with an electronic bracelet, which subjected them to global positioning system (GPS) tracking. Of the 74% of the cases that were prosecuted in criminal court, there was no trial in 71% of them because they were resolved by guilty pleas and no trial in 13% of the cases because they were dismissed. Only 12% of the cases actually went to trial. Of the 83 accused abusers who pleaded guilty or were found guilty at trial, 60% were incarcerated, 40% were required to participate in a batterer's intervention program, and 20% of them were required to wear an electronic bracelet.

Creators of HRTs claim individualized, coordinated continuing victim support, lethality risk assessment, perpetrator-focused coordinated community/criminal justice response by HRTs, arrest, dangerousness hearings, preventive detention, and GPS monitoring prevent male intimate partner homicide by containing and monitoring the only person who could prevent intimate partner homicide: the perpetrator.

Evidence supporting the claim that HRTs prevent domestic abuse cases from escalating to domestic homicide cases takes the form of presenting the results of a before-and-after comparison. In Amesbury, Massachusetts, a domestic homicide was recorded "nearly every year" during a 10-year period, 1992–2002, but after the establishment of an HRT in Amesbury in 2005, "not one single abuse case ended in homicide" (Snyder, 2013, pp. 40–41).

The evidence cited here is not persuasive because it was produced by the use of the simple before-and-after study design that does not include at least one other HRT-free town as a comparison group. Consequently, we cannot eliminate the possibility that the rates of one or more of the factors positively associated with domestic violence homicide were higher during the 1992–2002 period (e.g., high rates of separating/separated couples, participation in adversarial separation/divorce proceedings, unemployed male partners, substance abuse) and lower during the 2005–2012 period, and/or factors negatively associated with domestic violence homicide, such as shelters for abused women, were absent during the "before" period and present during the "after" period. Although creators of HRT are dismissive of shelters—"they do save lives but they also isolate and penalize victims by disrupting their lives instead of containing and disrupting the lives of perpetrators and are also a ticket to welfare" (Dunne, in Snyder, 2013, p. 36)—no evidence supporting this conclusion is presented. On the other hand, evidence cited in the Maryland Network Against Domestic Violence report (2004) indicates that abused female partners using shelters experienced a 60% reduction in the risk of serious assault. Unfortunately, the authors did not specify this finding by reporting the proportion of abused women who were and were not seriously assaulted while they were residing in a shelter with the proportion of women who were seriously and not seriously assaulted after leaving a shelter.

Perusal of the Safety and Accountability Report (2005–2011) published by the Greater Newburyport Domestic Violence High Risk Team does not include findings from a formal evaluation of the effectiveness of HRTs in preventing domestic violence homicide in the more than 25 Massachusetts locations in which they are operational. A formal evaluation of a "joint LAP/HRT replication model on a national scale" will be forthcoming following the appointment of a Department of Justice–funded DVHRT Program Manager in 2013 by the Jeanne Geiger Crisis Center, Newburyport.

Factors facilitating the integration of the two programs include:

- The shared goal of preventing domestic homicide;
- The use of the same lethality assessment instrument (Danger Assessment);
- Using prediction to achieve prevention;
- Limiting the reach of their programs to victims of sublethal male partner violence "to a small fraction of victims"—those known to agents of the criminal justice system and/or local service providers (Mednick, 2013, p. 3);
- Collaborative, coordinated community/law enforcement efforts aimed at promoting the safety of abused female partners; and
- Funding of integrated LAP/DVHRT replications by the Department of Justice's Office on Violence Against Women.

Practitioners responsible for implementing the integrated LAP/HRT Model being validated nationally may want to consider the following unsolicited suggestions. First, in order to increase the predictive validity of the Danger Assessment and the effectiveness of interventions aimed at preventing femicide, only dynamic (changeable) causal risk factors supported by deductive theories of femicide and/or validated by prospective research findings should be included in the Danger Assessment administered to clients. Currently, all the risk factors included in the Danger Assessment are correlated with femicide and femicide–suicide whereas "[r]isk management and violence reduction require a clear understanding of causation" (Yang, Wong, & Coid, 2010, p. 760). Other researchers who reached the same conclusion include Buchanan (2008), Douglas and Skeen (2005), Ellis (2014), Kraemer and associates (1997), and Mullen (2000).

Eke and associates (2011) conclude their intimate partner homicide risk assessment and prediction study with the following observation: "If all the offenders (in the Extreme Danger Assessment risk category) received effective services, some homicides and many serious nonlethal assaults could be prevented … but what constitutes effective services … remains a question in need of research" (p. 215). We believe that implementing interventions derived from dynamic causal risk factors included in lethality risk assessments and/or revealed in interviews with female partners who were victims of near fatal assaults by male partners are likely to be effective in preventing some femicides, femicide–suicides, and serious assaults.

Second, practitioners using the Revised Danger Assessment to predict femicide should avoid misusing it. The misuse of domestic violence risk assessment instruments—including the Danger Assessment—is noteworthy (Messing & Thaller, 2013, p. 1543; Nicholls et al., 2013, pp. 149–150). One example of misuse is the failure of LAP and DVHRT to use all 20 items included in the Revised Danger Assessment. Specifically, the LAP uses 11 items excluding "physical violence is increasing in severity or frequency," whereas DVHRT uses 19 items in assessing risk but only seven of them are identified as "high risk indicators" with "physical violence is increasing in severity or frequency" eliciting a yes response from more than 80% of the abused female partners to whom the Danger Assessment was administered (Jeanne Geiger Crisis Center, 2012, p. 12).

We suggest that the Danger Assessment being used in the integrated LAP/DVHRT Model being validated should be administered to clients in the same way that Campbell and associates administered it to research subjects in their 2009 retrospective study. Specifically, the Danger Assessment, including 20 items, should be used and clients should be asked to complete a "calendar of harms" experienced during the preceding year (Nicholls et al., 2013, p. 136). As the Danger Assessment does not appear to have been empirically validated using femicide as an outcome or criterion variable by researchers using their own data—not data collected by Campbell and associates—it is important for LAP/DVHRT practitioners to replicate the administration of the Danger Assessment and validate it using their own data to predict femicide. When predictions of violence against female partners bring about significant unwanted and continuing changes in the quality of their lives and also results in the incarceration of male partners who have not been convicted of a crime (preventive detention) "a very high level of accuracy (predictive validity)" should be required for decisions resulting in preventive detention for the latter (Yang et al., 2010) and changes in location, identity, jobs, schools, shopping, and recreational activities, and purchasing guard dogs or other electronic alarm systems for victims (Hoyle, 2008).

Third, if pretrial preventive detention (i.e., incarcerating male batterers assessed as high risk for homicide without a trial for a homicide they may commit in the future—is retained), its use should be limited to highest risk male partners during the weeks immediately following contested separations initiated by female partners with children. Findings presented by Ellis, Sakinofsky, and Stuckless (2012) indicate that, on the average, 47% of femicides occur within three months of separation and 74% of them occur between two and six months after separation.

Reflecting our concern with the morality and legality of preventive detention on the one hand and the safety of female partners on the other, we suggest that in-house record keeping should reveal the proportion of abusive male partners experiencing and not experiencing preventive detention who are subsequently found not guilty at trial or those whose cases are dismissed. As plea bargaining is grounded in the presumption of guilt, we would also suggest that all high-risk male partners experiencing preventive detention should proceed to trial.

Fourth, we suggest that, in addition to women's shelters and other support services for abused women, referral to conflict resolution training and other treatment programs be included among the community service programs to which violent male partners can be referred. A study conducted by Dobash, Dobash, Cavanagh, and Lewis (2000) not only identifies profeminist programs that are effective in preventing future male partner violence, but they also identify the mechanism (learning) that brings about personal changes associated with preventing future male partner violence. Compared with "fear of sanctions" administered by the criminal justice system, learning was found to be far more strongly associated with preventing subsequent male partner violence (pp. 129–174).

The LAP and DVHRT programs were probably included in the "comprehensive literature review" conducted by Laura Richards, but she did not replicate either of them in England. Instead, she created the DASH an Honor Based Violence model (2009) currently being used by all police forces in England and Wales. In addition to the comprehensive literature review, the evidence base for DASH includes:

- The analysis of 56 murders, 240 attempted murders, and 106,000 assaults that inflicted minor or no physical injuries;
- Consultation with national and international academic experts and practitioners;
- Extensive piloting in several areas on more than four occasions;
- Police officer, practitioner, and victim focus groups;
- Evaluation;
- Continuous review.

Evidence from these sources led Richards to two apparently contradictory conclusions. First, she concluded that "Risk identification and assessment [are] not a predictive process and there is no existing accurate procedure to calculate or foresee which cases will result in homicide or further assault and harm" (Richards, 2009a). Her second conclusion was "the use of a common checklist (DASH) for identifying and assessing risk … (by well-trained police and practitioner professionals) will save lives" (2009b). The contradiction is resolved when we learn that the 27-item checklist is not used by professionals to predict which cases of DASH and honor-based violence will escalate to homicide, but to use professional judgment in interpreting the DASH checklist information and to take this information into account in making decisions aimed at preventing "serious harms" against women by male partners located in the "high-risk" category on the basis of their DASH scores (14 or more yes answers by female partners to 27 questions). Unlike users of the Danger Assessment in the LAP and DVHRT programs, professionals who use the DASH checklist cannot change the items/questions in it.

DASH is used by police officers and safety-promoting community-based agencies and programs. Police officers who respond to calls for service by victims of domestic abuse, stalking, or honor-based violence conduct an initial/partial risk assessment using DASH for screening followed by a second fuller risk assessment including additional questions about children, stalking, harassment, and abuse it if is disclosed. Victims will have completed DASH Partial (screening) administered by first responders and DASH Full (assessment) by officers in the domestic abuse unit. Taking DASH information and other information available to the police force into account, police officers make safety-promoting decisions based on their professional judgment. As we interpret Richard's instructions, the professional judgment of police officers rule when it is contradicted by or deviates from information provided by DASH (Richards, 2009b).

A variety of frontline practitioners who work with victims of domestic violence also use Coordinated Action Against Domestic Abuse (CAADA) DASH to identify high-risk cases following CAADA guidelines in interpreting DASH, explaining thresholds for referrals, instructions on the use of professional judgment in cases in which victims do not answer any or all DASH questions. Criteria for referring a case to a Multi-agency Risk Assessment Conference (MARAC) meeting include a DASH score of 14 or more (high-risk) and minor acts of violence against the female partner that are escalating in seriousness and/or increasing in frequency. One outcome of an information-sharing MARAC meeting is a more effective community/law enforcement response based on a better understanding of the actual facts of the case.

According to Richards, well-trained frontline domestic violence practitioners make a significant contribution to preventing homicide and serious violence because they are "able to identify risk factors associated with serious violence and murder … understand how they apply in each situation, know what needs to be done to keep the victim safe" and transform their knowledge into a coordinated community/law enforcement response that prevents homicide and serious violence against female partners who have been abused, stalked, or experienced family honor-based violence (Richards, 2009, p. 2).

A summary of the causal mechanisms explaining the association between the prevention models described in this chapter and the prevention of femicide is presented in Table 8.1.

All three models described here—DASH Risk Identification and Assessment and Management Model, LAP, and DVHRT Model—are similar to each other in as least five ways.

Table 8.1 Causal Mechanisms in Models for Preventing Femicide

Prevention Models	Causal Mechanisms
LAP	Deterrence/support/treatment
DVHRT	Incapacitation/deterrence/support/treatment
DASH	Deterrence/support/treatment

DASH, Domestic Abuse, Stalking, and Harassment; DVHRT, Domestic Violence High Risk Team; LAP, Lethality Assessment Program.

First, they ignore interventions based on causal mechanisms underlying correlations between risk factors and intimate partner violence in favor of using risk factor ratings as an *aide memoire* for police officers and service providers involved in assessing risk (Ellis, 2014; Ellis, Stuckless, & Smith, 2014, Chapter 3; Tilley & Paulson, 1997; Trabold, 2007). Second, they limit their reach to the fraction of abused/stalked female partners who contact law enforcement and front-line practitioners. Third, they aim at achieving the goal of preventing homicide and serious violence against female partners. Fourth, the degree to which they achieve their goals is unknown because they have not been validated. Fifth, criminal justice system interventions are an autonomous but collaborative part of the program (Buzawa & Buzawa, 1996).

In all three programs, the criminal justice system interventions of prosecution, trial, conviction, and sentencing start with the arrest of an alleged male perpetrator of a violent crime against a female partner. Arrest is hypothesized to prevent violence by deterring would-be perpetrators from repeating minor (misdemeanant) acts of violence and escalating violence to the point where female partners are seriously injured (require emergency treatment in a hospital and/or hospitalization) or killed.

Findings supporting the first part of this hypothesis are reported by the authors of the field experimental study of immediate arrest effects conducted in Minneapolis (Sherman & Berk, 1984). In this city, police statistics revealed that "randomized arrest and a night in jail cut the risk of repeat (minor) acts of violence against the same victim in half over a six month follow-up period from 20% to 10%" (Sherman, 1992, p. 2). Findings reported by Tauchen and Witte (1995) also found that arrest deterred repeat violence against the same female partner but only for two weeks.

On the other hand, findings from three replications of the Sherman and Berk study indicated that arrest escalated violence among the unemployed and deterred violence among the employed in all three cities (Omaha, Milwaukee, and Colorado Springs) where employment status was measured. When arrest effects were measured using official police statistics, findings indicate that repeat violence escalated between six and 12 months following arrest in Omaha, Charlotte, and Milwaukee and was deterred for 30–60 days in Minneapolis, Milwaukee, and Miami. Victim interview data indicated that repeat violence following arrest was deterred for six months in Colorado Springs, Miami, and Minneapolis and 30–60 days in Milwaukee, Minneapolis, and Miami (Sherman, 1992, p. 129, Table 6.1). The low response rate for abused females who completed the immediately/shortly-after-arrest and six-months-after arrest interviews (30%) raises questions about the stability of findings based upon victim interview data.

The creators of all three models draw attention to the fact that the assessment instruments they are using are "evidence-based." If the same criterion is being used for the criminal justice system response of arrest, evidence supporting the use of it should be cited because findings from studies using the methodologically soundest study design— field experimental method with random assignment of subjects to treatments—are not consistent. Instead, arrest effects (deter versus escalate violence) vary with the city and its racial composition, source of data (police versus victim interviews), time period in which repeat violence was measured, income, employment, and marital status.

Evidence cited by Sherman and supported by leading criminologists (1992, p. 2) indicates that employed, married, and higher-income suspects who remain at the scene are deterred by "arrest and spending a night in jail." However, when police officers arrive at the scene of a "domestic disturbance" call, they often discover that between 40% and 60% of the suspects have scarpered—left the scene (Ferraro, 1989; Sherman, 1992, p. 150).

The authors of the Omaha study—a methodologically sounder replication of the original Sherman and Berk study—randomly assigned misdemeanor assault suspects who were not present at the scene to a "no arrest warrant" and a "warrant arrest" group (Dunford, Huizinga, & Elliott, 1989). Suspects in the warrant arrest group were subsequently informed that an arrest warrant had been issued and full prosecution to the limits of the law (maximum incarceration time) was threatened. Sherman found the deterrent of the "Sword of Damocles" warrant strategy to be "substantial" based on findings indicating significant differences in the odds of being arrested—50% in the suspect absent–warrant group and 25% in the suspect absent–no warrant group—and significant differences in physical injuries reported by women in the no warrant and warrant groups—30% versus 16% at six months and 35% versus 19% at 12 months, respectively (Sherman, 1992, p. 151). If we assume that unmarried, unemployed, low-income individuals are likely to be concentrated among suspects who left the scene, then it may not be unreasonable to conclude that warrantless arrests also deter them.

A warrantless/warrant strategy for minor assaults by suspects who have left the scene is not legally mandated in Maryland and Massachusetts (Iyengar, 2008, Table 8.1) but may be legal in some or all of the states in which LAP/DVHRT will be operating in the future. In the description of the DASH Model, no reference is made to a warrantless mandatory strategy for minor (nonindictable) acts of criminal domestic violence by suspects who have left the scene.

Although legislation (Domestic Violence, Crime, and Victims Act, 2004, and the Human Rights Act, 1998) has expanded the types of offenses for which arrest is an option, DASH is operating in two countries (England and Wales) that do not have a mandatory arrest policy. In the description of the DASH model, no reference is made to a warrantless warrant strategy for minor (nonindictable) criminal acts of domestic violence (Parradine & Wilkinson, 2004; Ray, 2011).

The Minneapolis and Omaha field experimental studies cited here refer only to minor (misdemeanor) assaults. Sherman explicitly states that these studies were "limited to the risks for minor assault, with no separate data on homicides or serious injuries reported anywhere" (and there is no) direct evidence that arrests (for minor assaults) can prevent homicide (1992, p. 99). Notwithstanding this caveat, he reports that "lobbyists and legislators in many states (and the federal government's Violence Against Women Act, 1994) cited the Minneapolis experiment as providing support for mandatory arrest … in misdemeanor assaults" (1992, p. 99). Legislators and chiefs of police in England and Wales may have paid more attention to the caveat because mandatory arrest laws for minor (nonindictable) acts of criminal domestic violence have not been passed in England and Wales (Ray, 2011). The decision not to pass mandatory arrest laws is supported by evidence indicating that mandatory arrest for prior misdemeanor assaults increased the risk of intimate partner homicide in the United States.

Iyengar (2008) investigated the effect of mandatory arrest laws on misdemeanor assaults and intimate partner homicides. Intimate partner homicides were defined as "any homicide committed against a husband or wife, common-law husband or wife ex-husband or wife" (p. 11). Data on 36,442 intimate partner homicides were recorded between 1976 and 2003 in 50 states plus Washington, DC. States with mandatory arrest laws ($n = 15$) for misdemeanor assaults were compared with states where arrest was recommended ($n = 8$). Mandatory arrest states "have no discretion as to whether to make a warrantless arrest when an intimate partner assault is reported." Recommended states are states where "officers are instructed but not required to make an arrest" in the same circumstances (p. 31). When intimate partner homicides ($n = 992$) were regressed on type of state, the results revealed "a 54% increase in intimate partners homicides" in mandatory arrest states (p. 12).

Additional analyses indicated that the increase was a function of two factors. First was deterrence: Victims were deterred from reporting assaults. Findings reported by researchers in England strongly suggest that constraints and opportunities influencing the choices of female victims of male partner violence be taken into account in arresting their abusive partners and making plans promoting their safety. Hagerty (2003) notes that violence by ex-partners is only one of a number of risks that female victims must manage by balancing not only its probability and seriousness, but also how quickly harmful outcomes are likely to be experienced. Thus, a battered women may balance the arrest of her abusive male partner against the risk of being arrested herself and having her children cared for by child protection authorities, having her abusive partner arrested, or having him removed from the home against the risk of ending a relationship with a man she is still emotionally attached to; damaging the relationship she has with her children; and the loss of her home because she can no longer afford to pay the mortgage and other expenses on her own. After the batterer's release, she faces the financial cost of staying in her home but installing an expensive security system and/or buying a guard dog; changing her job and/or routes and time she goes to work in her present job; and avoiding places she used to enjoy going to but now avoids them in case she runs into her ex-partner.

Iyengar also found that decreases in reporting assaults following a mandatory arrest varied with race/ethnicity and income. Low-income African-Americans, who were most distrustful of the police and reluctant to have any contact with law enforcement officers, were least likely to report assaults against them following the mandatory arrest of an intimate partner perpetrator.

The second factor was abuser reprisal for being arrested. The following contradictory policy implication of victim deterrence from reporting and abuser reprisal is noted by Iyengar: Incapacitating the offender would prevent mandatory arrest–motivated homicides but mandatory arrests may increase the risk of homicide by deterring victims from reporting perpetrators of assault to the police in the first place (p. 19). Creators of the DVHRT Model have opted for the incapacitation-through-preventive detention option.

In addition to the criminal justice system, the adversarial family law system may also help increase the risk of domestic homicide by increasing the intensity of conflict between separating/divorcing couples (Arendell, 1995; Ellis, 2014; Logan et al., 2008; Mnookin, 2010; Pruett & Jackson, 1999; Spanier & Casto, 1979). In fact, the contribution made by mandatory arrest for misdemeanor assaults in the criminal justice system is paralleled by the contribution made by participation in the adversarial proceedings in the family law system (Logan et al., 2008; Mnookin, 2010; Pruett & Jackson, 1999; Spanier & Casto, 1979). Especially when children are present, participation in adversarial proceedings tends to increase the risk of femicide and femicide–suicide while participation in collaborative proceedings tends to decrease it (Ellis, 2014).

Separation is included as a risk factor in almost all domestic violence risk assessment instruments, including the Danger Assessment used in LAP/DVHRT and the 27-item DASH checklist, but the possibility of preventing homicides by diverting couples to participation in collaborative proceedings is an intervention that is unlikely to be implemented by creators of homicide prevention models who are unaware of the causal mechanisms underlying the association between separation and femicide.

In Ontario, Canada, resources have been devoted to the creation of a Mandatory Information Program (MIP) that is, or appears to be, grounded in three hypotheses. First, using a stream analogy, the hypothesis is that fully informed choice decisions will broaden the collaborative stream and narrow the adversarial stream, especially for couples with children. Second, the transaction costs (financial, psychological, relational damage, physical injuries/death, temporal) are less likely to be experienced by parties during and following participation in collaborative than in adversarial proceedings. Third, providing general information on matters, such as separation and divorce and the effects of conflict on children, will increase the likelihood that participants will make choices that serve the best interests of their children.

MIPs are available in family courts located in communities across the province. Under the legislation creating the MIP, parties who have initiated a family court case must obtain a Certificate of Attendance at a 2-hour MIP session as the first step in their court case. Since its inception in June 2011, MIP practice has changed to permit parties without children to attend only the first hour of the MIP. Parents with children are required to be present during the entire 2-hour MIP. Mandatory attendance at MIPs is not required for parties in cases:

- That are proceeding on consent (both parties have agreed to the order being requested); and/or
- Where the only claims made are for divorce, costs, or an order incorporating the terms of an agreement or prior court order.

Parties who have not started a family court case are not required to attend an MIP session but they can attend voluntarily. Applicants (mainly women) and respondents (mainly men) attend separate MIPs. MIPs are in the process of being evaluated.

In England, divorcing couples are required to participate in Mediation Information and Assessment Meetings (MIAMs) "in order to find out about alternatives to court (such as mediation, collaborative law, and arbitration) before being able to issue a court application in relation to their financial or children's issues" (Resolution, 2012, p. 1). Findings from a survey of 6,000 Resolution members who are family lawyers using MIAMs in more than 100 courts across England and Wales indicate that between 2011 and 2012 participation in divorce mediation increased by 51% among MIAM participants.

As the presenters at MIAMs are family lawyers committed to a collaborative/consensual (mediation/collaborative law) approach to settling family conflicts, this finding may not be surprising. However, as 90% of the MIAM attendees were referred to them by their lawyers, less than 10% were self-referrals, most of them had (presumably) already been informed about the benefits associated with being represented by collaborative lawyers. Under this condition, the 51% increase reflects informed choices by participants that support the first two interrelated hypotheses mentioned earlier. Moreover, during the two-year period in which this increase occurred, no increase was reported in the number of mediated agreements submitted for judicial review alleging they were unfair because they reflect power imbalances.

Resolution researchers report that the 51% increase in the use of mediation may have been significantly higher if they had not found that MIAMs "are not working as they should" because:

- 20% of MIAM respondents were either not informing or informing but not sending their clients to MIAMs; and
- family courts identified by 56% of the respondents stated they are not requiring parties filing an application to provide proof of attending an MIAM.

These findings are not surprising when we discover that the legislation establishing MIAMs simultaneously states that "every would-be litigant must attend an MIAM prior to initiating proceedings in family court but attendance at an MIAM is not compulsory" (2012, p. 2). In short, MIAMs operate in the shadow of a contradictory family law.

With MIPs and MIAMs in mind, creators of homicide prevention models, such as LAP/DVHRT and DASH, may also want to consider adding the diversion of separating/divorcing couples to participation in collaborative conflict resolution proceedings among the family law system interventions currently available to them.

Conflict Resolution Training

The inclusion of conflict resolution training is supported by theory and research indicating that the intensity of conflict is a causal mechanism for homicide, femicide, femicide–suicide, and suicide during and following separation (Ellis, 2014). The intensity of conflict tends to be relatively high among individuals who are emotionally attached to each other and the stronger the emotional bond the higher the intensity of conflict (Goode, 1971). The higher intensity of conflict the greater the likelihood that intimate partners will use emotionally and physically abusive tactics in attempting to settle conflicts between them. As contested unilateral decisions to separate tend to markedly increase the intensity of conflict, especially when the "custody" of dependent children is an issue, the use of emotionally and physically abusive conflict resolution tactics is likely to increase. Conflict resolution training is grounded in a conception of conflict as an opportunity for preventing the use of physically harmful tactics by discovering and reconciling the thoughts and feelings underlying their use.

The starting point for the conflict training module we shall describe is recognition and acknowledgment of the presence of feelings of mutual hostility between intimate partners involved in contested separations, especially when the "custody" of dependent children is an issue. The training model focuses on the self-help process of negotiating an agreement that is safe, peaceful, and durable because following (Fisher, Ury, & Patton, 1972) it:

- reconciles thoughts, feelings, and values underlying positions on substantive outcomes they want to obtain;
- does not further damage and may improve their relationship with each other and their children;
- results in an agreement they reached themselves (Fisher et al., 1972).

Negotiation is embedded in a "conflict resolution ladder" describing a variety of collaborative and adversarial proceeding options. Collaborative self-help options are located on the bottom rung of the ladder, and the most adversarial third party–involved option is located on the top rung. During the course of a separation, parties may move up or down one or more rungs of the ladder. Direct participant control over the process and outcomes of a conflict resolution proceeding decreases as participants ascend the ladder. Transaction costs (financial, temporal, psychological, and social) also increase for parties who ascend the following conflict resolution ladder:

> Adjudication/litigating lawyers
> Adversarial lawyer negotiators
> Collaborative lawyer negotiators
> Collaborative practice lawyer negotiators
> Mediators
> Principled negotiators

Readers of *Getting to Yes* (Fisher et al., 1972) will be familiar with the criteria used to define a "wise agreement"—we referred to two of their criteria earlier—and the definition of principled negotiation (PN) as negotiation in which outcomes reflect the relative merits of each party's case and a process that helps both parties reconcile their interests while behaving decently toward each other. Communication skills are essential to effective communication in general and the achievement of a wise agreement through PN in particular. For this reason, the first segment of the training model deals with communication skills training.

Communication Skills

Segments taken from Bennett and Hughes (2005, pp. 88–106) are used to teach communication skills. Each of the skills taught must be demonstrated in sequenced, cumulative coaching sessions. The specific communication skills taught in the Communication Skills Module are:

- Attentive listening, which can be demonstrated in subsequent accurate paraphrasing and summarizing;
- Effective integrative ways of asking questions;
- Paraphrasing important points of information in a message immediately after it has been communicated;
- Accurate summarizing of a larger amount of information on an issue or topic;
- Sending clear messages and clarifying messages received if they are not clear;
- Reframing—changing a destructive communication into a constructive one. Example: "You are a liar. You broke the promise you made to share custody of the children" is reframed as "You are right so I am willing to keep my promise by withdrawing my motion for sole custody filed in family court and send proof of its withdrawal to you before we meet for our next negotiation session on a parenting plan."

Segments taken from Gottman and associates (2002) are used to teach separating parties involved in a relationship in which negative reciprocity (harm-for-harm exchanges) has become the only way the couple attempts to overcome problems in communication that undermine attempts to settle conflicts between them that may arise during negotiations. The conflict resolution dynamics observed by Gottman and associates are described in terms of the identification of three communication problems (meta-communications, negative sentiment override, and fundamental attribution error) that undermine attempts to settle conflicts (repair attempts).

Negative reciprocity is an absorbed state (state in which the intensity of conflict is high) that would not have been achieved if repair attempts made by intimate partners had been successful. Repair attempts aimed at settling conflicts include verbal statements explicitly aimed at settling the conflict that are accompanied by a nonverbal emotional message. They tend to fail because one or both of the parties attend to the nonverbal message (meta-communication) that is perceived as negative and ignore the verbal message aimed at ending the conflict. For example: "Please stop interrupting me. I am trying to tell you I agree with you" is stated in a manner that conveys irritation or exasperation (arms waving/eyes rolling) and the listening partner attends to the meta-communication and ignores the communication. Attending to the communication and responding to it with a communication accompanied with a positive meta-communication is a skill participants are asked to demonstrate in coaching sessions.

Intimate partners on the road to separation tend to respond to negative and neutral meta-communications negatively because of negative sentiment override (NSO). NSO refers to the tendency to interpret a positive statement as neutral and a neutral statement as negative. Couples involved in a relationship in which negative reciprocity has become an absorbed state commit a fundamental attribution error (FAE) more frequently than couples in friendly, caring relationships. FAE refers to the tendency to attribute their partner's negativity to something stable or internal to him/her (e.g., personality or ego) and to attribute to their partner's positive statements and contributions to transient situational factors or moods. Using role scripts from actual cases, participants are asked to demonstrate a nuanced or balanced sentiment override and *Fundamental Attribution Correctness* during coaching sessions.

Principled Negotiation Training

The statement introducing participants to principled negotiation (PN) training includes defining PN as a collaborative decision-making method in which the parties are expected to treat each other with respect and that the settlement package they agree to should reflect the relative merits of each party's case. Parents with children are informed that the criterion used by family court judges in determining the relative merits of each party's case is what in the best interests of the child(ren). The context for participation in PN is described as a continuing, changing relationship in which some events may be under the control of one party, some may be under the control of the other party, some will be controlled by both parties, and others will be under the control of neither party.

In terms of content, training in PN teaches participants how to implement the four principles of PN that result in a wise agreement. In our modified definition, a wise agreement:

- Reconciles underlying values thoughts and feelings underlying the positions on a "settlement package" that includes the primary residence of children and responsibility for making legal decisions affecting them, financial support, division of property, and the payment of family debt;
- Does not damage and may improve relationships between intimate partners and other family members;
- Is reached by the parties themselves with relatively small transaction costs (e.g., financial, temporal, psychological, social); and
- Is durable.

Intimate partners who are separating tend to blame each other for the problems that led to the separation as well as the problems they experience in attempting to settle conflicts associated with separation by negotiating an agreement themselves. Consequently, the positions on outcomes (e.g., parenting plans, financial support) tend to be rejected not on their merits but because they were stated by the other party whom "everyone knows is greedy/a liar/an unfit parent/out for revenge." In other words, angry intimate partners tend to integrate the person and the problem of achieving a "settlement package" that each party feels is the best they could achieve under the circumstances. The first principle of PN is to separate the person from the problem.

Problem-solving skills (skills aimed at solving the substantive problems included in settlement packages) are different from person problem-solving skills, but the two skill sets are related to each other in the PN rule, which states "be soft on the person and hard on the problem, and the harder you are on (solving) the substantive problem the softer you should be on the person if the person is not going to get in the way of solving the substantive problem" (Video: *Getting to Yes*). Each set of skills is taught to participants who are expected to demonstrate them in coaching sessions.

Positions on outcomes that are ultimately included in a settlement package are usually stated by the parties during the opening phases of the negotiation; however, the values underlying them (e.g., autonomy, security, justice, health, best interest of children) may not be. When they are not disclosed, they have to be discovered. Participants are taught to ask questions, such as "why is (this outcome) so very important to you" that reveal underlying ultimate, fundamental, or proximal values underlying positions. Each of these values is defined. Then, value conflicts and examples of ultimate, fundamental, and proximal value conflicts are presented.

The discovery of values, feelings, and thoughts underlying stated positions is the first step in the direction of attempting to reconcile them by creating mutual gain options. The third principle is creating options for mutual gain. Participants learn three approaches to creating options for mutual gain. If the underlying values are complementary (e.g., survival is the value and I have more food and less water than I need to survive and you have more water but less food than you need to survive), trading is called for. If the underlying values are not complementary (e.g., survival is the value and both parties have enough food but in order to survive they need greater access to a limited supply of river water), rule-governed brainstorming involving trusted third parties may reveal a feasible mutual gain option.

When creation of mutual gain options, reconciling values, and underlying stated positions on outcomes included in a settlement package lead to an agreement, the agreement itself needs to be evaluated using legal rights and/or widely accepted social norms using child development research findings criteria as standards. The fourth principle of PN is using independent, objective standards to evaluate agreements. Participants will receive a handout identifying current applicable independent standards that can be used for this purpose.

Balancing Power Imbalances

The starting point for training in power balancing is an observation and a caveat. The observation communicated to participants is that the process of negotiation itself makes a significant positive contribution to power balancing because it requires joint decision-making. The caveat communicated to them verbally and in writing is that the joint decision to use one or more of the struggle tactics listed below tend to increase the intensity of conflict to the point where the parties abuse each other emotionally and physically and/or experience the adverse consequences of jointly deciding to hire highly adversarial lawyers to represent them. Tactics that increase the intensity of conflict include negative stereotyping, use of threats, proliferating issues, personal attacks, excessive stonewalling, expressions of contempt, and extreme defensiveness (Bennett & Hughes, 2005; Gottman, 2002; Pruitt & Rubin, 1986).

Separating parties rarely bring equality in interpersonal power to the process of negotiating a separation agreement. In the third segment of the training program, participants are taught how to balance an imbalanced interpersonal power relationship and then asked to demonstrate their ability to balance an imbalanced power relationship in coaching sessions. Interpersonal power is defined as a relationship in which differences in the resources controlled by the other party and the willingness and ability of the parties to use them effectively are reflected in their ability to achieve desired outcomes. Power-balancing tactics that are derived from the process theory of interpersonal power created by Gulliver (1979) and modified by Ellis and Anderson (2005) are illustrated in Figure 8.1.

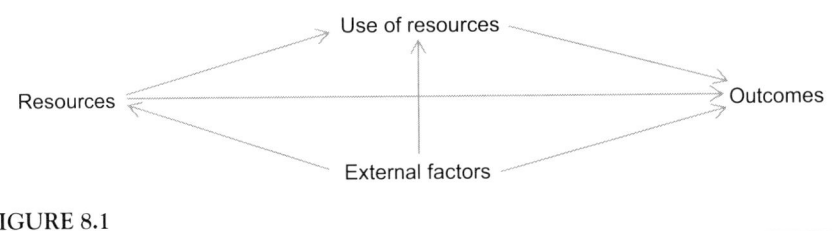

FIGURE 8.1

Process theory of interpersonal power.

Resources are the first variable interrelated in this theory. Resources are defined as "anything that, in context, contributes to the achievement of desired outcomes." Better alternative to a negotiated agreement (referred to by the acronym BATNA) is a potent resource. It is defined for participants who are taught how to improve their BATNAs in preparation for negotiations.

Use of resources is defined as "persuasive strength or the degree to which the resources used by one party move the other party toward an agreement." Outcomes (agreement) refer to the results of using resources. Outcomes can be positive-sum, zero-sum, or negative-sum. External factors refer to factors within the wider social setting (community or society) that influence the outcomes of negotiations directly or indirectly by "augmenting, depleting, and modifying the resources available to the parties."

SHELTERS AND DOMESTIC VIOLENCE ABUSE COURTS

A worldwide concern is the number of women who are murdered by their abusive partners. Intimate partner violence takes a physical and psychological toll including posttraumatic stress disorder (PTSD), depression, and suicide attempts (Perez, Johnson, & Wright, 2012). Over 30 years in Canada, women are three to four times as likely to be killed by their spouses as are men (Sinha, 2012) and in more than one in five spousal homicides, the perpetrator committed suicide (more than 25% were men and 3% were women between 1991 and 2000) (Banks, Crandall, Sklar, & Bauer, 2008; Bunge, 2002).

On average, every six days a woman in Canada is killed by her intimate partner and, in 2009, 67 women were killed by a current or former intimate partner (Beattie & Cotter, 2009). These murders and subsequent suicides happen even after frightened women have complained to the police about beatings and threats (Montgomery, 2013). In 2011, from the 89 police-reported spousal homicides, 76 of the victims (over 85%) were women. Although the number of intimate femicides/homicides had been dropping (Rennison & Welchans, 2000), a troubling trend was the reversal in the number of femicides (Farmer & Tiefenthaler, 2003), for example, in Ontario, where spousal homicides rose from 68 (2000) to 86 (2002) (Thomas, 2002). Ways to prevent this carnage must be explored.

A suggested way of preventing femicide/femicide–suicide is to stop all contact between an abused woman and her abusive partner. Yet, in the United States and Canada, a man who beats and rapes his female partner is able to stay in his own home while the woman and children must sometimes move to a shelter. This disrupts their lives and work, and the children must change schools to avoid being traced by their father (Trainor, 1999). Abused women facing injury or possibly death at the hands of their partners attempt to escape by fleeing their relationship (Dobash & Dobash, 1992). However, this often exacerbates their situation because the most dangerous time for women is in the days or months after they have either said they were going to leave or have left the abusive relationship (Crawford & Gardner, 1992; Sullivan & Bybee, 2000; Wells, Ren, & DeLeon-Granados, 2010). A further problem for the women is that they most often do not have funds or family and friends' support to be able to obtain a safe place to live (Stuckless & Toner, 1998).

One remedy, albeit usually short-term, appears to be the establishment of abused women shelters to provide protection and services for those who are fortunate enough to obtain a place (Sev'er, 2002). However, although there is anecdotal evidence of the benefits of these shelters, far less is known about the relationship between staying in, and subsequently leaving, shelters and further danger to the women.

The contribution made by shelters in preventing femicide will be explored. To this end, we will address the following:

- A discussion of shelters, including numbers, history, and types.
- Do shelters help prevent women being abused by their partners?
- Do shelters prevent femicide?
- Do other services or policies prevent femicide?

Battered women's alternatives are improved by providing shelters, hotlines, and other services that help make it possible to leave their relationships. Shelters provide abused women and their children with a place of safety, services, and opportunities for child care, job preparation, group meetings, and counseling (Stuckless & Toner, 1998). Over the past 25 years, numerous nonprofit groups have augmented the funds supplied by various levels of government that contribute to increasing the availability of services for battered women (Farmer & Tiefenthaler, 2003).

Why Shelters?

During three months in 2002, a great number of femicides were committed by current or estranged partners (Sev'er, 2002). Sev'er concluded that, although steps were taken to prevent abuse by police questioning and arresting the abusers, and by peace bonds being issued, numerous women were murdered because they did not have a place to go where they would be safe. Commenting on the situation of women who are forced to leave their abusive partners, Morrow (2002) argued that "Women can't leave if there's nowhere to go and no way to look after their children. They need shelters and affordable housing. ... BC [British Columbia] will see an increase in spousal murders if there continues to be less and less support for women who are forced to leave their homes" (Thomas, 2002). Rodgers and MacDonald (2000) reported that 29% of women in 1998 who were residing in shelters at the time had contacted the police about the last incident that caused them to go to the shelter and that arrests were made in 86% of the cases. Unfortunately, women who had to leave shelters after a short or medium-length stay often had to return to the abusive relationship because of lack of affordable housing and jobs because waiting times for battered women can range from three weeks to five years, even though they are given priority for housing (OAITH, 1998).

History of Shelters

A number of shelters were opened by feminists in the United States in the 1970s to protect abused women fleeing their abusive partners (Gengler, 2012), although Haven House opened in California as early as 1964. The funding is mostly provided by the federal government (40–50%). Most states have cut their funding for shelters and other initiatives responding to domestic violence (DV), leaving many abused women with no place to escape the violence (Dunivan, 2011; Galen, 2012). Chiswick Women's Aid was opened in London in 1971 (Tierney, 1981); Ishtar Transitional House, the first transition house in Canada, was opened in British Columbia in 1973; while others were opened in Christchurch, New Zealand, and Sydney, Australia. Although in most places shelters are exclusively for women, in the United Kingdom, a number of places were opened for abused men. Even so, whereas 7,500 places were available for women abused by their intimate partners, only 60 places were available for abused men (Campbell, 2010).

The abused women reported that abuse was a common reason for their admissions (71%). Most of them (67%) were looking for shelter from current partners, and most (60%) had not reported the abuse to police (Campbell & Wolf, 2012). A very disturbing statistic, however, was that in Oregon, in 2011, 20,681 requests for shelter were unable to be met (Striving to Meet the Need, 2012).

Shelters provide abused women and their children with a place of safety, services, and opportunities. Many women in a study conducted by Stuckless and Toner (1998) reported that, in addition to child care and job preparation, their most valuable times were in group meetings and counseling. Shelters help women in other ways, including helping women through the legal proceedings when they apply for restraining orders and also providing counseling services. Shelters are servicing more women; however, once again, requests for shelter are often unable to be met (Kay, 2013). Part of this problem arises from the fact that some shelters allow women to stay longer because they have nowhere else to go to prevent returning to the violent relationship. This limits access to other women seeking shelter. A nationwide survey in the United States in 2013 by Mary Kay showed that more than 800 shelters shared this concern.

Types of Shelters

Marta Burczycka and Adam Cotter (2011) administered the Transition Home Survey to abused women who were asked to select the type of shelter they use. They described the types of shelters as transition home/shelter, which is short-term or moderate-term (one day–11 weeks) secure housing for abused women with or without children (also referred to as first-stage emergency housing); second-stage housing, which is long-term (three–12 months) secure housing with support and referral services for women who can search for permanent housing; women's emergency center/shelter, which is short-term (one–21 days) respite for women and their dependent children; and emergency shelter, which is short-term (one–three days) respite for a wide population range, not exclusively abused women.

An International Need for Shelters

The need for shelter is international. In 2010, Statistics Canada revealed that the number of shelters and beds in Canada had increased slightly (by 24) since 2008 (Burczycka & Cotter, 2011): There were 593 shelters for abused women in operation. The larger increases were found in the number of second-stage housing facilities (up 11%, or 11 shelters) and transition homes (up 8%, or 22 facilities). On any given day in Canada, more than 3,300 women (along with their 3,000 children) are forced to sleep in an emergency shelter to escape DV. Yet, every night, about 200 women are turned away because the shelters are full (Burczycka & Cotter, 2011). In 2010, there were 11,461 beds available in shelters across Canada, an increase of 7% from two years earlier. "Between April 1, 2009, and March 31, 2010, there were over 64,500 admissions of women to shelters across Canada ... up 2% from 2007/2008" (p. 4). Almost one-third (31%) of these women had stayed at the shelter before, up from one-quarter (25%) in 2007/2008.

In Asia, Panchanadeswaran and Koverola (2005) found that there was a great need for safety for assaulted women in India from their abusive husbands and their families. The women reported that women's shelters and counseling centers were the most effective way of preventing death at the hands of their husbands or his family. Similarly, in Baghdad, underground shelters are the only hope for Iraqi women abused by their intimate partners (Badkhen, 2009). Women in Lahore, Pakistan, often must spend extended times in the shelters because women who have left the shelters have been murdered (Dastak, 2013).

Who Uses Shelters?

The first thing an abused woman needs is to be safe. More women, of all races, are killed by partners or former partners than by anyone else. This carnage is reported worldwide, although there are differences. For example, 4,000 (more than three a day) are killed by their partners in the United States yearly (Domestic Abuse Shelters, 2014; Domestic Violence Resource Center, 2013), most often by guns (Aldridge & Browne, 2003). In the United Kingdom, reports are that "37% of all women were killed by their current or former intimate partners compared to 6% of men" (Aldridge & Browne, 2003, Abstract). In the U.K., the cause of death was most often a sharp instrument or strangulation. In 2000, 1,247 women were killed by an intimate partner compared to 400 men. This accounts for 30% of all women murdered and 5% of all men (Domestic Violence Resource Center, 2013).

Leaving the Abusive Relationship

Although most research is on pre-separation violence, less attention is paid to what happens after women leave their abusive relationships (Anderson & Saunders, 2003; Fleury, Sullivan & Bybee, 2000). "Clearly, process studies highlight the courage, determination, and persistence involved in leaving an abusive partner" (Anderson & Saunders, 2003, p. 176). In qualitative interviews with 20 shelter residents looking at the needs of shelter users, 84% of the women said that they were fleeing abuse, 65% physical abuse and/or 79% psychological abuse, and 14% sexual abuse (Stensrud, 2005). Another study involving interviews with abused women residing in shelters revealed a number of factors about why the women took a long time before they left the violent, abusive relationship (Stuckless & Toner, 1998). These included distrust of the criminal justice system, the fact that they most often do not have funds or family and friends' support to be able to obtain a safe place to live, and fear of retribution by their abusive partner. Financial dependence on their partner is a common reason for staying in the abusive relationship because more than 1.22 million Canadian women and their children live in poverty. Women who raise children on their own are five times more likely to be poor than if they stayed with their partner (Townson, 2009). There are also psychological and material (employment and income) factors predicting leaving the partner (Anderson & Saunders, 2003). Women's needs for intervention and protection most often increase after they leave the abusive partner. Karen Nelson Grundy (2003) made a very thorough discussion of the possible consequences for a battered woman if she decides to leave the batterer or if she decides to stay with her partner. She said the battered woman had two choices, both bad. If she decides to leave the batterer, she may lose economic security for herself and her children; lose her position in her community; lose the partner whom she loves despite his cruel behavior; lose the support of traditional-minded family and church members who believe she should endure all things to keep her family together. Because battered women are in the greatest danger when they leave their batterer, she may be stalked, threatened, attacked, and even murdered.

If she decides to stay with her partner, she may risk losing her children; losing even more of her self-esteem; painful, terrifying, and humiliating abuse; and ultimately losing her life (Grundy, 2012).

Although a woman will leave her abuser an average of seven times before the final break (Domestic Abuse Shelters of the Florida Keys, 2014), fear for their children was usually the "last straw," the reason why they finally end the abusive relationship (Stuckless & Toner, 1998). There are instances where leaving the abusive home, and subsequently the shelter, can lead to increased safety because the opportunity for physical violence decreases. However, leaving the abusive partner may initiate violence for the first time or aggravate existing violence (Fleury, Sullivan, & Bybee, 2000).

Leaving is the most dangerous time for abused women. Leaving a violent relationship or saying she is leaving is the most dangerous time for a woman (Campbell et al., 2003; DeKeseredy, 2011; Ellis & Stuckless, 1996). Seventy-five percent of women killed by their batterers are murdered when they attempt to leave or after they have left an abusive relationship (Domestic Abuse Shelters of the Florida Keys, 2014). One in five women who reported abuse said that violence occurred after or during separation, and in one-third of the cases, the violence increased in severity on separation. Separated women are about 25 times more likely to be assaulted by their former intimate partners (Bachman & Saltzman, 1995) and five times more likely to be murdered (Wilson & Daly, 1993). Although Block et al. (2000) found that 40% of femicides were precipitated when "the woman is leaving or trying to leave the abusive relationship" (p. 242), Campbell, Rose, Kub, and Nedd (1998) countered that staying is always unhealthy.

The most dangerous time for an abused woman is the first 12 months after separation. Forty-seven percent (15 of 38) of slain wives in Australia were killed within the first two months and 91% (29 of 38) within the first year (Statistics Canada, 2009). Statistics Canada reported in 2001 that almost half (49%) of women killed by their spouses are killed within two months of separation (Domestic Abuse Shelters of the Florida Keys, 2014). This rate was consistent in 2006, with half of the murdered women killed within two months Canadian Women's Foundation, 2012; Fleury, Sullivan, & Bybee, 2000). Another 32% of murdered spouses are killed within two to 12 months after separation.

The question then arises: Can shelters prevent femicide?

Do Shelters Benefit Abused Women and Their Children?

Stout (1989) outlines four ways in which shelters benefit battered women: (1) providing safety from immediate danger; (2) allowing women to recover from the abuse; (3) giving women the opportunity to assess their situation and investigate their options; and (4) introducing women to other women facing the same ordeals (p. 25). Shelters provide means for women to work toward gaining independence in a safe location. In their study, with 227 residents of two shelters for abused women, Perez, Johnson, and Wright (2012) reported that the initial separation from the violence and fear perpetrated by the abuser was the most important variable for the women. The study also found evidence of the effect of empowerment on the reduction of PTSD symptoms for the abused women. As a result, they suggest that psychotherapeutic interventions developed to foster empowerment of the abused women could be added to the shelter services. Shelters provide many services for the abused women after they leave their partners, including a safe place to live, counseling, housing support, job readiness training, child care, and legal support (Redwood, 2013).

As we stated earlier, abused women reported that abuse was a common reason for admissions, with most of them looking for shelter from current partners (Campbell & Wolf, 2012). Yet every night women and their children are turned away because of lack of space (Burczycka & Cotter, 2011; Kay, 2013).

Many women in the study conducted by Stuckless and Toner (1998) reported that, in addition to child care and job preparation, their most valuable times were in group meetings and counseling. Shelters help women in other ways, including helping women through the legal proceedings when they apply for restraining orders and also providing counseling services. However, proponents of the HRT program organized by the Jeanne Geiger Center in Newburyport, Massachusetts (discussed earlier) are dismissive of the value of shelters. They concede that shelters do save lives, but argue that shelters primarily have negative effects as they "also isolate and penalize victims by disrupting their lives instead of containing and disrupting the lives of perpetrators and are also a ticket to welfare" (Dunne, in Snyder, 2013, p. 36). It must be noted that they do not offer evidence to support this conclusion.

The Efficacy of Shelters in Reducing Spousal Violence

There is evidence that shelters can be effective in preventing women from being abused by their partners or ex-partners. Evidence cited in the Maryland Network Against Domestic Violence report (2004) indicates that abused female partners using shelters experienced a 60% reduction in the risk of serious assault. Unfortunately, the authors did not specify this finding by reporting the proportion of abused women who were and were not seriously assaulted while they were residing in a shelter with the proportion of women who were seriously and not seriously assaulted after leaving a shelter.

Campbell and Wolf (2012) reported a 60–70% reduction in the incidence and severity of re-assault during the three–12 month follow-up time after access to shelter services was compared to those women who were not in shelters. The shelter services were more effective in reducing assault than was moving or court or law enforcement protection. Unfortunately, the need for beds and other services meant that the women could only stay for a short period of time. Alternate accommodations were found for a small number of the women, but most were forced to look for other shelters or to return to their abusive partner after a short period of time. Because many women are threatened, stalked, and killed by their former partner, shelters often have a policy to keep the location a secret to prevent the abusive partner from contacting his partner or children. This, however, can be difficult for the children and their schooling and friends (Shelters & Safehouses, 2003).

Bunge (2002) believes that the increasing availability of shelters and other services for spousal violence victims could have contributed to the declines in nonlethal and lethal spousal violence. However, with the exception of legal services, none of the services specifically designed to help victims of DV appear to impact the likelihood of abuse. Many countries have a number of services, including shelters, hotlines, programs for batterers, children's programs, and counseling. Women accessing these services do not report significantly less spousal violence than women in countries that do not have these services. An interesting finding is that when women live in countries where there are legal assistance programs to help battered women, they are significantly less likely to report abuse. It appears that the support battered women receive from legal services about matters such as protective orders, custody, and child support gives them other ways to deal with their relationships (Farmer & Tiefenthaler, 2003; Stout, 1989).

What Happens after Leaving the Shelter?

Although there is ample anecdotal evidence of the benefits of these shelters, far less is known about how staying in a shelter can affect the possibility of further danger to the women after they leave the shelter. "The majority of the process studies on battered women either ignore or downplay the importance of the post-separation period, including the violence and other stressors that often occur then" (Anderson & Saunders, 2003, p. 178). In fact, those who had been in shelters were more likely to experience new violence (Bowker, 1983; Davis, 1988). Tutty's (1998) study revealed that half the women reported feeling threatened by their partners even though at least 4–6 months had passed after they left DV shelters. Similarly, Stover, Meadows, and Kaufman (2009) saw little change in the abuse suffered by women in their study after they left the shelter.

Bowker (1983) interviewed 150 former victims of intimate partner abuse who were free from abuse for over a year and found that, although the shelters were valuable, they were not as effective as other interventions such as restraint orders. There are variables that may help predict greater abuse (Dobash & Dobash, 1992; Kay, 2013). Women who are not able to obtain resources are less likely to leave the abusive relationship. Second, women who are in male-dominated marriages that they are highly dependent on may suffer more violence, and, finally, gender inequality, in general, is linked to greater abuse.

In Fleury, Sullivan, and Bybee's study on post-relationship (2000), one-third of the women reported being assaulted by their abusive partners two years after they left the shelter. They reported a number of variables related to violence by an ex-partner after the women left the shelter. These were (p. 1375):

- Threats against women prior to assault, $p < 0.01$;
- Length of relationship prior to first assault, $p < 0.05$;
- Batterer's extreme jealousy prior to shelter entry, $p < 0.05$;
- Batterer's proximity (same city as woman or not), $p < .001$;
- Is survivor currently in another relationship, $p < 0.02$.

For some women, leaving the abusive relationship did lead to greater safety after leaving the shelter. More than one-half the women in Fleury, Sullivan, and Bybee's study (2000) who had left their abusive relationship reported greater feelings of safety after leaving the shelter. However, this depended on whether or not "the batterer currently lived in the same city as the woman" (p. 1375). As they reported, "If the batterer and the woman no longer lived in the same city, she was less likely to be assaulted by her ex-partner (odds ratio = 4.64). It should be noted that the majority of women stayed in the same city; the difference seemed to be whether batterers moved out of the area" (p. 1376).

Why Return Home?

A study of battered women (Tutty, 1998), based on data collected from 77 shelters (9,000 shelter stays) after the women left the shelters, found that 44% returned home. Of these, 27% returned to an unchanged situation whereas 17% returned to a situation that included counseling and perhaps court orders. An interesting note is that women who had previously been physically abused were less likely to return to the abuser than those who had suffered "psychological, emotional, or financial abuse" (p. 14). The question arose as to why almost half of the women returned home. For some women, attachment to their spouses led to the return, whereas for others, lack of resources, including failure to find housing, forced the return. Abuse often continues post-separation and the women may feel that their best chance to avoid the threats of violence is to return to the abuser. It was suggested that this is not considered to be a failure on behalf of the shelter or the women but rather that the process of ending the relationship can be very difficult (Anderson & Saunders, 2003).

Decline in Intimate Partner Abuse and Mortality Rates

There is evidence that there is a reduction in intimate inter-partner violence (IPV). In particular, there has been a decrease in the rate of both men and women being killed by their partners.

In a press release dated May 17, 2000, the Bureau of Justice Statistics (BJS) reported that violence against women by intimate partners fell by 21% from 1993 through 1998. This statistic was calculated from the National Crime Victimization Survey (NCVS), an annual survey on the incidence of all types of crimes, including violence by intimates (current or former spouses, girlfriends, or boyfriends). National estimates on the rate of DV are available only from 1993 because the NCVS (formerly called the National Crime Survey) was significantly redesigned in 1992. Previous estimates of intimate partner abuse were found to suffer from a serious problem of underreporting, but the redesigned survey includes several questions concerning specifically intimate partner abuse. However, trend data are available on intimate partner homicide since the 1970s, and these data support a long-term decline in DV. The BJS reports that between 1976 and 1998, the number of male victims of intimate partner homicide declined an average 4% per year and the number of female victims declined an average 1% per year (Farmer & Tiefenthaler, 2003, p. 4).

The irony for those who are advocating against violence against women is that the greatest decline is in the number of men being killed by their female partners (Campbell, 2003; Davis, 1988). Intimate partner homicide accounts for approximately 40–50% of U.S. femicides but only a relatively small proportion of male homicides (5.9%). The percentage of intimate partner homicides involving male victims decreased between 1976 and 1996, whereas the percentage of female victims increased from 54% to 72% (Campbell et al., 2003).

Farmer and Tiefenthaler (2003) discuss factors that may explain the recent decline. They suggest that economic models of DV predict that violence against women will decline as women's alternatives outside their relationships improve. Providing shelters, hotlines, and other services improves alternatives that help make leaving their relationships possible for these women. Numerous non-profit groups augment federal, state, and local governments' contributions for available services for battered women throughout the United States (Farmer & Tiefenthaler, 2003).

Do Shelters Prevent Femicide?

Intimate partner homicides declined over the past 30 years in California but the role of shelters in this decline is not well known. Women who accessed shelters as well as other services had the greatest success. The drop was not consistent, with urban centers showing the drop but rural centers not doing so (Well, Ren, & DeLeon-Granados, 2010). "Our results indicate that there are three important factors that likely contribute to the decline: (1) the increased provision of legal services for victims of intimate partner abuse, (2) improvements in women's economic status, and (3) demographic trends, most notably the aging of the population" (Farmer & Tiefenthaler, 2003, p. 19). Twenty-nine percent of shelter residents in 1998 had called the police about abuse and arrests were made in 86% of the cases (Rodgers & MacDonald, 2000). As noted earlier, after short or medium-length shelter stays, many women had to return to the abusing partner because they could not get housing or jobs (OAITH, 1998).

Can Availability for Access to Shelters Prevent Femicide?

Every six days, on average, a woman is killed by her intimate partner. From the 89 police-reported spousal homicides in 2011, 76 of the victims (more than 85%) were women. Although there is some evidence for the reduction of nonlethal violence, there appears to be little support for the role of shelters in the reduction of lethal violence against women by their intimate partners. The question of whether the ability of an abused woman to access a shelter will prevent her from being killed by an intimate partner is far from clear (Wells, Ren, & DeLeon, 2010). Although there has been a reduction in the number of intimate femicides and homicides over the past number of years, there has been little research on the question of whether the availability of services in shelters for abused women is responsible for this reduction.

There was only one study (Stout, 1989) that supported the role of shelters in reducing femicide and homicide. She looked at the rate of intimate femicide in the 50 states, the availability of shelters and rape crisis centers, and legislation concerning violence against women. The results indicated negative correlations between the number of shelters per million and the number of intimate femicides (-0.52, $p = 0.001$), and the number of rape control centers per million (-0.40, $p = 0.005$), indicating that availability of shelters appeared to lessen the likelihood of women being killed by their intimate partners. By contrast, other more recent studies have found that the resources in DV shelters do not show efficacy in preventing women being killed by their spouses (DeLeon-Granados & Wells, 2003).

Prevention of Homicide

There appears to be efficacy in reducing intimate partner homicide for women killing their male partners but not for men killing their female partners. A study by DeLeon-Granados and Wells (2003) indicated that hotlines and legal services impact negatively on the rate at which wives murder their husbands but not on the rate at which men murdered their female partners. Shelters did not lessen the rate of female victimization. Ironically, for those who advocate for protection for women, it appeared that men were made safer and women were not. Wells, Ren, and DeLeon-Granados (2010) analyzed a set of county-level data that indicated that the shelter-based service availability did not show an effect for the shelter-based services on the rate of intimate femicide. They suggest that there may be problems with the measures reporting intimate partner homicides, questioning their reliability and validity. Farmer and Tiefenthaler (2003) confirm the reduction of the rate at which men are killed by their intimate partners.

Although the empirical literature supports the importance of women's economic alternatives as a determinant of DV, there is little empirical work that examines the effect of service provision on the rate of female abuse. However, one study does examine the effect of service provision on the rate at which women kill their husbands. Dugan et al. (1998) examine the effects of domesticity, women's economic power, and resources for battered women on intimate partner homicides in 29 U.S. cities over four biannual periods. The results indicate that both women's economic power and services provided for battered women lower the rate at which women kill their husbands. The authors contend that women with better alternatives are more likely to use them rather than resort to killing their abusers to protect themselves (Farmer & Tiefenthaler, 2003, p. 6).

Sev'er (2002) reported that, in a three-month period in 2002, a large number of women were murdered by their current or estranged partners. He concluded that, although steps were taken to prevent abuse by police questioning and arresting the abusers, and by peace bonds being issued, numerous women were murdered because they did not have a place to go where they would be safe. He contends that vulnerable women are being shortchanged and that shelters that protect the women from their abusers are "in a state of crisis" (p. 21). Shelters then may reduce the chance of women's being battered, but this benefit does not appear to carry over to prevent their being murdered. Wells, Ren, and DeLeon-Granados (2010) conducted analyses looking at the effect of federally funded shelters' availability on the frequency of intimate partner homicides. They did not find that the availability/non-availability of access to shelters or criminal justice responses affected or predicted the rate of intimate partner homicides.

Evaluation

The literature indicates that there are mixed messages regarding the efficacy of shelters in preventing violence. There is evidence that nonlethal violence is prevented, or at least reduced, while women are in shelters. Shelters help prevent women from being killed during the "most dangerous time after leaving the abusive relationship." There is also ample evidence of services provided by shelters for abused women and their children. However, the evidence does not support the efficacy of shelters in preventing violence after the women leave the shelter or femicide. The rate of men murdered by their intimate partners was reduced, but not women by their intimate partners. Shelters that offer access to legal services to shelter residents will make a greater contribution toward prevention than providing other kinds of services. One serious failing in the literature is that there has been no empirical program evaluation of the efficacy of shelters.

Over and beyond trying to increase availability in shelters (Badken, 2009; Sev'er, 2002), there are public policies and treatments for abusers that are designed to help protect battered women and their children.

THE ROLE OF PUBLIC POLICIES AND PROGRAMS IN PREVENTING FEMICIDE

We now examine the efficacy of public policies and programs in preventing women being abused or killed by their current or ex-partners. Criminal charges related to DV and other forms of sexual harassment have been passed in the United States (Stout, 2011) and in Canada (Bunge, 2002) over the past number of years. Other policies and programs, ranging from counseling programs for the abusers (York Region Violence Against Women Coordinating Committee, 2009), civil protection orders (POs) (Durfee & Messing, 2012), restraining orders (Safrath, 2013), Postshelter Advocacy Intervention Programs, legal aid, anger management therapy, and courts restricted to DV cases. The question arises as to how effective are they in preventing both nonlethal and lethal violence against women.

Protection Orders and Restraining Orders

A resource in the United States for victims of IPV is the use of DV civil protection orders (POs), orders that forbid contact between the victim and the abuser. The number of POs increased by 35% from 1994 to 2003 (Durfee & Messing, 2012).

A number of factors predicted when POs would be used by IPV victims seeking shelter services. These include previous contact with medical authorities and police, the level of education, income, age, race, and children who live with their mothers in the shelter. Another resource for abused women is the issuance of restraining orders (ROs).

Safrath (2013) explains the differences between POs and ROs. "Orders of protection and restraining orders are two options for people being threatened or physically abused. The two orders are similar in whom they protect, but are different in how long they are good for and the penalties for violation."

POs issued by the courts to DV victims demand that their abusive partner stop threatening, stalking, or physically assaulting the victim. Often, orders may also demand that an abuser stop all contact with the victim, in person, by phone, or by mail. POs are usually in effect for at least one year, but the court can issue them for longer periods or renew them if a request is made. All 50 states have legislation enabling POs (Logan & Walker, 2011).

A restraining order is issued by a court to protect someone from threats or physical abuse. They differ from POs because ROs may also include requirements for property, child support and custody, and spousal support when these issues arise during a divorce or separation. The court sets the length of the ROs on a case-by-case consideration, usually for at least six months, but they may extend for several years. If the woman wishes an extension, that must be requested and approved before the expiration of the initial RO.

An important distinction between POs and ROs is the penalties for violation of the restrictions imposed by the court. An abuser who violates an RO will face only a contempt charge and be required to pay a fine. However, an abuser violating a PO can face criminal charges, which can range from a misdemeanor to a felony, "depending upon the circumstances of the violation and the number of violations already against the abuser" (Safrath, 2013).

There is considerable disagreement over the effectiveness of POs. Benitez, McNiel, and Binder (2010) contend that the answer depends on understanding the question that is asked. Most often the measure of success is the rate of violation of the abuser of the restrictions imposed by the courts, and conclusions based on those rates. However, these rates vary widely. Spitzberg's (2002) meta-analysis of 23 studies that were published prior to 2002 showed rates of violation ranging from 3% to 79% (mean = 40).

Keilitz, Davis, Efkeman, Flango, and Hannaford (1998) maintain that how effective civil POs are depends on how "specific and comprehensive they are and how well they are enforced." That leaves bigger questions to be answered. Specifically, for whom do POs work best and under what circumstances?

Recent National Institute of Justice–sponsored research, conducted by the National Center for State Courts and involving interviews with women who filed POs, concluded that victims' views on the effectiveness of POs vary with how accessible the courts are for victims and how well established the links are between public and private services and support resources for victims. In addition, violations of the protection order increase and reported effectiveness decreases as the criminal record of the abuser becomes more serious. In the majority of cases, victims felt that civil POs protected them against repeated incidents of physical and psychological abuse and were valuable in helping them regain a sense of well-being. A PO alone, however, was not as likely to be effective against abusers with a history of violent offenses; women in these cases were more likely to report a greater number of problems with violations of the PO. The researchers noted that criminal prosecution of these individuals may be required to curb such behavior (National Institute of Justice, 1998).

Albrecht (2012) suggests that, on the average, ROs work about half the time, and the other half, they do not. The problem is that far too often the issuance of an RO makes a bad situation much worse. In an analysis of 231 women killed by their intimate partners, Vittes and Sorenson (2008) reported that 11% of the murdered women had been issued ROs, yet one-fifth of the IPV victims had been murdered within two days of the issuance of the orders and one-third were killed within a month. Nearly half of those with ROs had been protected by multiple orders. An interesting fact is that not one of the seven men who were killed by their female intimate partners had ROs. Vittes and Sorenson concluded that the abused women expected that the ROs would protect them when, in fact, the orders may have had the opposite effect. These women need protection from the abuser, but they and the staff were frustrated over how ineffective the peace bonds or ROs were.

Men who ignore the orders rarely are meaningfully penalized so women have little motivation to report the abuse because they do not feel they would be protected and the abuser might become angry (Stensrud, 2005). Stensrud proposed that abused women who are shelter residents should be provided with legal representation to help them with the separation from their abuser. In a clip service involving articles about women who were killed by their intimate partners, a great number of the men who killed their partners were under an RO (Kingston Frontenac Anti-Violence Coordinating Committee, 2010).

Post-shelter Advocacy Intervention Programs

Post-shelter advocacy intervention programs appear to have some success in ameliorating the conditions facing shelter residents after they leave the shelters. A study by Sullivan and Bybee (1999) demonstrated this. As they left their shelter, 278 women indicated the issues they would like to address with professionals if they were randomly selected to receive the counseling and support in a 10-week advocacy program intervention of four to six hours per week. The results of this qualitative study indicated that the women who were randomly selected to participate in the treatment condition, receiving the counseling and support, reported fewer incidents of abuse, greater quality of life, and greater access to resources than the women who were not selected and did not receive the counseling and support (Anderson & Saunders, 2003).

Another post-shelter program with encouraging results used the services of trained professionals who provided practical and psychological support (Anderson &

Saunders, 2003; Tutty, 1998). A self-assessment instrument was administered to 76 women before, immediately after, and six months after attending any of 12 selected support groups. The women had low self-esteem, clinical levels of marital dysfunction, and had suffered spousal violence. Changes were noted in each individual's responses at each time period. The women who participated in the support groups reported significant improvements in a number of variables including self-esteem, less traditional attitudes toward marriage and the family, perceived stress, and their relationships with their partners. Those who were living with their partners reported unexpected significant decreases in abuse (Tutty, 1993).

Programs for Abusers

Specific programs are developed that offer counseling and therapy for men. "Some programs try to educate the men about their abusive behavior and alternatives to it: others are more intent on healing and changing them" (Gondolf, 2002, p. 1). "[M]ost programs for abusive men are informed by the Duluth Model, suggesting that male violence against women is influenced by the dictates of patriarchy and sexism. Accordingly, this model promotes the importance of educational groups, which aim to debunk men's stereotypical beliefs about women. Thus, men's early abuse history, which also contributes to the use of violence, is omitted from service delivery" (Aymer, 2008, Abstract).

The Efficacy of Intervention Programs and Policies in Preventing Intimate Violence and Femicide

Re-assault is a measure of outcome evaluating the efficacy of the programs and policies. More than one-third of the men re-assaulted their partners during the 15 months following program intake, and the proportion increases to almost one half by the end of four years. "The trend of re-assaults shows that the vast majority of men have sustained a cessation of violence (for a year or more) at the two and one-half year follow-up. About 20% of the men, however, repeatedly and severely assaulted their partners" (Gondolf, 2002, p. 22).

A treatment review by Stover, Meadows, and Kaufman (2009) based on IPV treatment studies with randomized case assignment found that the interventions have limited effect on whether violence is repeated. Most treatments reported minimal benefit above arrest alone. In particular, "there is a lack of research evidence for the effectiveness of the most common treatments provided for victims and perpetrators of IPV, including the Duluth Model for perpetrators and shelter–advocacy approaches for victims. Rates of recidivism in most perpetrator- and partner-focused treatments are approximately 30% within six months, regardless of intervention strategy used" (p. 223).

Additionally, the availability and services for abusers are not adequate. In the York region (Canada), yearly 3,200 women are abused, 1,000 men are charged with DV, and yet only 500 men are given services (York Region Violence Against Women

Coordinating Committee, 2009). They may also not be effective. In her study on the efficacy of shelters and programs designed to protect abused women, Karen Stout (1989) looked at the rate of intimate femicide in the 50 states, and the number of programs designed for men who batter (p. 27). She found that there was no correlation between the number of programs designed for men who batter, per million, and the rate of intimate femicide (0.12, not significant). The programs did not protect battered women.

One particular program is anger management. "Anger control no doubt contributes to the redirection or reduction of anger and of aggression in many individuals. The question is how well suited is it for batterers. Does it help end wife abuse, as opposed to only reduce dysfunctional anger? Two, does it lend itself to misuse by counselors and batterers? In other words, is anger control effective if properly used, and is it likely to be properly implemented by this particular population?" (Gondolf & Russell, 1986, p. 2).

The effectiveness of anger management programs in stopping the violence against battered women is being questioned (Gondolf, 2012). The findings from a meta-analysis raise questions about the value of these programs. Although additional research is needed, the meta-analysis does not offer strong support that the court-mandated treatment of anger management therapy for DV offenders reduces the likelihood of further re-assault (Feder & Wilson, 2005). Holly (2012) reported that men who abuse and who complete anger management programs do not stop abusing. They just choose another way to reach the same end less violently (Gondolf & Russell, 1986).

Domestic Violence Courts

A final major program in the United States and Canada for attempting to protect abused partners and prevent re-assault or femicide is the establishment of domestic violence courts (DVCs), designed solely for charges related to intimate partner abuse. In the United States, there are more than 200 DVCs, representing an important strategy for handling DV cases flooding the state courts. The courts handle a jurisdiction's DV cases on a separate calendar and are presided over by specially assigned judges with expertise in the unique legal and personal issues that these cases pose (Cissner, Labriola, & Rempel, 2013). Generally, there are two types of courts, one for first offenders and the other for serious offenders. The first ones in Canada were set up in Winnipeg, in 1990 and in Ontario, which has DVCs in each court jurisdiction, and in other provinces as well. The purpose of these courts is to make it more efficient to prosecute domestic assault cases, have earlier trials, and provide more support to the victims (Bunge, 2002). The following is a brief look at three jurisdictions where DVCs are established.

In Idaho in the United States, the DVCs are successful in that they are superior to the traditional courts' handling of DV cases, but further steps are needed to realize their full potential (Hovda, 2012). When comparing the DVC offenders to the traditional court offenders, the evaluation report showed just nominal differences in both completion of treatment and compliance. The report showed that 79% of DVC offenders had completed, or were currently attending, treatment, compared to 54.5% of offenders in traditional court. However, no statistically significant differences in outcomes related to compliance with court-ordered treatment were found in comparisons between randomly selected subsets of offenders from the two courts. A difficulty arises in that no research exists regarding recidivism rates of participants in the DVCs because the authorities said that measuring recidivism was "beyond the scope" of the evaluation of any DVC in Idaho.

In New York State in the United States, examination made of the impact of the DVCs on re-arrest revealed that the DVCs did not reduce re-arrests overall. However, they did significantly reduce re-arrest on DV charges (29% versus 32%). In this state, different DVCs were established to deal with different aspects of the judicial system. Courts that emphasized deterring men from re-offending by including policy measures that are designed to penalize noncompliant offenders and address victim safety and service needs were compared to courts that focused less on these issues. The courts that focused on the deterrence and safety measures reported significantly fewer re-arrests on DV charges (Cissner, Labriola, & Rempel, 2013).

In Ontario in Canada, Johnson and Fraser (2011) examined whether the DVCs can make women safer. Focus groups and a workshop with women who had experience with the courts revealed that the participants had positive experiences with elements of the DVC program. However, it found that women felt that they lack choice and control over critical decisions during court proceedings. They also reported problems with court delays despite recent attempts to shorten time delays in court with the Ontario government's "Justice on Target" initiative, and a lack of awareness among some court personnel about how IPV affected women.

That being said, Johnson and Fraser (2011) reported positive benefits of the DVC system: "an increase in the number of cases reported to the police and an increase in arrest rates; a reduction in attrition (or dropping off) as cases flow through the criminal justice system; a speedier response to these cases in court; better supports available for victims throughout the criminal justice process, and better referrals to community agencies, and improved risk assessment" (p. 7).

The various policies and programs were shown to be ineffective in reducing femicide. However, there has been limited success in reducing nonlethal violence. DV civil POs are criminal-based orders and have varied results reported in different jurisdictions. There are many problems with making charges, enforcing, and following up on POs. However, positive results have been reported in reduced re-assaults. On the other hand, ROs are civil orders and while they may prevent assault at times, they were often not proven to be effective in preventing further violence or femicide, and actually could be a factor in this increased violence against women because the women may have a false sense of security.

Programs for abusers, including anger management therapy, also had little success in preventing further abuse. Post-shelter advocacy intervention programs, however, did appear to have some success in ameliorating the conditions facing shelter residents after they leave the shelters. Abused women reported both positive and negative aspects of the DVCs. These specialized courts did appear to have limited success in reducing the number of re-arrests on DV. However, overall results in preventing women being abused by their partners have not been recognized.

Questions arise as to the efficacy of the various interventions we have reviewed. There are some interventions that make the greatest contribution toward preventing violence against female and male partners. First, our review showed that violence is largely prevented when a woman and her abusive partner live in different cities. Although most often it is the abusive partner who moved out of the city, this is self-help intervention when the woman moves herself and her children to another city. Second, because legal services help women with practical matters, such as protective orders, custody, and child support, they appear to actually present women with real long-term alternatives to their relationships that make them independent of their abusive partner. These alternatives may also give women an alternative to killing an abusive spouse. Finally, results from various post-shelter intervention programs indicate that many of the women reported fewer incidents of abuse, greater quality of life, and greater access to resources after the counseling and support.

However, there are other interventions that actually may increase the risks of violence against female partners. What happens when the abused women do leave their relationship? First, because the time of greatest danger to women is shortly after they leave the abusive relationship, shelters with short occupancy times that require women to leave during that high-risk period after they are separated from their abusive male partners expose the women to increased danger. Second, ROs, which motivate female partners to take risks they would not otherwise have taken, also expose the women to the chance of further violence.

Violence against women and femicide are increasingly important matters of concern worldwide. Often, women are murdered because they have no safe place to go to escape the abusive partner. Women have many reasons for staying in the abusive relationship, but when they finally leave, DV shelters are a refuge for many of these women, providing safety and many services. However, as we have seen, the need for a safe shelter far outweighs the availability. Research has shown that the most dangerous time for abused women is shortly after they leave the abusive relationship and that although shelters may stop women being harmed initially, they do not prevent the women from being murdered. Shelter and post-shelter contributions toward preventing violence against female partners are restricted to preventing nonlethal violence. Shelters and other interventions prevent violence against male and female partners, both the leaver and the one left behind. However, there is one difference. Providing alternatives to abused women reduces the risk of homicide against men, and the rate of men murdered by their spouses has decreased far more than that of women murdered by their current or ex-partners.

A number of programs and policies have been developed to stop the violence. The results are mixed. POs, which are imposed in criminal courts, have shown some preventive results in fewer re-assaults. Although ROs may have some positive results, their issuance often leads to further abuse of the women who applied for the issuance of the orders. Anger management therapy has not been proved to be effective. Decisions on the effectiveness of DVCs depend on the various jurisdictions where they are established. It is important to note the contribution made by opportunity (shelters in the short term after the women leave their abusive relationship, and living in a different city than the abuser in the post-shelter period) to preventing post-separation violence against women. We strongly suggest empirical program evaluations of shelters and programs designed to prevent femicide.

RISK ASSESSMENT

The purpose of this section is to describe the processes, practitioners, and tools involved in risk assessment for IPV, to examine the direct and indirect benefits of using these tools, to explore how their effectiveness has been measured and the limitations of the tools, and to provide recommendations regarding future research on risk assessment instruments for IPV. A review of the relevant literature reveals the presence of these recurring questions:

- How can we define risk assessment?
- Why are risk assessments important?
- What are the major approaches to risk assessment?
- Who is involved in the assessment process?
- What formal assessments exist to evaluate risk of intimate partner violence?
- What formal assessment exists to evaluate risk of lethal intimate partner violence?
- Each of these questions is answered in the pages that follow.

Risk Assessment for Intimate Partner Violence

A risk assessment is a qualitative or quantitative evaluation of the probability or likelihood of future harm in a given situation in the context of DV. The term "risk assessment" often describes a process of identifying factors in the life of the subject that are known to be associated with re-assault. After collection and consolidation of these details, the results may be utilized by legal, community, or health-related agencies to help prevent IPV. Results help to identify the most effective types of services for the individual's specific situation, as well as help to determine the frequency of those services. It is important to acknowledge that the IPV literature has largely focused on violence perpetrated by men on female partners, and the same is true of risk assessment research. In this section, we generally refer to male perpetrators and female victims because the majority of the literature to date has explored this form of violence in the context of heterosexual relationships. This is not to minimize female-perpetrated violence or violence in LGBT (that is, lesbian, gay, bisexual, and transgender) relationships, but that parameters in the study of IPV must be expanded to reflect contemporary society.

This definition of risk assessment is limited to evaluation of the likelihood (probability) of future harm, unlike Hart (1998), who extends the definition to include prevention. Rather, we would situate risk assessments as components of a larger process of risk management, which is inclusive of the broad array of decisions and protective actions taken by both the victim and perpetrator of abuse, health, and community services providers, and the criminal justice system.

The risk assessment literature for IPV and femicide has largely restricted itself to prediction of re-assault. Particularly when severe or lethal violence is a factor, accurate and defensible assessment of the risk of repeated violence is essential to inform the actions taken through risk management efforts. However, determining the value of risk assessment tools in the prevention of violence is meaningless when the broader context is not taken into consideration. To date, there is no literature that supports the notion that risk assessments translate into better risk management decisions, and, hence, the prevention of violence. Yang et al. (2010, p. 759) argue "building a better model of violence prediction should not be the sole aim of risk prediction research, which is just one link in the risk assessment–prediction–management triad that aims to achieve violence reduction and improved mental health. Risk management could be achieved by providing better treatment and continuity of care, but it must rely on good risk assessment."

Approaches to Risk Assessment

Historically, unstructured professional judgment (UPJ) was the most common approach to violence risk assessment. With this form of risk assessment, the potential for future violence is determined based on the impression and opinion of individuals considered to have relevant expertise without formal guidelines or constraints defining the evaluation process (Doyle & Dolan, 2007; Nicholls et al., 2013). This approach has the advantage of being flexible, allowing the professional or clinician to explore and focus on relevant case-specific details and risk factors (Douglas, Hart, Groscup, & Litwack, 2014; Doyle & Dolan, 2007). However, UPJ assessments have been criticized as being unacceptably informal and subjective (Doyle & Dolan, 2007, p. 409). The limitations of unstructured assessments with respect to validity, reliability, and accountability have been widely addressed in violence risk assessment literature (Douglas et al., 2014; Harris, Rice, & Cormier, 2006; Nicholls et al., 2013; Quinsey, Nicholls, Desmarais, Douglas, & Kropp, 2007).

In the interest of improving "transparency, replicability, and validity" of violence risk assessment, many jurisdictions and agencies are now favoring the use of empirically validated measures over the traditional UPJ (Nicholls et al., 2013, p. 80). To this end, research has turned toward the development and validation of tools that fall (loosely) into two categories: actuarial risk assessment (ARA) and structured professional judgment (SPJ) instruments.

ARA instruments are developed using statistical techniques to select and weight risk factors based on associations with outcomes in representative samples (Hilton, Harris, Rice, Lang, Cormier, & Lines, 2004). Actuarial assessments represent the most formalized approach to risk assessment, using fixed and explicit procedures to limit the discretionary nature of the assessment. These instruments involve the administrator determining the absence or presence of a defined list of conditions and provide formal guidelines in scoring the items to produce a measure that corresponds to "a specific level of risk for future violence (e.g., 50%) over a given period (e.g., the next 5 years)" (Nicholls et al., 2013, p. 81).

SPJ assessments are thought to be a compromise between the UPJ and ARA approaches (Douglas & Kropp, 2002; Hart, 1998). Structured assessments endeavor to preserve the ability of expert administrators to integrate their judgment and expertise into the evaluation, while providing a framework for the process and ensuring information on critical risk factors (determined through literature, research, and theory) is at minimum considered and documented. Instruments of an SPJ nature generally lend themselves to calculation of a total score by summing or otherwise combining items, a step that may or may not be explicitly recommended in the instrument documentation. However, these tools generally allow the assessor to make the final determination of risk (e.g., low, moderate, or high risk) on the basis of the items deemed to be most pertinent to the case being considered, and to incorporate additional considerations not explicitly defined by the instrument (Douglas & Kropp, 2002; Hart, 1998; Kropp & Hart, 2000; Nicholls et al., 2013).

Risk Assessment Instruments for Predicting Assault

Over the past few decades considerable interest has formed around the development and implementation of risk assessment instruments for the evaluation of IPV (not excluding but rarely inclusive of lethal violence). Many instruments intended for use in assessment of the risk of DV have been published in peer-reviewed publications, but research evaluating the performance of these instruments remains limited. A recent meta-analysis by Nicholls et al. (2013) identified 17 IPV risk-assessment tools evaluated in 39 validation studies published through December 2011. Of these measures, eight had been evaluated in three or more published studies and are no longer considered pilot instruments for IPV (see Table 8.2). These instruments are two structured professional judgment inventories (Danger Assessment (DA); Spousal Assault Risk Assessment (SARA)); three actuarial risk assessments (Ontario Domestic Assault Risk Assessment (ODARA); Domestic Violence Screening Instrument (DVSI); Propensity for Abusiveness Scale (PAS)); and three general violence actuarial risk assessments (Level of Service Inventory-Ontario Revision, LSI-OR; Psychopathy Checklist Revised (PCL-R); Violence Risk Appraisal Guide).

It should be noted that these inventories vary widely along a number of dimensions, including number of items; recommended training, experience and qualifications of administrators; access to case files and criminal and medical records; and access to victims and offenders for interview/self-report. A brief description of each inventory and a summary of its intended usage, as described in the accompanying manuals or publications, are also provided in Table 8.2.

Notably, none of the instruments has complete statistical information with respect to reliability and validity. In many cases, the interrater reliability, degree of agreement among administrators completing the same inventory with respect to the same case, and test-retest reliability, repeatability of an instrument over multiple

Table 8.2 Summary of Studies Evaluating the Danger Assessment.

Author	DA Variant	Sample	Outcome	Design	Pre/Postdictive Validity
McFarlane, Parker, and Soeken (1995)	Original DA	1203 Pregnant women United States	Physical abuse (self-report)	Prospective cohort study (3 assessments over course of pregnancy)	Mean DA scores significantly higher for women abused than women who did not report abuse.
McFarlane, Soeken, Campbell, Parker, Reel, and Silva (1998)	Original DA (items 2–15)	199 Pregnant women screened positive for abuse United States	Not applicable	Cross-sectional (reporting data from first interview of a prospective study)	Not applicable
Goodman, Dutton, and Bennett (2000)	Original DA	92 Women recruited/49 women completed follow-up (identified via DVC cases) United States	Physical abuse or threat (self-report)	Prospective study (initial assessment, 3-month follow-up)	Unadjusted odds ratio = 4.18 (with 1 SD increase in DA score)
Weisz, Tolman, and Saunders (2000)	Original DA (11 items coded through secondary analysis of an existing dataset)	177 Women completed (identified via DVC cases) United States	Incident(s) of severe violence (self-report)	Prospective study (initial assessment shortly after case disposition, 4-month follow-up)	Items from DA were included as binary predictors in a regression model. Available Danger Assessment items did not significantly predict repeat violence ($R^2 = 0.09$).
Heckert and Gondolf (2004)	Original DA ("simulated" version of risk assessment instrument used; 13 of 15 items)	840 Men were recruited and 662 female partners participated. Some women were new partners (identified via batter program evaluation) United States	Men classified into categories: repeat physical re-assault; one-time physical re-assault; threatening re-assault; controlling behavior or verbal abuse; no abuse	Prospective study (intake, follow-up every 3 months over 15 months)	ROC AUC = 0.70 for repeat re-assault, 66% sensitivity, 33% false positives

Continued

Table 8.2 Summary of Studies Evaluating the Danger Assessment—cont'd

Author	DA Variant	Sample	Outcome	Design	Pre/Postdictive Validity
Hilton, Harris, Rice, Lang, Cormier, and Lines (2004)	Original DA (15 items, scored where possible from case files)	598 Male offenders from police records + 100 cases for cross-validation Ontario, Canada	Any subsequent violent assault against an (ex-) wife or (ex-) common-law wife known to police	Retrospective (mean follow-up period 4.8 years)	ROC AUC = 0.59
Roehl, Sullivan, Webster, and Campbell (2005) RAVE study	Revised DA (current version 20 items, weighted scoring)	1307 Women completed baseline interviews, 782 women completed follow-up (RAVE study) United States	8 Abuse outcome severity categories: none; verbal abuse; stalking and threats; and physical abuse low, medium, high, and very high	Prospective (baseline and follow-up between 6 and 12 months)	Correlation between baseline DA score and severity of abuse (excluding cases with no potential contact) r = 0.328 The four categories of danger based on the DA were highly associated with the level/type of abuse
Glass, Perrin, Hanson, Bloom, Gardner, and Campbell (2008)	Modified version of revised DA (abusive female same-sex relationships, 8 original and 10 new items)	93 Women completed baseline interviews and 84 completed the 1-month follow-up United States	Threatened or actual physical or sexual violence	Prospective study baseline and 1-month follow-up)	Each additional point on the modified DA odds of threatened or actual violence increased by a factor of 1.3 mean for no repeated violence was 9.05 vs 11.25 for those who experienced violence
Hilton, Harris, Rice, Houghton, and Eke (2008)	Original DA (15 items, scored where possible from case files)	Sample 1: 303 male offenders from police records (subsample Hilton et al., 2004) Sample 2: 346 male offenders identified through police records Ontario, Canada	Subsequent assaults against a current or former wife or common-law wife	Retrospective (mean follow-up period 5.1 years)	Combined sample: ROC AUC = 0.56 Dichotomous wife assault recidivism r = 0.17, number of incidents r = 0.24

Campbell, Webster, and Glass (2009)	Revised DA (current version 20 items, weighted scoring)	310 Femicide cases (proxy informants), 324 abused controls, and 194 attempted femicide victims, United States (11 cities)	Femicide (attempted or completed) vs abuse	Retrospective (12 months prior to focal incident)	DA score significantly higher in attempted femicide group (M = 18.7) than abused control (M = 7.7) Attempted femicide vs abused control ROC AUC = 0.916 Maximized sensitivity (0.863) and specificity (0.788) with "severe danger" as threshold (3rd of 4 classification levels) Predictive value of DA score not reported
McFarlane, Campbell, Sharps, and Watson (2002)	*Modification of original DA (questions were rephrased. Item #2 and item #7 separated ir to 4 items, for a total of 17 items)*	*263 Femicide cases (proxy informant), 174 attempted femicides, 384 abused women as control group. Only women who reported ever having been pregnant were included (subsample Campbell et al., 2009) United States (10 cities)*	*Femicide (attempted or completed) vs abuse*	*Retrospective (12 months prior to focal incident)*	
Glass, Laughon, Rutto, Bevacqua, and Campbell (2008)	Original DA (15 items)	23 Young adult female femicide victims (proxy informants) and 53 abused controls (subsample Campbell et al., 2009) United States (10 cities)	Femicide vs abuse	Retrospective (12 months prior to focal incident)	DA score significantly higher in femicide group (M = 5.4) than abused control (M = 3.8)

Entries in Italics Represent Analyses Conducted on Subsamples of a Database Reported in Other Publications. AUC, area under the curve; DA, Danger Assessment; DVC, domestic violence court; RAVE, risk assessment validation study; ROC, receiver operating characteristic.

administrations, have not been reported in the literature. Measures of internal consistency are obtained by assessing the covariance of items within the same instrument in a single administration, and are based on the assumption that the items are measuring the same underlying construct (Mead, 2005). Internal consistency of a test should be high, and reported values are generally acceptable (Kline, 2000, p. 13) for the DA, SARA, DVSI, PAS, and LSI-OR. The internal consistency of the ODARA, at $\alpha = 0.65$, is rather low. The concurrent validity of an inventory is typically ascertained by correlating scores with a "gold standard" test. In DV risk assessment, there presently is no single inventory that may be considered a benchmark, and, as such, the recommended practice is to correlate inventories with other available measures with moderate correlations of 0.4–0.5 considered evidence of construct validity (Klein, 2000, p. 21). Nicholls et al. (2013) summarized concurrent validity measures, and when reported, they appear to show reasonably good construct validity across inventories.

Of particular interest is the predictive validity of an instrument, that is, its ability to predict a target criterion. A major issue in risk assessment evaluation for IPV is that outcome criteria vary considerably from study to study, ranging from verbal threats to femicide. As such, comparison across studies are challenging, and aggregates of predictive efficiency measures must be considered judiciously. Messing and Thaller (2013) conducted a review of the predictive validity of four of the IPV risk assessment tools included in Table 8.2, producing aggregate receiver operating characteristic area under the curve (ROC AUC) scores for each. ROC AUCs are a useful measure of predictive validity for violence risk assessment instruments because they are independent of base rates of violence in the population and the cutoff score selected to classify cases as high risk (Dolan & Doyle, 2000; Messing & Thaller, 2013; Rice & Harris, 1995). ROC AUC scores can range from 0 to 1, indicating perfect prediction, and 0.5, indicating prediction consistent with chance (Dolan & Doyle, 2000; Mossman, 1994). As a heuristic, an ROC AUC of 0.715 can be considered a large effect (Rice & Harris, 2005); however, one ought to carefully consider the context-specific severity of misclassification when characterizing effect sizes as "small" or "large."

Messing and Thaller (2013) reported small average ROC AUCs for the DA, SARA, and DVSI, and a medium ROC AUC for the ODARA. In general, a frequent finding of the recent review literature is that several IPV risk assessment instruments demonstrate only modest ability to predict harmful outcomes, but that the methods used for assessing predictive ability are highly inconsistent (Hanson, Bourgon, & Helmus, 2007; Messing & Thaller, 2013; Nicholls et al., 2013; Yang, Wong, & Coid, 2010).

In summary, there remains considerable work left to be done in order complete evaluation of the reliability, validity, and especially predictive efficacy of IPV risk assessment instruments and ascertain the superiority of any one instrument (Hanson, Bourgon, & Helmus, 2007; Messing & Thaller, 2013; Nicholls et al., 2013; Yang, Wong, & Coid, 2010). As a more rigorous body of research on IPV risk assessment is developed, users should select instruments appropriate to the particular setting in which they are to be used (Messing & Thaller, 2013) and are warned against making criminal justice decisions based exclusively on the results of the available tools (Yang, Wong, & Coid, 2010).

At present, there is insufficient evidence-based research on risk assessment for IPV, and the methodological limitations of the studies that have been conducted to date preclude drawing strong conclusions with respect to clinical implications (Hanson, Bourgon, & Helmus, 2007; Messing & Thaller, 2013; Nicholls et al., 2013; Yang, Wong, & Coid, 2010). Conducting research on DV is a challenging enterprise. Evaluation studies require careful development of protocols and training of personnel in order to protect the safety and privacy of participants. Large samples are required for prospective studies in order to capture low-frequency occurrences, such as incidents of severe violence, and to offset loss to follow-up that must be anticipated in these populations. Nevertheless, more high-quality research is essential in order to continue making progress in this important domain. A number of recommendations for future studies have been presented:

1. *Study Design.* The gold standard in predictive research is blind (or masked) follow up of high-risk populations (Hilton & Harris, 2005), and there remains a shortage of prospective, longitudinal studies in the field (Nicholls et al., 2013).
2. *Administration of Inventories.* In many of the existing studies, the risk assessment inventories were not administered in the way they were intended to be used (e.g., retrospectively coded from case files) and items were rephrased or omitted (Messing & Thaller, 2013; Nicholls et al., 2013). In order to fully validate and allow for fair comparison of instruments, there is a great need for studies in which multiple risk assessment tools are administered in their entirety, without altering language or administration protocols.
3. *Outcome Measures.* Future research will be more versatile if more nuanced outcome measures are recorded, such as severity and frequency of recidivistic offenses (Hilton & Harris, 2005; Messing & Thaller, 2013). Furthermore, a persistent problem is reliance on criminal records to assess recidivism, which is likely to underestimate actual rates. In addition to official records, victim and collateral reports should be used where possible to ascertain re-assault (Nicholls et al., 2013).
4. *Assessing the Broader Context.* Domestic assault is unusual among violent crimes in the sense that it typically involves known victims. The actions of courts, services, and agencies with respect to both offenders and victims, as well as the protective actions taken by victims themselves, must be known in order to properly evaluate the predictive efficacy of risk assessment instruments (Gondolf, 2001; Messing & Thaller, 2013). For example, repeat violence might be very likely for a particular offender or victim, but if the offender is incarcerated or the victim goes to extraordinary lengths to protect himself/herself (e.g., going into hiding), additional incidents of violence may not be possible during the follow-up timeframe. Future research must endeavor to capture the broader context, not simply the absence or occurrence of incidents of violence. This will also improve our understanding of what combinations of assessment and protective responses may actually serve to prevent violence.

5. *Increasing Diversity of Populations.* To date, the majority of IPV risk assessment literature has focused on male-perpetrated violence with female victims, with a few exceptions (e.g., female same-sex relationships in Glass et al., 2008). Future research should extend to include male victims/female perpetrators, advance understanding of domestic violence in LGBT communities, and capture differences across cultural, ethnic, and age groups (Nicholls et al., 2013).
6. *Novel Approaches to Risk Assessment.* It has been argued that the efficiency of the present style of risk assessment instrument, namely inventories by which an evaluation of risk is arrived at by summing a set of predictors, may have reached a plateau at levels of predictive accuracy that are unacceptably low (Yang, Wong, & Coid, 2010). New statistical techniques (e.g., neural network models) should be explored for identifying optimal risk factors, including situational or dynamic predictors, with a wider variety of nuanced outcome criteria (Yang, Wong, & Coid, 2010).

Risk Assessment Instruments for Predicting Lethal Violence

Homicide represents the most severe potential outcome in DV. Although many of the risk factors for IPV are also risk factors for lethal or potentially lethal outcomes, some differences do exist (Campbell, 1995; Campbell et al., 2003a, 2003b; Koziol-McLain et al., 2006). For example, women whose partner threatened or assaulted them with a gun or other weapon were found to be 20 times likely to later be killed than other women, and women whose partners threatened them with murder were 15 times more likely to be killed (Campbell et al., 2003a).

Only two instruments have been developed with assessment of intimate partner femicide in mind and will therefore be reviewed in more depth in this section, the Method of Assessment of Domestic Violence Situations or Domestic Violence Method (DeBecker, 1997; DV-MOSAIC) and the Danger Assessment Scale (Campbell, 1986; Campbell, Webster, & Glass, 2009). To our knowledge, no instruments have yet been developed for evaluation of risk for intimate partner homicide involving violence against a male partner by a female partner. The discussion in this section is therefore restricted to male-on-female lethal violence, with the understanding that the reverse, as well as homicide in same-sex relationships, is equally serious and represents an important area for future research.

Given the scarcity of quality research in DV risk assessment, it should come as no surprise that risk assessment for lethal violence is extremely limited. Base rates for intimate partner femicide are low, even among the highest-risk populations. Although 25–30% of IPV cases result in repeated incidents of violence, intimate partner femicide occurs in only 0.04% of cases (Campbell et al., 2009, p. 657). Several large prospective studies have been published, following hundreds of IPV cases for months or years, without incidents of femicide being captured (e.g., Campbell et al., 2009; Heckert & Gondolf, 2004; McFarlane, Parker, & Soeken, 1995; Roehl, Sullivan, Webster, & Campbell, 2005). Furthermore, any validation of a homicide prediction tool has considerable ethical considerations, as intervention must be made available to individuals who are at high risk of committing or falling victim to homicide.

Because prospective studies on intimate partner femicide are generally infeasible for practical reasons, research on lethality assessments has had to rely on prospective research using other outcomes (e.g., incidents of severe violence) or retrospective designs using proxy respondents or the researchers coding instruments from available records. Neither is ideal, as the former does not directly address the outcome of interest, whereas the latter may introduce bias as the informants do not have complete information but are necessarily aware of the outcome.

Domestic Violence-MOSAIC

The MOSAIC is a family of computer-assisted instruments developed by Gavin de Becker & Associates to assess escalated risk and danger (de Becker, 2000). Among the MOSAIC inventories is the DV-MOSAIC, with versions for male and female offenders, which was constructed based on cases of intimate partner homicide from the Los Angeles Police Department (Roehl et al., 2005). Its authors maintain that it is not intended primarily as a predictive instrument but as a tool to aid police officers in fully documenting and investigating DV situations (Roehl et al., 2005). However, the confidential MOSAIC manual does state that the assessment process is designed to assess "the likelihood of escalation of violence between the person being pursued and the person under assessment" (Roehl et al., 2005). The instrument is therefore designed to evaluate the risk of escalation, including homicide, and emphasizes that dangerousness is situational and not a permanent or stable attribute (Roehl et al., 2005).

The DV-MOSAIC consists of a 46-item inventory with multiple response categories, often covering complex patterns rather than single features of the perpetrator or relationship (Roehl et al., 2005). The DV-MOSAIC should be completed by a trained assessor with access to criminal justice records as well as opportunity to interview both the perpetrator and the victim; as such it is relatively time-intensive to complete. Two measures are produced by the DV-MOSAIC, an Information Quotient score indicating the amount of information available for the assessment and a 1 to 10 rating indicating the level of risk (Roehl et al., 2005). The developers emphasize that assessment practitioners are meant to use all information available when making case management decisions, rather than prescribe specific case management responses following a specific level of risk rating, suggesting that the DV-MOSAIC might best be characterized as a structured professional judgment tool. The program is "described as using a case-matching or template-matching procedure to produce the rating of risk," assigning values to factors by comparing them to cases where the outcome is known (Roehl et al., 2005, p. 23).

Very little published research has included evaluation of the DV-MOSAIC, likely because it is a privately published and licensed assessment inventory. The exception to this was the large prospective Risk Assessment Validation Study (RAVE) validation study conducted by the U.S. Department of Justice (Roehl et al., 2005), which compared performance of the DV-MOSAIC, Danger Assessment, DVSI, and Kingston Screening Instrument for Domestic Violence.

This study followed 1,307 battered female partners during a one-year follow-up period, and found the DV-MOSAIC was most strongly associated with victim perceptions of risk and risk of serious harm, yielded risk scores (categories) that were most strongly associated with subsequent experience of serious harm, did better in classifying as "high-risk" all 38 women who sought safety in a women's shelter after experiencing serious/near lethal violence by their male partners, and correctly classified over 80% of the women who were re-assaulted during the follow-up year (Ellis, Sakinofsky, & Stuckless, 2012; Roehl et al., 2005). The ROC AUC for predicting severe abuse was 0.647 when controlling for potential confounds (significantly higher than chance 0.50), which was slightly lower than that found for the Danger Assessment (0.687) and higher than the other instruments evaluated.

Given the performance of the DV-MOSAIC in the U.S. Department of Justice RAVE study and its apparent widespread use in criminal justice systems (Roehl et al., 2005), it is important that future research continue to evaluate this assessment method. In particular, further assessment of the predictive efficacy of the DV-MOSAIC in predicting lethal outcomes is essential, as is a better understanding of the instrument's interrater reliability.

The Danger Assessment Scale

The Danger Assessment Scale (Campbell, 1986, 1995; Campbell et al., 2009), known as the Danger Assessment, was developed in consultation with "battered women, shelter workers, law enforcement officials, and other clinical experts on domestic violence with the primary objective being creation of a tool to assist battered women in assessing their danger of being murdered (or seriously injured) by their intimate partner or ex–intimate partner" (Campbell et al., 2009, p. 658). The Danger Assessment is generally administered in a victim services setting and is intended to empower women in abusive relationships to make self-care decisions (Messing, Amanor-Boadu, Cavanaugh, Glass, & Campbell, 2013, p. 264).

The Danger Assessment is administered in two parts. Initially, the woman is presented with a calendar and asked to assess the severity and frequency of battering over the course of the past year. The woman records the approximate dates when physically abusive incidents occurred and rates each occurrence on a 1-to-5 scale (1 = slap, pushing, no injuries, and/or lasting pain, through 5 = use of weapon, wounds from weapon) (Campbell et al., 2009, p. 658). The aim of the calendar portion of the Danger Assessment is to decrease the typical minimization of IPV by female victims. The authors report that in the 38% of women who initially reported no increase in the severity or frequency of violence changed their response to "yes" after completing the calendar exercise (Campbell, 1986, 1995).

The second portion of the original Danger Assessment Scale was a 15-item inventory of risk factors associated with intimate partner femicide presented in a yes/no format (Campbell, 1995). The original Danger Assessment was scored by simply counting the number of "yes" answers, with a higher score indicating that more risk factors for lethal intimate partner violence are present in the relationship (Campbell et al., 2009, p. 658).

The Danger Assessment Scale was revised following an 11-city case–control study that compared victims of femicide (via proxy informants), victims of attempted femicide, and abused controls (Campbell et al., 2009). Multivariate analysis was conducted to test the predictive ability of the risk factors, and the results were used to revise the original Danger Assessment by adding four additional items and separating one "double-barreled" item into two, producing the current 20-item instrument with a weighted scoring algorithm. In addition, some items were reworded for clarity. The authors also produced recommended thresholds for levels of risk (variable danger, increased danger, severe danger, and extreme danger).

The Danger Assessment Scale has been the most widely studied risk assessment inventory in the IPV literature; however, there are considerable methodological limitations in this body of work that limit the conclusions that can be drawn. A summary of research studies conducted evaluating the original and revised Danger Assessment is summarized in Table 8.2. In the overwhelming majority of studies, the 15-item Danger Assessment was used, but not administered in the way it was intended (e.g., coding from case files), and often items were omitted or rephrased. There are, in fact, only two large studies conducted using the revised 20-item Danger Assessment: Campbell, Webster, and Glass (2009) and Roehl, Sullivan, Webster, and Campbell (2005).

There has been only one database in which femicide was used as a primary outcome (Campbell et al., 2009; Glass, Laughon, Rutto, Bevacqua, & Campbell, 2008; McFarlane, Campbell, Sharps, & Watson, 2002), and the same 11-city data were used for the development of the revised 20-item Danger Assessment (Campbell et al., 2009). This study was retrospective in nature, meaning risk assessment instruments were completed after the fact, and proxy informants provided information on behalf of femicide victims ($n = 373$). The revised Danger Assessment was cross-validated using the attempted femicide ($n = 194$) and abused controls ($n = 324$) from this sample, and the resulting ROC AUC was very high at 0.916. Unfortunately, no other risk assessment instruments were included for comparison in this study.

The second large-scale study evaluating the revised Danger Assessment was the Department of Justice RAVE study (Roehl, Sullivan, Webster, & Campbell, 2005). As mentioned, this prospective study followed 1,307 women over a one-year follow-up period in which incidents of violence was the criterion measure, including severe potentially lethal abuse. The authors reported that Danger Assessment categories of risk (variable danger, increased danger, severe danger, and extreme danger) were highly and significantly associated with the level of abuse reported during follow-up (Roehl, Sullivan, Webster, & Campbell, 2005). The ROC AUC for the Danger Assessment predicting severe abuse was 0.670, significantly better than chance (0.50) and higher than the other instruments evaluated (e.g., DV-MOSAIC ROC AUC = 0.589). However, note that this value is considerably lower than the ROC AUC reported in the 11-city retrospective study of femicide (Campbell et al., 2009).

Messing and Thaller (2013) produced an aggregate predictive efficacy by taking weighted averages of ROC AUC scores from four prospective studies in which the Danger Assessment was evaluated (Heckert & Gondolf, 2004; Hilton et al., 2004;

Hilton et al., 2008; Roehl, Sullivan, Webster, & Campbell, 2005). In only one of these four studies was the Danger Assessment correctly administered, and the outcome criteria was re-assault, as opposed to severe or potentially lethal violence. The weighted average ROC AUC was 0.618.

The test-retest reliability (the consistency of a test across time) of the Danger Assessment has not been reported for either the original or the revised instrument. Interrater reliability has not been reported; however, given that the inventory is based on victim appraisals, this measure of reliability would not be meaningful for the test's intended application. Internal consistency (Cronbach's Alpha) for the original 15-item Danger Assessment has been reported, ranging from $\alpha=0.72$–0.84 in battered women, $\alpha=0.74$ in attempted femicide victims, and $\alpha=0.80$ for proxy report on behalf of femicide victims (see Table 8.2). Internal consistency for the 20-item Danger Assessment was reported to be $\alpha=0.74$ among abused women, $\alpha=0.75$ in attempted femicide victims, and $\alpha=0.80$ for femicide victims (Campbell et al., 2009). The original 15-item Danger Assessment has been shown to have reasonably good convergent validity with the SARA ($r=41$, Hilton et al., 2004; $r=0.61$, Hilton et al., 2008), ODARA ($r=0.43$, Hilton et al., 2004), DVSI ($r=0.36$, Hilton et al., 2008), and PCL-R ($r=0.36$, Hilton et al., 2008). Convergent validity for the revised 20-item Danger Assessment has not been reported.

Like the DV-MOSAIC, validation of the Danger Assessment Scale is presently incomplete and there remains considerable need for further evaluation of the current 20-item Danger Assessment. Given the discrepancy in predictive ability reported in the two primary studies evaluating this instrument, further independent evaluation of predictive efficacy of this instrument with respect to lethal or potentially lethal violence is essential.

Summary of Lethality Instruments

The Danger Assessment and the DV-MOSAIC are, at present, the only risk assessment instruments developed to address severe, potentially lethal violence. They are, however, intended for use in rather different contexts. The DV-MOSAIC was constructed to use as a tool to aid police officers in investigation and documentation of DV cases (Roehl et al., 2005), whereas the Danger Assessment was developed primarily for use in victim services settings to assist battered women in evaluating their situation and empowering them to make informed self-care choices (Campbell et al., 2009). We would argue that both tools are worthwhile for their intended primary applications, but there remains insufficient evidence of predictive efficacy to recommend their use in criminal justice decisions.

LETHALITY RISK ASSESSMENT AND SEPARATION

Separation is a known risk factor for lethal DV and is included as a risk factor in both the Danger Assessment and the DV-MOSAIC. As we have noted, the period immediately following a separation is the most likely time for a femicide to occur, and, as such, the temptation may exist to implement formal risk assessments as part of standard protocol in civil (family) law proceedings, particularly in cases in which a history of DV exists. However, a number of issues have been raised in adoption the Danger Assessment or the DV-MOSAIC for the purpose of preventing estrangement-associated lethal DV in this context (Ellis, Sakinofsky, & Stuckless, 2012).

As the Danger Assessment was developed specifically for use with female victims of abuse, items on this instrument are gendered and implicitly assume that perpetrators are men and victims are women. It would therefore not be possible to administer the same instrument to both men and women participating in separation and divorce proceedings. The DV-MOSAIC does offer versions for both male and female offenders, but there has been no published validation of the female offender version of this instrument. The unilateral administration of a risk assessment may undermine trust in mediation processes or provide a power resource for adversarial lawyers that are available only to female participants (Ellis, Sakinofsky, & Stuckless, 2012).

The subject of risk assessment in the context of separation and divorce proceedings reflects another area in which further research is warranted. The development of tools that will support, rather than hinder, mediation processes has been proposed and should be explored (Ellis et al., 2012).

COMMENT

Considerable work remains in the evaluation of existing risk-assessment instruments for the prediction of re-assault and lethal violence, and we have highlighted some of the missing information and made recommendations for extending and improving future research. However, it would appear from the current body of research that the predictive efficacy of available tools is fairly modest (Messing & Thaller, 2013; Yang, Wong, & Coid, 2010). Until predictive efficacy can be improved, heavy reliance on test scores without supporting evidence should be avoided when determining permanent or long-term legal situations. Selection of one inventory over another should be based on the "intended setting, outcome, and skills of the assessor as well as access to the victim, offender, and case files" (Messing & Thaller, 2013, p. 1545).

Despite the limited predictive value of these inventories, they offer considerable value in facilitating the development of safety plans for victims, for example, with regard to their living situation, finances, and personal support. Inventories can raise valuable awareness among police and health-care professionals of the risk factors for IPV, ensuring that DV cases are adequately documented while developing professional understanding of the issues involved in the intricate cases. Last, inventories also assist in the development of rehabilitation supervision and support planning for offenders (Millar, 2009). Rather than viewing risk assessment instruments as a means of collapsing a complex and dynamic relationship into a single numeric score, we should instead use them as a tool to guide administrators, victims, and perpetrators in exploring the options and services available to them. Instruments can then indirectly ameliorate the circumstances of the individuals involved and improve their outlook for the future (which includes, but is not limited to, the domains of safety, emotion regulation, employment, and finances). Risk assessment inventories should be considered the first step in a longer process of risk management and safety planning (Dutton & Kropp, 2000).

DISCUSSION QUESTIONS

1. Evaluate this statement: Use of the Danger Assessment instrument in the LAP and DVHRT prevention models is justified on the ground that it makes a significant contribution toward preventing intimate partner femicide following separation. Do you agree or disagree? Give reasons for your answer.

2. Evaluate this statement: Shelters for abused women should be included in the integrated LAP/DVHRT femicide prevention models described in this chapter because of the contribution they make to preventing femicide following separation. Do you agree or disagree? Give reasons for your answer.

3. Compare and critically evaluate the contribution made by DASH and DVHRT to preventing femicide following separation.

4. Evaluate this statement: Criminal justice system interventions should be included in all three of the femicide prevention models described in this chapter because of the significant contribution they make to preventing femicide following separation. Do you agree or disagree? Give reasons for your answer.

References

Adams, D. (2009). Predisposing childhood factors for men who kill their intimate partners. *Victims and Offenders*, 4, 215–229.

Adams, J. S. (2007). *Why do they kill? Men who murder their intimate partners*. Nashville: Vanderbilt University Press.

Adler, J. S. (1999). "If we can't live in peace, we might as well die": Homicide-suicide in Chicago, 1875–1910. *Journal of Urban History*, 26, 3–21.

Adler, J. S. (2010). "Bessie done cut her old man": Race, common-law marriage and homicide in New Orleans, 1925–1945. *Journal of Social History*, 44, 38–54.

Afifi, T. O., MacMillan, H., Cox, B. J., Asmundson, G. J., Stein, M. B., & Sareen, B. J. (2009). Mental health correlates of intimate partner violence in marital relationships in a nationally representative sample of males and females. *Journal of Interpersonal Violence*, 24, 1398–1417.

Agnew, R. (1992). Foundation for a general strain theory of crime and delinquency. *Criminology*, 30, 47–87.

Albrecht, S. (2012). The act of violence: Do domestic violence restraining orders ever really work? *Psychology Today* (July 27, 2012).

Alderbigee, Y. A. (1997). Violence in America: A survey of suicide linked to homicides. *Journal of Forensic Science*, 42, 662–665.

Aldridge, M. L., & Browne, K. D. (2003). Perpetrators of spousal homicide: A review. *Trauma, Violence & Abuse*, 4, 265–276.

Allen, N. H. (1983). Homicide followed by suicide: Los Angeles, 1970–1979. *Suicide and Life-threatening Behavior*, 13, 155–165.

Ambert, A.-M. (2001). *Families in the new millennium*. Needham Heights, MA: Allyn and Bacon.

American Psychological Association (2013). *The diagnostic and statistical measurement handbook-5*. (Washington, D.C).

Anand, U. (April 15, 2013). Khaps to SC: Honour killings only by peace-loving families. *The Indian Express*.

Anderson, D. K., & Saunders, D. G. (2003). Leaving an abusive partner: An empirical review of predictors, the process of leaving and psychological well-being. *Trauma, Violence & Abuse*, 4, 163–191.

Archer, J. (2000). Sex differences in aggression between heterosexual partners: A meta-analytic review. *Psychological Bulletin*, 126, 651–680.

Arendell, T. (1995). *Fathers and divorce*. Thousand Oaks, CA: Sage.

Asian Human Rights Commission (2010). *Acid attacks a serious concern in Pakistan*. Statement, STM-018-2010.

Associated Press (March 27, 2013). Why Ruth shot Eddie. *The Globe and Mail*. S.3.

Aston, C., & Bunge, P. V. (2005). Family homicide–suicides. In K. Aucoin (Ed.), *Family violence in Canada: A statistical profile*. Statistics Canada, Canadian Centre for Justice Statistics.

Atkinson, J. M. (1971). Societal reactions to suicide: The role of coroner's definitions. In S. Cohen (Ed.), *Images of deviance* (pp. 165–191). Harmondsworth: Penguin.

Aubert, V. (1963). Competition and dissensus: Two types of conflict resolution. *Journal of Conflict Resolution*, 7, 26–42.

Aymer, S. R. (2008). Beyond power and control: Clinical interventions with men engaged in partner abuse. *Clinical Social Work Journal*, 36(4), 323–332.

Bachman, R., & Saltzman, L. (1995). *Violence against women: Estimates from the redesigned survey*. Washington, DC: U.S. Department of Justice.

Badkhen, A. (2009). Baghdad's underground shelters, Ms Magazine (Summer, 2009). www.msmagazine.com/summer/2009/baghdad_underground.asp.

Baechler, J. (1980). A strategic theory. *Suicide and Life-threatening Behavior, 10*, 70–97.

Baker, N. V., Gregware, P. R., & Cassidy, M. A. (1999). Family killing fields: Honor rationales in the killing of women. *Violence Against Women, 5*, 164–184.

Bancroft, L. (2002). *Why does he do that? Inside the minds of angry and controlling men*. New York: Berkley Books.

Bandura, A. (1973). *Aggression: A social learning analysis*. Englewood Cliffs, NJ: Prentice Hall.

Bandura, A. (1989). Frustration-aggression hypothesis: Examination and reformulation. *Psychological Bulletin, 106*, 59–73.

Banks, l., Crandall, C., Sklar, D., & Bauer, M. (2008). A comparison of intimate partner homicide to intimate partner homicide-suicide. *Violence Against Women, 14*, 1065–1078.

Barber, C. W., Hemenway, D., Olson, L. M., Nie, C., Schaechter, J., & Walsh, S. (2008). Suicide and suicide attempts following suicide: Victim-suspect relationships, weapon type and presence of antidepressants. *Homicide Studies, 12*, 285–297.

Barker, L. (2006). Homicides and suicides: National violent death reporting system, United States, 2003–2004. *Morbidity and Mortality Weekly Report, 7*, 26–42.

Barker, L. (July 6, 2006). Homicides and suicides: National violent death reporting system, United States, 2003–2004. *Morbidity and Mortality Weekly Report*.

Barnard, G. W., Vera, H., & Newman, G. (1982). Till death do us part: A study of spouse murder. *Bulletin of the American Academy of Psychiatry and Law, 10*, 271–280.

Barraclough, B., & Harris, E. C. (2002). Suicide preceded by murder: The epidemiology of homicide-suicide in England and Wales 1988–1992. *Psychological Medicine, 32*, 577–584.

Beattie, S., & Cotter, A. (2010). Homicide in Canada, 2009. *Juristat, 30*(3). Statistics Canada. 85-002-X.

Belknap, J., Larson, D. L., Abrams, M. L., Garcia, C., & Anderson-Block, K. (2012). Types of intimate partner homicides committed by women: Self-defence, proxy/retaliation and sexual proprietariness. *Homicide Studies, 16*, 358–379.

Benitez, T., McNiel, D. E., & Binder, R. L. (2010). Do protection orders protect? *Journal of American Academy Psychiatry and the Law, 38*(3), 376–385.

Bennett, M. D., & Hughes, S. (2005). *The art of mediation*. Notre Dame, IN: National Institute of Trial Advocacy, University of Notre Dame.

Bergman, B., & Brismar, B. (1991). Suicide attempts by battered wives. *Acta Psychiatrica Scandanavia, 83*, 380–384.

Berkowitz, L. (1989). Frustration-aggression hypothesis: Examination and reformulation. *Psychological Bulletin, 106*, 59–73.

Berman, A. L. (1996). Dyadic death: A typology. *Suicide and Life-threatening Behavior, 26*, 342–350.

Bernal, M., & ESEMED/MHEDEA Investigators. (2007). Risk factors for suicidality in Europe: Results for the ESEMED study. *Journal of Affective Disorders, 101*, 27–34.

Bernard, J. (1972). *The future of marriage*. New York: Dial Press.

Bhargava, N., Chand, R., Ranjan, S., & Pratyush, A. (2013). *Honour killings in modern India*. New Delhi, India: Indian Institute of Technology.

Black, D. (1983). Crime as social control. *American Sociological Review, 48*, 30–45.

Black, D. (1998). *The structure of right and wrong*. San Diego, CA: Academic Press.

Black, D. (2004). Violent structures. In M. Zahn, H. Brownstein, & S. Jackson (Eds.), *Violence: From theory to research*. Cincinnati OH: Anderson.

Blair-West, G. W., Cantor, C. H., Mellsop, G. W., & Everson-Annan, M. L. (1999). Life-time suicide risk in major depression: Sex and age determinants. *Journal of Affective Disorders*, 55, 171–178.

Block, C. (June 2000). *The Chicago women's health risk study: A collaborative research project*. Revised Report. Chicago: Illinois Criminal Justice Information Authority.

Block, C. R., & Christakos, A. (1993). Intimate partner homicide in Chicago over 29 years. *Crime and Delinquency*, 41, 496–526.

Block, C. R., Devitt, C. O., Fugate, M., Martin, C., Pasold, T., Fonda, D., et al. (2000). *The Chicago women's health risk study: Risk of serious injury or death in intimate violence or death: A collaborative research project*. NCJ 184511. Chicago: Illinois Criminal Justice Information Authority.

Bloom, B. L., White, S. W., & Asher, S. J. (1979). Marital disruption as a stressful life event. In G. Levinger, & O. C. Moles (Eds.), *Divorce and separation: Context, causes and consequences* (pp. 181–183). New York: Basic Books.

Bograd, M. (1988). Feminist perspectives on spouse abuse: An introduction. In K. Yllo, & M. Bograd (Eds.), *Feminist perspectives on wife-abuse* (pp. 11–27). Newbury Park, CA: Sage.

Boles, S. M., & Miotto, K. (2003). Substance abuse and violence: A review of the literature. *Aggression and Violent Behavior*, 8, 155–174.

Bourget, D., & Gagne, P. (2012). Women who kill their mates. *Behavioral Science and the Law*, 1–10.

Bourget, D., Gagne, P., & Moamai, J. (2000). Spousal homicide and suicide in Quebec. *Journal of the American Academy of Psychiatry and Law*, 28, 179–182.

Bowker, L. H. (1983). *Beating wife-beating*. Lexington, MA: D.C. Heath.

Bowlby, J. (1977). The making and breaking of affectional bonds. 1. Aetiology and psychopathology in the light of attachment theory. *The British Journal of Psychiatry*, 130, 201–210.

Bramachari, R. (2010). *Islamic barbarism: Disfiguring women by acid attack. Part 2*. www.islam-watch.org/authors/73-bramachari/493.

Braver, S. L., & O' Connell, D. (1998). *Divorced dads: Shattering the myths*. New York: Penguin Putnam.

Brinig, M. F., & Allen, W. (2000). "These boots are made for walking": Why most divorce filers are women. *American Law and Economics Review*, 2, 126–129.

Brodsky, B., Malone, K., Ellis, S., & Mann, J. J. (1997). Characteristics of borderline personality disorder associated with suicidal behavior. *American Journal of Psychiatry*, 154, 1715–1729.

Browne, A. (1987). *When battered women kill*. New York: Free Press.

Browne, A., & Williams, K. (1993). Gender intimacy and lethal violence: Trends from 1976 through 1987. *Gender and Society*, 7, 78–98.

Brownridge, D. A. (2006). Violence against women post-separation. *Aggression and Violent Behavior*, 11, 514–530.

Bunge, V. P. (2002). National trends in intimate partner homicides, 1974–2000. *Statistics Canada – catalogue no. 85-002-XIE*, 22(5).

Burch, T. K. (1983). The impact of forms of families and sexual unions and dissolution of unions on fertility. In R. D. Lee (Ed.), *Determinants of fertility in developing countries* (pp. 532–561). New York: Academic Press.

Burczycka, M., & Cotter, A. (2011). *Shelters for abused women in Canada, 2010*. Statistics Canada, catalogue no. 85-002-X Juristat.

Burns, S. (2013). *Amicus brief affirming the rights of pregnant women*. Reproductive Justice Clinic, NYU LAW.

Buss, D. (2002). *Core premises of evolutionary psychology*. www.davidbuss.com.

Buss, D. M. (2005). *The murderer next door; why the mind is designed to kill*. New York: Penguin.
Buss, D. M., & Duntley, J. D. (2011). The evolution of intimate partner violence. *Aggression and Violent Behavior, 16*, 411–419.
Buteau, J., Lesage, A. D., & Kiely, M. C. (1993). Homicide followed by suicide: A Quebec case series. *Canadian Journal of Psychiatry, 38*, 552–556.
Buzawa, E. S., & Buzawa, C. G. (1996). *Domestic violence: The criminal justice system response*. Thousand Oaks, CA: Sage.
Campbell, D. (2010). *More than 40% of domestic violence victims are male, report reveals*. http://guardian.co.uk/society/2010/sep/05/men-victims-domestic-violence (*The Observer*).
Campbell, J. (1992). "If I can't have you, no one can": Power and control in homicide. In J. Radford, & D. E. H. Russell (Eds.), *Femicide: The politics of woman killing* (pp. 99–113). New York: Twane.
Campbell, J. (1995). Prediction of homicide of and by battered women. In J. Campbell (Ed.), *Assessing dangerousness: Violence by sexual offenders, batterers and child abusers* (pp. 68–95). Thousand Oaks, CA: Sage.
Campbell, J. C. (2004). *Danger Assessment*. Baltimore, Maryland: Johns Hopkins School of Nursing.
Campbell, J., Rose, L., Kub, J., & Nedd, D. (1998). Voices of strength and resistance: A contextual and longitudinal analysis of women's responses to battering. *Journal of Interpersonal Violence, 13*(6), 743–762.
Campbell, J. C., & Runyan, C. W. (1998). Femicide: Guest editor's introduction. *Homicide Studies, 2*, 347–352.
Campbell, J. C., Webster, D., Kozial-Maclean, J., Block, C., Campbell, D., Curry, M. A., et al. (2003). Risk factors for femicide in abusive relationships: Results from a multisite case control study, control study. *American Journal of Public Health, 97*(7). PMC1447915.
Campbell, J. C., Webster, D., Koziol-Mclain, J., Block, C., Campbell, D., McFarlane, J., et al. (2003). Intimate partner homicide: Review and implications for research and policy. *Trauma, Violence & Abuse, 8*, 246–269.
Campbell, J. C., Webster, D. W., & Glass, N. (2009). The danger assessment: Validation of a lethality risk assessment instrument. *Journal of Interpersonal Violence, 24*, 653–674.
Campbell, J. C., & Wolf, A. D. (2012). *Protective action and re-assault: Findings from the RAVE study*.
Canadian Panel on Violence Against Women (1993). *Changing the landscape: Ending violence-achieving equality*. Ottawa: Ministry of Supply and Services. Cat: SW45-1/1993E.
Canadian Women's Foundation (2012). *Measuring violence against women: Statistical trends 2006*. www.canadianwomen.org/facts-about-violence.
Cantor, C., & Slator, P. (1995). Marital breakdown: Parenthood and suicide. *Journal of Family Studies, 1*, 91–102.
Caputi, J., & Russell, D. E. (1992). Femicide: Speaking the unspeakable. *MS Magazine*. September–October.
Carcach, C., & Grabosky, P. N. (March 1998). *Murder-suicide in Australia. Trends and issues in criminal justice*. Canberra, Australia: Australian Institute of Criminology aicpress@aic.gov.au.
Carnevale, P. J., & Pruett, D. G. (1992). Negotiation and mediation. *Annual Review of Psychology, 43*, 941–951.
Cavan, R. (1928). *Suicide*. Chicago: University of Chicago Press.
Centers for Disease Control and Prevention (2011). *Self-directed violence: Uniform definitions and recommended data elements*. Atlanta, GA.

Centers for Disease Control and Prevention (2012). *National violent death reporting system report on violent deaths reported by 18 states*. Atlanta, GA.

Chan, C. Y., Beh, S. L., & Broadhurst, R. G. (2003). Homicide-suicide in Hong Kong, 1989-1998. *Forensic Science International, 137*, 165–171.

Chaucer, G. (1380–1382). The Canterbury tales. Published by William Caxton, Westminster, (1477).

Cherlin, J. (2009). *The marriage- go-round: The state of marriage and the family in America today*. New York: Alfred J. Knopf.

Chimbos, P. (1976). Marital violence: A study of husband-wife homicide. In K. Ishwaran (Ed.), *The Canadian family revised* (pp. 580–599). Toronto: Holt, Rinehart and Winston.

Choice, P., Lamke, L. K., & Pittman, J. F. (1995). Conflict resolution strategies and marital distress as mediating factors in the link between witnessing inter-parental violence and wife battering. *Violence and Victims, 10*, 107–119.

Cissner, A. B., Labriola, M., & Rempel, M. (2013). *Testing the effects of New York's domestic violence courts: A statewide impact evaluation*. A project of the Fund for the City of New York.

Civil Service India (2013). *Honour killing in India*. www.civilserviceinindia.com/subject/Essay/honor-killing-in-india.html.

Coleman, D. H., & Straus, M. (1986). Marital power, conflict and violence in a nationally representative sample of American couples. *Violence and Victims, 1*, 141–146.

Conner, K. R., Duberstein, P. R., Conwell, Y., Seidlitz, L., & Caine, E. D. (2001). Psychological vulnerability to completed suicide: A review of empirical studies. *Suicide and Life-threatening Behavior, 31*, 367–385.

Cooney, M. (2011). Beyond patriarchy: Third parties and honor killings. In *Paper presented at the annual meeting of the American Society of Criminology*, Washington, DC. (November 15).

Cooper, M., & Eaves, D. (1996). Suicide following homicide in the family. *Violence and Victims, 1*, 99–112.

Coser, L. A. (1956). *The functions of social conflict*. New York: The Free Press.

Costa, P. T., Jr., & McRae, R. R. (1992). *Revised NEO and NEO five factor inventory professional manual*. Odessa, Florida: Psychological Assessment Resources.

Crawford, M., & Gartner, R. (1992). *Woman killing: Intimate femicide in Ontario, 1974-1990*. (Report prepared for the Women We Honour Action Committee. Toronto.)

Crawford, M., Gartner, R., & Dawson, M. (1997). *Woman killing: Intimate femicide in Ontario, 1991–1994*. (Report prepared in collaboration with Women We Honour Action Committee, Toronto.)

Crimmins, S. (1991). Parricide or suicide: The dilemma of them or me. In A. V. Wilson (Ed.), *Homicide: The victim-offender connection*. Cincinnati, OH: Anderson.

Cross, S. E., & Madson, L. (1997). Models of self: Self-construals and gender. *Psychological Bulletin, 122*, 5–37.

Culotta, E. (2013). Latest skirmish over ancestral violence strikes blow for peace. *Science, 341*, 224.

Cummings, E. M., & Davies, P. (1994). *Children and marital conflict: The impact of family dispute resolution*. New York: The Guilford Press.

Daly, M., Singh, L. S., & Wilson, M. (1993). Children fathered by previous partners: A risk factor for violence against women. *Canadian Journal of Public health, 84*, 209–210.

Daly, M., & Wilson, M. (1988). *Homicide*. New York: Aldine de Gruyter.

Daly, M., & Wilson, M. (1991). A reply to Gelles: Stepchildren are disproportionately abused and diverse forms of violence can share causal factors. *Human Nature, 2*, 419–426.

Daly, M., & Wilson, M. (1995). Evolutionary perspective on male sexual proprietariness. In R. Rubach, & N. Weiner (Eds.), *Interpersonal violent behaviors: Social and cultural aspects* (pp. 109–133). New York: Springer.

Daly, M., & Wilson, M. (1998). Violence against stepchildren. *Current Directions in Psychological Science, 5*, 77–81.

Daly, M., Wilson, M., & Weghorst, S. J. (1982). Male sexual jealousy. *Ethology and Sociobiology, 3*, 11–27.

Danigelis, N., & Pope, W. (1979). Durkheim's theory of suicide applied to the family: An empirical test. *Social Forces, 57*, 1081–1106.

Dastak (2013). *The woman's shelter/cause of death: Woman*. http://www.causeofdeathwoman.com/the-womens-shelter.

Davies, M., & Mouzos, J. (2007) Homicide in Australia: 2005–2006: National homicide report moniprogram annual report. Canberra, Australia: Australian Institute of Criminology. *Research and Public Policy, 77*.

Davis, N. J. (1988). Shelters for battered women: Social policy response to interpersonal violence. *The Social Science Journal, 25*(4), 401–419.

Dawkins, R. (2009). *The greatest show on earth: The evidence for evolution*. London: Free Press.

Dawson, M. (2005). Intimate femicide followed by suicide: Examining the role of premeditation. *Suicide and Life-threatening Behavior, 35*, 76–90.

Dawson, M., & Gartner, R. (1998). Differences in the characteristics of intimate femicides: The role of relationship state and relationship status. *Homicide Studies, 2*, 378–399.

DeBecker, G. (2000). *Domestic Violence method (DV-MOSAIC)* www.mosaicsystem.com/dv.htm.

Dee, T. S. (2003). Until death do you part: The effects of unilateral divorce on spousal homicides. *Economic Inquiry, 41*, 163–182.

DeKeseredy, W. (2011). *Violence against women: Myths, facts, controversies*. Toronto: University of Toronto Press.

DeLeon-Granados, W., & Wells, W. (2003). *The reliability and validity of measures of domestic violence resources as used in intimate partner homicide research, Violence Against Women.* 9(2), 148–162.

DeMaris, A. (2004). Till discord do us part: The role of physical and verbal conflict in union disruption. *Journal of Marriage and the Family, 62*, 683–692.

Denney, J. T. (2010). Family household formations and suicide in the United States. *Journal of Marriage and the Family, 72*, 202–213.

Denver Metro Domestic Fatality Review Committee (2012). Annual report. Denver, Colorado.

Diserood, D., Loeb, M., & Ekeberg, O. (2000). Suicidal behavior in the municipality of Baerum, Norway: A 12 year prospective study of parasuicide and suicide. *Suicide and Life-threatening Behavior, 30*, 61–73.

Diserood, G., Roysamb, E., Braverman, N., Dalgard, O., & Ekeberg, O. (2003). Predicting repetition of suicide attempts: A prospective study of 50 suicide attempters. *Suicide and Life-threatening Behavior, 7*, 1–15.

Dixon, L., Hamilton-Giachritsis, C., & Browne, K. (2008). Classifying partner homicide. *Journal of Interpersonal Violence, 23*, 74–93.

Dobash, R. E., & Dobash, R. P. (1979). *Violence against wives*. New York: The Free Press.

Dobash, R. E., & Dobash, R. P. (1992). *Women/violence and social change*. Florence, KY: Routledge.

Dobash, R. E., & Dobash, R. P. (2010). What were they thinking? Men who murder an intimate partner. *Violence Against Women, 20*, 1–24.

Dobash, R. E., Dobash, R. P., & Cavanagh, K. (2009). Out of the blue: Men who murder an intimate partner. *Feminist Criminology, 4*, 194–225.

Dobash, R. E., Dobash, R. P., Cavanagh, K., & Lewis, R. (2000). *Changing violent men*. Thousand Oaks, CA: Sage.

Dobash, R. E., Dobash, R. P., Cavanagh, K., & Medina-Ariza, J. (2007). Lethal and non-lethal violence against an intimate partner: Comparing male murderers to nonlethal abusers. *Violence Against Women, 13*, 329–353.

Dollard, J., Doob, L. W., Miller, N., Mowrer, O. H., & Sears, R. F. (1939). *Frustration and aggression*. New Haven, CT: Yale University Press.

Domestic Abuse Shelters of the Florida Keys. A New Beginning (2014). www.domesticabuseshelter.org/Infodomesticviolence.htm.

Domestic Violence Resource Center (2013). *Domestic violence statistics*.

Domestic Violence Resource Center (2014). *Domestic abuse shelters of the Florida keys: A new beginning*.

Douglas, J. D. (1967). *The social meanings of suicide*. Princeton, NJ: Princeton University Press.

Douglas, J. D. (1969). The rhetoric of science and the origins of statistical thought; the case of Durkheim's suicide. In A. Tiryakian (Ed.), *The phenomenon of sociology*. New York: Appleton-Century-Crofts.

Dugan, L., Nagin, D. S., & Rosenfeld, R. (2000). *Exposure reduction or backlash? The effects of domestic violence resources on intimate partner homicide: Final report*. Washington, DC: Department of Justice, National Institute of Justice.

Dugan, L., Nagin, D. S., & Rosenfeld, R. (2003). Explaining the decline in intimate partner homicide. *Homicide Studies, 3*, 187–214.

Dunford, F., Huizinga, D., & Elliott, D. S. (1989). *The Omaha domestic violence experiments* (Final report to the National Institute of Justice, Washington, DC).

Dunivan, C. (2011). *The bully pulpit: State to eliminate domestic violence shelters*. Caseyspulpit.blogspot.com.

Duntley, J. D., & Buss, D. M. (2008). The origins of homicide. In J. D. Duntley, & T. K. Shackleford (Eds.), *Evolutionary forensic psychology: Darwinian foundations of crime and law* (pp. 41–46). Oxford: Oxford University Press.

Durfee, A., & Messing, J. T. (2012). Use among victims of intimate partner violence. *Violence Against Women, 18*(6), 701–710.

Durham Response to Woman Abuse (2007). *Task force report on court, police and legal issues*. Report presented to the Status of Women Canada and the Ontario Women's Directorate. www.durhamrespomsetowomanabuse.com.

Durkheim, E. (1952). *Suicide: A study in sociology*. Translated by Spaulding, J., & Simpson, G. London: Routledge and Kegan Paul. Orig. published in 1875.

Durrant, R. (2009). Born to kill? A critical evaluation of homicide adaptation theory. *Aggression and Violent Behavior, 14*, 374–381.

Dutta, S., & Stancati, M. (January 16, 2013). Why honour killings happen. *Wall Street Journal*.

Dutton, D. G. (2006). *Rethinking domestic violence*. Vancouver, BC: UBC Press.

Dutton, D. G. (2003). *The abusive personality*. New York: The Guilford Press.

Dutton, D., & Browning, J. J. (1988). Power struggles and intimacy anxiety as causative factors in wife assault. In G. Russell (Ed.), *Violence in intimate relationships* (pp. 166–175). Great Neck, NY: PMA Publishing.

Dutton, D., & Kerry, G. (1999). *Modus operandi* and personality disorder in incarcerated spousal killers. *International Journal of Law and Psychiatry, 22*, 287–299.

Easteal, P. W. (1993). *Killing the beloved*. Canberra: Australian Institute of Criminology (ACT).

Eke, A. W., Hilton, N. Z., & Harris, G. T. (2011). Intimate partner homicide: Risk assessment and prospects for prediction. *Journal of Family Violence, 26*, 211–216.

Elias, N. (2000). *The civilizing process: Sociogenetic and psychogenetic investigations*. Cambridge, MA: Blackwell.

Eliason, S. (2009). Murder-suicide: A review of the recent literature. *Journal of the American Academy of Psychiatry and Law, 37*, 371–376.

Ellis, D. (1994). *Family mediation pilot project.* (Report submitted to the Attorney general of Ontario.)

Ellis, D. (2014). Marital separation, conflict resolution and lethal male partner violence. *Violence Against Women* (Forthcoming).

Ellis, D., & Anderson, D. (2005). *Conflict resolution: An introductory text*. Toronto: Emond-Montgomery.

Ellis, D., & De Keseredy, W. (1996). *The wrong stuff: An introduction to the sociological study of deviance*. Scarborough, Toronto: Allyn & Bacon.

Ellis, D., Sakinofsky, I., & Stuckless, N. (2012). *Estrangement associated lethal male partner violence: Risk factors and prevention*. Report submitted to the Department of Justice (Family Violence Prevention Division), Ottawa.

Ellis, D., & Stuckless, N. (1996). *Mediating and negotiating marital conflicts*. Thousand Oaks, CA: Sage.

Ellis, D., & Stuckless, N. (2006). Separation, domestic violence and divorce mediation. *Conflict Resolution Quarterly, 23*, 461–486.

Emery, R. (2012). *The truth about children and divorce*. New York: Viking-Penguin.

Emery, R. E., Lauman-Billings, L., Waldron, M. C., Sbarra, D. A., & Dillon, O. (2001). Child custody mediation and litigation: Custody, contact and co-parenting 12 years after initial dispute resolution. *Journal of Consulting and Clinical Psychology, 69*, 323–332.

Emery, R. E., Matthews, S. G., & Kitzmann, K. (1991). Child custody mediation and litigation: Parents satisfaction and functioning a year after settlement. *Journal of Consulting and Clinical Psychology, 62*, 124–129.

Ettlinger, R. W., & Flordah, P. (1955). Attempted suicide. *Acta Psychiatrica Scandinavica, 103*, 45–56.

European Parliament (2007). *Honour killing—its causes and consequences; suggested strategies for the European parliament*. Brussels: Directorate General External Policies of the Union. http://europarl.europa.eu/activieies/expert/e.Studies.do?LanguageEN.

Family Conflict Resolution Services (2013). *Family conflict relating to separation and divorce: The causes and solutions*. Toronto, Ontario, Canada. htpp//.camadacourtwatch.com/fjrc/causes_solutions.htm.

Farmer, A., & Tiefenthaler, J. (2003). Explaining the recent decline in domestic violence, contemporary economic policy. *A Journal of Western Association International, 21*(2), 158–172.

Feder, L., & Wilson, D. B. (2005). A meta-analytic review of court-mandated batterer programs: Can courts affect abusive behaviour? *Journal of Experimental Criminology, 1*, 239–262.

Federal Bureau of Investigation (2011). *Uniform crime reports*. Washington, DC: Government Printing Office.

Felder, R. (1996). *Getting away with murder: Weapons for the war against domestic violence*. New York: Simon and Schuster.
Felson, M. (1987). Routine activities and crime prevention in the developing metropolis. *Criminology, 25*, 911–931.
Felson, R. B., & Messner, S. F. (2000). The control motive in intimate partner violence. *Social Psychology Quarterly, 63*, 86–94.
Ferarro, K. J., & Johnson, M. (1983). How women experience battering: The process of victimization. *Social Problems, 30*, 325–339.
Ferraro, K. J. (1989). Policing woman battering. *Social Problems, 36*, 61–74.
Fine, M. A. (2001). Marital conflict in stepfamilies. In A. Booth, A. C. Crouter, & M. Clements (Eds.), *Couples in conflict* (pp. 363–385). Mahwah, NJ: Lawrence Erlbaum and Associates.
Fisher, R., Ury, W., & Patton, W. (1992). *Getting to yes*. Toronto: Penguin.
Fleury, R. E., Sullivan, C. M., & Bybee, D. I. (2000). When ending the relationship does not end the violence: Women's experience of violence by former partners. *Violence Against Women, 6*, 1363. 10.1177/10778010022183695.
Flynn, S., & Graham, K. (2010). Gender differences in reasons for intimate partner violence. *Aggression and Violent Behavior, 15*, 239–251.
Flynn, S., Swinson, N., While, D., Hunt, I. M., Roscoe, A., Rodway, C., et al. (2009). Homicide followed by suicide: A cross-sectional study. *The Journal of Forensic Psychiatry and Psychology, 20*, 306–321.
Foucault, M. (1982). The subject and power. *Critical Inquiry, 8*, 777–795.
Fountoulakis, K. N., Leucht, S., & Kaprinis, G. (2008). Personality disorders and violence. *Current Opinion in Psychiatry, 21*, 84–92.
Frances, A., Fryer, M., & Clarkin, J. (1986). Personality and suicide. In J. J. Mann, & M. Stanley (Eds.), *Psychobiology of suicidal behavior*. New York: New York Academy of Sciences.
Fry, D. P., & Soderberg, P. (2013). Lethal aggression in forager bands and implications for the origins of war. *Science, 341*, 270–271.
Fryer, M., Frances, A. J., Sullivan, T., Hurt, S. W., & Clarkin, J. (1988). Comorbidity of borderline personality disorder. *Archives of General Psychiatry, 45*, 348–352.
Gabriel, T. (November 24, 2013). Custody battle raises questions about rights of women. *New York Times*, 18–22.
Galen, E. (2012). *U.S. budget cuts devastate shelters for victims of domestic violence*. http://www.wsws.org/articles/2012/jan.2012/viol-j25.shtml.
Garcia, L., Soria, C., & Hurwitz, E. L. (2007). Homicides and intimate partner violence: A literature review. *Trauma, Violence & Abuse, 8*, 370–383.
Gartner, R., Dawson, M., & Crawford, M. (1999). Woman killing: Intimate femicide in Ontario, 1974-1994. *Resources For Feminist Research, 26*, 151–173.
Gauthier, D. K., & Bankstron, W. B. (2004). "Who kills whom" revisited: A sociological study of variation in the sex ratio of spouse killings. *Homicide Studies, 8*, 96–122.
Gauvreau, D. (2012). *Mediation versus litigation: Examining differences in outcomes amongst the children of divorce*. Toronto: University of Western Ontario. Paper presented to Family Law Alternative Resolution.
Gavigan, S. (2013). Something old, something new?: Re-theorizing patriarchal relations and privatization from the outskirts of family law. *Theoretical Inquires in Law, 13*, 271–301.
Gelles, R. (1991). Physical violence, child abuse and child homicide: A continuum of violence or distinct behaviors? *Human Nature, 2*, 59–72.

Gengler, A. M. (2012). Defying (Dis) empowerment in a battered women's shelter: Moral, rhetorics, intersectionality, and processes of control and resistance. *Social Problems, 59*, 501–521.

Gibbs, J. P., & Martin, W. T. (1964). *Social integration and suicide: A sociological study*. Eugene, OR: University of Oregon Press.

Giddens, A. (1993). Domination and power. In P. Cassell (Ed.), *The Giddens reader* (pp. 212–283). London: Macmillan.

Gillespie, C. (1989). *Justifiable homicide: Battered women, self defence and the law*. Columbus, OH: Ohio State University Press.

Gillespie, M., Hearn, V., & Silverman, R. A. (1998). Suicide following homicide in Canada. *Homicide Studies, 2*, 46–63.

Gillis, A. R. (1996). So long as they both shall live: Marital dissolution and the decline of domestic homicide in France, 1852–1909. *American Journal of Sociology, 101*, 1273–1305.

Glass, N., Perrin, N., Hanson, G., Bloom, T., Gardner, E., & Campbell, J. C. (2008). Risk for re-assault in abusive female same-sex relationships. *American Journal of Public health, 98*, 1021–1027.

Glass, N., Laughon, K., Rutto, C., Bevacqua, J., & Campbell, J. C. (2008). Young adult intimate partner femicide: An exploratory study. *Homicide Studies, 12*, 177–187.

Godbole, A., & Kukde, H. G. (2007). Suicidal and homicidal deaths: A comparative and circumstantial approach. *Journal of Forensic Legal Medicine, 14*, 253–260.

Goetting, A. (1987). Homicidal wives: A profile. *Journal of Family Issues, 8*, 332–341.

Goetting, A. (1995). *Homicide in families and other special populations*. New York: Springer.

Gold, M. (1958). Suicide, homicide and the socialization of aggression. *American Journal of Sociology, 63*, 651–661.

Golding, J. M. (1999). Intimate partner violence as a risk factor for mental disorders: A meta-analysis. *Journal of Family Violence, 14*, 99–132.

Gondolf, E. W. (2002). *Batterer intervention systems, issues, outcomes and recommendations*. Thousand Oaks, CA: Sage.

Gondolf, E. W. (2012). *The future of batterer programs: Reassessing evidence-based practice*. Boston, MA: Northeastern University Press of New England.

Gondolf, E. W., & Russell, D. (1986). The case against anger control treatment programs for batterers. *Response, 9*(3), 2–5.

Goode, W. J. (1971). Force and violence in the family. *Journal of Marriage and the Family*, November, 624–635.

Gottman, J. M., Murray, J. D., Swanson, C. C., Tyson, R., & Swanson, K. R. (2002). *The mathematics of marriage: Non-linear dynamic models*. Cambridge, MA: MIT Press.

Gould, S. J. (1992). Male nipples and clitoral ripples. In *Bully for Brontosaurus: Further reflections in natural history*. New York: Norton.

Gould, S. J., & Lewontin, R. C. (1979). The spandrels of San Marco and the panglossian paradigm: A critique of the adapationist programme. *Proceedings of the Royal Society of London, 205*, 581–598.

Goussinsky, R., & Yassour-Borochowitz, D. (2012). "I killed her, but I never laid a finger on her"-a phenomenological difference between wife-killing and wife-battering. *Aggression and Violent Behavior, 17*, 553–564.

Gove, W. R. (1973). Sex, marital status and morality. *American Journal of Sociology, 79*, 45–67.

Grant, B. C. (1983). Till death do us part: A social psychological analysis of women who kill their partners. Ph.D. Dissertation, Department of Sociology, Mississippi State University.

Gruber, S., & Szoltzysek, M. (2012). *Quantifying patriarchy: An explorative comparison of two joint family societies*. Working Paper, Rostock, Germany: Max Planck Institute for Demographic Research. www.demogr.mpg.de.

Grundy, K. N. (June 24, 2012). *Why didn't she just leave?* Wichita Falls: First Step, Inc.

Gulliver, P. (1979). *Disputes and negotiations: A cross-cultural perspective*. New York: Academic Press.

Gunderson, J. G. (1984). *Borderline personality disorder*. Washington, DC: American Psychiatric Press.

Gunderson, J. G. (2009). Borderline personality disorder: Ontogeny of a diagnosis. *American Journal of Psychiatry, 166*, 530–539.

Guttmacher, M. S. (1955). Criminal responsibility in certain homicide cases involving family members. In P. H. Hoch, & J. Zubin (Eds.), *Psychiatry and the law* (pp. 73–96). New York: Grune & Stratton.

Hagerty, K. D. (2003). From risk to precaution: The rationalities of personal crime prevention. In R. Erickson, & R. A. Doyle (Eds.), *Risk and morality* (pp. 193–214). Toronto: University of Toronto Press.

Hall Smith, P., Moracco, K. M., & Butts, J. (1998). Partner homicide in context: A population-based perspective. *Homicide Studies, 2*, 400–421.

Hamberger, L. K., Lohr, J. M., Bonge, D., & Tolin, D. F. (1997). An empirical classification of motivations for domestic violence. *Violence Against Women, 3*, 401–423.

Hamlett, N. (1998). *Women who abuse in intimate relationships*. Minneapolis, MN: Domestic Abuse Project.

Harper, D. W., & Voight, L. (2007). Homicide followed by suicide: An integrated theoretical perspective. *Homicide Studies, 11*, 295–318.

Harris, E. C., & Barraclough, B. (1997). Suicide as an outcome of mental disorders. *British Journal of Psychiatry, 170*, 205–228.

Hart, B. (2010). Battered women-suicide. *Fatality Revue Bulletin* ((Winter). National Domestic Violence Fatality Revue Initiative).

Hassan, R. (1995). *Suicide explained*. Melbourne, AU: Melbourne University Press.

Hawkins, D. (1983). Black and white homicide differentials: Alternatives to an inadequate theory. *Criminal Justice and Behavior, 10*, 407–440.

Hawton, K., Houston, K., Haw, C., Townsend, E., & Harris, L. (2003). Co-morbidity in axis I and II disorders in patients who attempted suicide. *American Journal of Psychiatry, 160*, 1494–1500.

Hedeem, T., & Salem, P. (2006). What should family lawyers know? Results of a survey of practitioners and students. *Family Court Review, 44*, 601–611.

Hegerl, U., Rummel-Kluge, C., Varnik, A. M., Arensman, E., & Koburger, N. (February 21, 2013). Alliances against depression-A community based approach to target depression and to prevent suicidal behaviour. *Neuroscience Biobehaviour Review*, 1–16.

Heider, F. (1958). *The psychology of interpersonal relations*. New York: Psychology Press.

Heikkinen, M., Aro, H., & Lonnqvist, J. (1992). Recent life events and their role in suicide as seen by the spouses. *Acta Psychiatrica Scandinavica, 86*, 489–494.

Henry, A. F., & Short, J. F. (1954). *Suicide and homicide*. Glencoe, IL: Free Press.

Hetherington, E. M., Law, T. C., & O'Connor, G. O. (2001). Divorce: Challenges, changes and new chances. In A. S. Skolnick, & J. Skolnick (Eds.), *Family in transition* (pp. 222–230). Toronto: Allyn and Bacon.

Hirschi, T., & Gottfredson, M. (1983). Age and the explanation of crime. *American Journal of Sociology, 89*, 552–584.

Hobbes, T. (1651/1957). *Leviathan*. New York: Oxford University Press.

Hoffman, K., Demo, D. H., & Edwards, J. N. (1994). Physical wife abuse in a non-western society: An integrated theoretical approach. *Journal of Marriage and the Family, 56*, 131–146.

Holly, K. J. (2012). Anger management likely to increase domestic abuse. *Healthy Place. America's Mental Health Channel*, (January 5, 2012). http://www.healthyplace.com/blogs/verbalabuseinrelationships/2012/01/anger-management-likely-to-increase-domestic-abuse/.

Holmes, T. H., & Rahe, R. H. (1967). The social adjustment rating scale. *Journal of Psychosomatic Research, 11*, 213–218.

Holtzworth-Munroe, A., & Stuart, G. L. (1994). Typologies of male batterers: Three sub-types and differences among them. *Psychological Bulletin, 116*, 476–497.

Hotton, T. (2001). *Spousal violence after marital separation. Juristat, 21, # 7. Canadian Centre for Justice Statistics*. Ottawa: Statistics Canada.

Hovda, J. (2012). The efficacy of Idaho's domestic violence courts: An opportunity for the court system to effect social change. *Idaho Law Review, 48*, 587.

Hoyle, C. (2008). Will she be safe: A critical analysis of risk assessment in domestic violence cases. *Children and Youth Services Review, 30*, 323–337.

Huer, L. B., & Penrod, S. (1986). Procedural preferences in relation to conflict intensity. *Journal of Personality and Social Psychology, 51*, 700–710.

Hughes, F. H., Stuart, G. L., Gordon, K. C., & Moore, T. M. (2007). Predicting the use of aggressive conflict tactics in a sample of women arrested for domestic violence. *Journal of Personal and Social Relationships, 24*, 155–176.

Hunnicutt, G. (2009). Varieties of patriarchy and violence against women: Resurrecting "patriarchy" as a theoretical tool. *Violence Against Women, 15*, 553–573.

Ide, N., Wyder, M., Kolves, K., & De Leo, D. (2010). Separation as an important risk factor for suicide: A systematic review. *Journal of Family Issues, 31*, 1689–1716.

International Herald Tribune (November 28, 2011). *Acid attacks: The burning sting of rejection*.

Isacsson, G., & Rich, C. L. (2003). Getting closer to suicide prevention. *The British Journal of Psychiatry, 182*, 457–458.

Iyengar, R. Does the certainty of arrest reduce domestic violence? Evidence for mandatory and recommended arrest laws. Harvard University, unpublished paper.

Jacobson, G. F., & Portuges, S. H. (1978). Relation of marital separation and divorce to suicide: A report. *Suicide and Life-threatening Behavior, 8*, 217–224.

Jeanne Geiger Crisis Center, Inc. (2011). *Greater Newburyport domestic violence high risk team: Safety and accountability report*. Newburyport, MA.

Jensen, V. (2001). *Why women kill: Homicide and gender equality*. Boulder, CO: Lynne Reinner Publishers.

Jiwani, Y. (2000). *Spousal abuse: A fact sheet from the department of justice Ottawa, ON, Canada, 2001*.

Johnson, H., & Dawson, M. (2011). *Violence against women in Canada: Research and policy perspectives*. Toronto: Oxford University Press.

Johnson, H., & Fraser, J. (2011). *Specialized domestic violence courts: Do they make women safer?* University of Ottawa. Community Report Phase I.

Johnson, H., & Hotton, T. (2003). Losing control: Homicide risk in estranged and intact intimate relationships. *Homicide Studies, 7*, 8–54.

Jones, A. (1994). *Next time she'll be dead: Battering and how to stop it*. Boston: Beacon Press.

Jurik, N. C., & Wynn, R. (1990). Gender and homicide: A comparison of men and women who kill. *Violence and Victims, 5*, 227–242.

Kaighobadi, F., & Shackleford, T. (2009). From mate retention to murder: Evolutionary psychological perspectives on men's partner-directed violence. *Review of General Psychology, 13*, 327–334.

Kalmuss, D. S. (1984). The intergenerational transmission of marital aggression. *Journal of Marriage and the Family, 46*, 11–19.

Kandiyoti, D. (1988). Bargaining with patriarchy. *Gender and Society, 2*, 274–290.

Kandiyotti, D. A. (1987). Emancipated but un-liberated: Reflections on the Turkish case. *Feminist Studies, 13*, 317–338.

Kay, M. (2013). *Annual survey reveals cycle of domestic violence continues in generation Y, Share Inc.* http://www.sharemorgancounty.org/page/2/.

Keilitz, S. L., Davis, C., Efkeman, H. S., Flango, C., & Hannaford, P. L. (1998). *Civil protection orders: Victims views on effectiveness.* National Institute of Justice Research Review.

Kellerman, A. l., Rivara, F. P., Rushforth, M. B., Banton, J. G., Reay, D. T., Francisco, J. T., et al. (1993). Gun ownership as a risk factor for homicide in the home. *The New England Journal of Medicine, 329*, 1084–1091.

Kelley, H. H. (1967). Attribution theory in social psychology. In D. Levine (Ed.). *Nebraska symposium on motivation, 15*, pp. 192–238. Lincoln: University of Nebraska Press.

Kelly, J. B., & Johnson, M. P. (2008). Differentiation among different types of intimate partner violence: Research update and implications for prevention. *Family Court Review, 46*, 47–499.

King, D. (2008). The personal is patrilineal: *Namus* as sovereignty. *Identities, 15*, 317–342.

Kingston Frontenac Anti-Violence Coordinating Committee (2010). *Women/Children Murdered Since 1990.* Media Clipping Service.

Kobler, A. L., & Stotland, E. (1964). *The end of hope.* Glencoe, IL: Free Press.

Kolves, K., Ide, N., & De Leo, D. (2010). Suicidal ideation and behaviour in the aftermath of marital separation; gender differences. *Journal of Affective Disorders, 120*, 48–53.

Kolves, K., Varnik, A., Schneider, B., Fritze, J., & Allik, J. (2006). Recent life events and suicide: A case-control study in Tallinn and Frankfurt. *Social Science and Medicine, 62*, 2887–2896.

Kowalski, M. (2005). Spousal homicides. *Family Violence in Canada: A Statistical Profile.* Statistics Canada, 85–204. Cat, # 85-224.

Koziol-McLain, J., Webster, D., McFarlane, J., Block, C., Ulrich, Y., Glass, N., et al. (2006). Risk factors for femicide-suicide in abusive relationships: Results from a multi-site case control study. *Violence and Victims, 21*, 3–21.

Kposowa, A. J. (2000). Marital status and suicide in the national longitudinal study. *Journal of Epidemiology Community Health, 54*, 254–261.

Kposowa, A. J., Singh, G. K., & Breault, K. D. (1994). The effects of marital status and social isolation on adult male homicides in the United States: Evidence from the national longitudinal mortality study. *Journal of Quantitative Criminology, 10*, 277–289.

Kressel, G. M. (1981). Soroicide/filiacide homicide for family honour. *Cultural Anthropology, 22*, 141–158.

Kruk, E. (1993). *Divorce and dis-engagement: Patterns of fatherhood within and beyond marriage.* Halifax: Fernwood Publishing.

Kulwicki, A. (2002). The practice of honour crimes: A glimpse of domestic violence in the Arab world. *Issues in Mental Health Nursing, 23*, 77–87.

Kurz, D. (1995). *For richer, for poorer: Mothers confront divorce.* New York: Routledge.

Kurz, D. (1996). Separation, divorce and woman abuse. *Violence Against Women, 2*, 063–081.

Lakoff, G., & Johnson, M. (1980). *Metaphors we live by*. Chicago: University of Chicago Press.
Landenburger, K. (1998). The dynamics of leaving and recovering from an abusive relationship. *Journal of Obstetric, Gynecologic and Neonatal Nursing, 27*, 700–706.
Large, M. N., Smith, G., & Nielson, O. (2009). The epidemiology of homicide followed by suicide: A systematic and quantitative review. *Suicide and Life-threatening Behavior, 39*, 294–306.
Lecomte, D., & Fornes, P. (1998). Homicide followed by suicide: Paris and its suburbs, 1991–1996. *Journal of Forensic Science, 43*, 76–85.
Leon, A. C., Friedman, R. A., Sweeney, J. A., Brown, R. P., & Mann, J. J. (1990). Statistical issues in the identification of risk factors for suicidal behavior: The application of survival analysis. *Psychiatry Research, 31*, 316–326.
Leone, J. M. (2011). Suicidal behavior among low-income African American female victims of intimate terrorism and situational couple violence. *Journal of Interpersonal Violence, 26*, 2568–2591.
Lester, D. (1987). Benefits of marriage for reducing the risk of violent death from suicide for white and non-white persons: Generalizing Gove's findings. *Psychological Reports, 61*, 193–199.
Levi, K. (1981). Homicide as a form of conflict resolution. *Deviant Behavior, 1*, 281–307.
Liao, M. S. (2006). Domestic violence among South Asian immigrant women: Risk factors, acculturation and intervention. *Women and Therapy, 29*, 23–39.
Liem, M. (2010). Homicide-parasuicide: A qualitative comparison with homicide and parasuicide. *The Journal of Forensic Psychiatry and Psychology, 21*, 247–263.
Liem, M., Hengeveld, M., & Koenrdraat, F. (2009). Domestic homicide followed by parasuicide: A comparison with homicide and parasuicide. *International Journal of Offender Therapy and Criminology, 10*, 1177. /0306624X09334646.
Liem, M., & Nieubeerta, P. (2010). Homicide followed by suicide: A comparison with homicide and suicide. *Suicide and Life-threatening Behavior, 40*, 133–145.
Liem, M., Postulart, M., & Nieuwbeerta, P. (2009). Homicide-suicide in the Netherlands: An epidemiology. *Homicide Studies, 13*, 99–120.
Liem, M., & Roberts, D. W. (2009). Intimate partner homicide by presence or absence of a self-destructive act. *Homicide Studies, 13*, 339–354.
Linehan, M. (1993). *Cognitive behavioral treatment of borderline personality disorder*. New York, NY: Guilford.
Linehan, M. (2012). Dialectical behavior therapy (DBT) for borderline personality disorder. *The Journal, 8*(1), 1–5.
Linehan, M., Camper, P., Chiles, J. A., Strosahl, K., & Shearin, E. (1987). Interpersonal problem solving and parasuicide. *Cognitive Therapy and Research, 11*, 1–12.
Lofland, J. (1969). *Deviance and identity*. Englewood Cliffs, NJ: Prentice-Hall.
Logan, J., Hill, A., Black, M. L., Crosby, A. E., Karch, D. L., Barnes, J. D., et al. (2008). Characteristic of perpetrators in homicide-suicide incidents: National violent death reporting system -17 US States, 2003–2005. *American Journal of Epidemiology, 168*, 1056–1064.
Logan, T. K., & Walker, R. (November 3, 2011). *Civil protective order effectiveness: Justice or just a piece of paper?* Carsey, Policy Brief No. 18.
Longman, J., & Barnes, T. (2013). A yellow card, then blood. *New York Times*. Sports, pages 1 and six.
Lund, L. E., & Smorodinsky, S. (2001). Violent death among intimate partners: A comparison of homicide and homicide followed by suicide in California. *Suicide and Life-threatening Behavior, 31*, 451–459.

MacCharles, T. (January 19, 2013). Supreme court frees battered woman. *Toronto Star*, A6.

Mahoney, M. (1991). Redefining the issue of separation. *Michigan Law Review*, 90, 1–94.

Makin, K. (January 18, 2013). Supreme court will lay out self defence guidelines for abused women. *The Globe and Mail*, A5.

Malone, K. M., Ocquendo, M. A., Haas, G. L., Ellis, S. P., & Mann, J. J. (2000). Protective factors against suicidal acts in major depression: Reasons for living. *American Journal of Psychiatry*, 157, 1084–1088.

Marcott, A. (2013). *Simple solution for preventing domestic violence*. The Slate Group: A Division of the Washington Post Company.

Maris, R. W. (1969). *Social forces in urban suicide*. Belmont, CA: Dorsey Press.

Marsiglio, W., & Pleck, J. H. (2005). Fatherhood and masculinities. In M. S. Kimmel, J. Hearn, & R. W. Connell (Eds.), *The handbook of studies on men and masculinities* (pp. 249–269). Thousand Oaks, CA: Sage.

Maryland Network Against Domestic Violence (2004). *Report to the lethality assessment committee concerning the pilot of the lethality screen for first responders and the protocol*. Bowie, MD.

Marzuk, P. M., Tardiff, K., & Hirsch, C. S. (1992). The epidemiology of murder-suicide. *Journal of the American Medical Association*, 267, 3179–3183.

McCrae, R. R., & Costa, P. T. (1999). A five factor theory of personality. In L. A. Pervin, & O. P. John (Eds.), *Handbook of personality: Theory and research* (2nd ed.) (pp. 139–153). New York: The Guilford Press.

McFarlane, J., Campbell, J. C., & Watson, K. (2001). The use of the justice system prior to intimate partner femicide. *Criminal Justice Review*, 26, 193–2080.

McFarlane, J., Campbell, J., & Watson, K. (2002). Intimate partner stalking and femicide: Urgent implications for women's safety. *Behavioral Sciences and the Law*, 20, 51–68.

McGirr, A., Paris, J., Lesage, A., Renaud, J., & Turecki, G. (2007). Risk factors for suicide completion in borderline personality disorder: A case control study of cluster comorbidity and impulsive aggression. *Journal of Clinical Psychiatry*, 721–729.

Megargee, E. (1966). Under-controlled and over-controlled person in extreme anti-social aggression. *Psychological Monographs*, 80. #3.

Mercy, J. A., & Saltzman, L. E. (1989). Fatal violence among spouses in the United States, 1976-1985. *American Journal of Public Health*, 79, 595–599.

Merton, R. K. (1957). *Social theory and social structure* (pp. 96–97). New York: Free Press.

Messing, J., & Thaller, J. (2013). The average predictive validity of intimate partner violence risk assessment instruments. *Journal of Interpersonal Violence*, 28, 1537–1558.

MIAMS (2005). *Family Law in Partnership*. www.twitter.com/resfamilylaw.

Miller, N. (1941). The frustration-aggression hypothesis. *Psychological Review*, 48, 337–342.

Millon, T. (1987). *Manual for the MCMI-II*. Minneapolis: National Computer Systems.

Milroy, C. M. (1998). Homicide followed by suicide: Remorse or revenge? *Journal of Clinical Forensic Medicine*, 5, 61–64.

Miner, E. J., Shackleford, T. K., Block, C. R., Starratt, V. C., & Weekes-Shackleford, V. A. (2012). Risk of death or life threatening injury for women with children not sired by the abuser. *Human Nature*, 23, 89–97.

Mnookin, R. (2010). A devilish divorce. In R. Mnookin (Ed.), *Bargaining with the devil: When to negotiate, when to fight* (pp. 209–231). New York: Simon and Schuster.

Montgomery, S. (2013). Seven cases where women died in Quebec despite police being warned about conjugal violence. *The Gazette* (May 28, 2013).

Morrow, E. (October 16, 2002). In S. Thomas (Ed.), *Ontario rise in spousal murders sign of things to come in B.C.* Vancouver Courier Newspaper.

Mortensen, P. B., Agerbo, E., Erikson, T., Qin, P., & Westergaard-Neilson, N. (2000). Psychiatric illness and risk factors for suicide. *Lancet, 355,* 9–12.

Morton, E., Runyan, C., Moracco, K. E., & Butts, J. (1998). Partner homicide-suicide involving female victims: A population-based study in North Carolina, 1988–1992. *Violence and Victims, 13,* 91–106.

Mosiciki, E. K. (1997). The identification of suicide risk factors using epidemiological studies. *Psychiatric Clinics of North America, 20,* 499–517.

National Institute of Justice (1997). *Civil protection orders: Victims' views on effectiveness.* Washington DC: U.S. Department of Justice. Available at: https://www.ncjrs.gov/pdffiles/fsWashington000191.pdf.ed. Accessed 10.06.14.

National Violent Death Reporting System (2012). *Surveillance summaries, 16 states, 2009.* Atlanta, GA: Centers for Disease Control and Prevention.

Nicholls, T. L., Pritchard, M. M., Reeves, K. A., & Hilterman, E. (2013). Risk assessment in intimate partner violence: A systematic review of contemporary approaches. *Partner Abuse, 4,* 76–168.

Nye, J. (2013). *Olympic skier Bose Miller accused of legally changing son's first name without mother's permission in latest swipe in bitter custody battle.* Mail Online. www.dailymail.co.uk/news/article.

OAITH (1998). *Falling through the gender gap: How Ontario government policy continues to fail abused women and their children.* Ontario Association of Interval and Transition Houses.

Odoms, T. (2001). Policy responses to couple conflict and domestic violence: A framework for discussion. In A. Booth, A. C. Crouter, & M. Clements (Eds.), *Couples in conflict* (pp. 227–239). Mahwah, NJ: Lawrence Erlbaum.

Ogle, R. S., & Jacobs, S. (2002). *Self defence and battered women who kill: A new framework.* Westport, CT: Praeger.

Ogle, R. S., & Jacobs, S. (2012). *Self defence and battered women who kill.* Belmont, CA: Greenwood Publishing.

Ogle, R. S., Katkin, D. M., & Bernard, T. J. (1995). A theory of homicidal behavior among women. *Criminology, 33,* 173–193.

Ogrodnik, L. (2009). *Fact sheet—Police reported spousal violence in Canada. Family violence in Canada: A statistical profile* (pp. 24–30). Ottawa: Statistics Canada.

Oklahoma Domestic Violence Fatality Review Board. (2011). *Domestic violence homicide in Oklahoma, 2001-2011.* Annual Report.

Okun, L. (1986). *Woman abuse: Facts replacing myths.* Albany: State University of New York Press.

Oliver, W. (2006). "The streets": An alternative black male socialization institution. *Journal of Black Studies, 36,* 918–937.

Ontario Domestic Violence Death Review Committee (2009/2010). Annual reports. Toronto: Ontario.

Oquendo, M. A., Bongiovi-Garcia, M. E., Galfalvy, H., Gruenbaum, M. F., Burke, A. K., & Mann, J. J. (2007). Sex differences in clinical predictors of suicidal acts after major depression. *American Journal of Psychiatry, 164,* 134–141.

Oquendo, M. A., Ellis, S. P., Greenwald, S., Malone, K. M., Weissman, M. M., & Mann, J. J. (2001). Ethnic and sex differences in suicide rates relative to major depression in the United States. *American Journal of Psychiatry, 158,* 1652–1658.

Oyserman, D., Coon, M. H., & Kemmelmeier, M. (2002). Rethinking individualism and collectivism: Evaluations of theoretical assumptions and theoretical analysis. *Psychological Bulletin, 128,* 3–72.

Palermo, G. B. (1984). Murder-suicide: An extended-suicide. *Journal of Offender Therapy and Comparative Criminology, 38*, 205–216.

Palmer, S., & Humphrey, J. A. (1980). Offender-victim relationships in criminal homicide followed by the offender's suicide. *Suicide and Life-threatening Behavior, 10*, 106–110.

Panchanadeswaran, S., & Koverola, C. (2005). The voices of battered women in India. *Violence Against Women, 11*, 736.

Paradine, K., & Wilkinson, J. (2004). *Protection and accountability: The reporting, investigation and prosecution of domestic violence cases*. A Research and Literature Review prepared for The National Centre for Policing Excellence, CENTREX, Central Police Training Development, Ashford, Kent, England.

Paykel, E. S., Myers, J. K., Klerman, M. N., Lindenthal, G. L., & Pepper, M. P. (1969). Life events and depression: A controlled study. *Archives of General Psychiatry, 21*, 753–760.

Pearson, J., & Thonnes, N. (1984). *Mediating and litigating custody disputes: A longitudinal evaluation*. Denver, CO: Center for Policy Research.

Pence, E., & Paymar, M. (1993). *Education groups for men who batter: The Duluth model*. New York: Springer.

Perez, A., Johnson, J. M., & Wright, C. V. (2012). *Violence Against Women, 18*, 102. DOI: 1177/1077801212437348.

Peterson, E. S. (1999). Murder as self-help: Women and intimate partner homicide. *Homicide Studies, 3*, 30–46.

Pinchevsky, G. M., & Wright, E. M. (2012). The impact of neighbourhoods on intimate partner violence and victimization. *Trauma, Violence & Abuse, 13*, 112–132.

Pinker, S. (2011). *The better angels of our nature: Why violence has declined*. New York: Viking/Penguin.

Polk, K. (1994). *When men kill*. New York: Cambridge University Press.

Polk, K., & Ransom, D. (1991). Patterns of homicide in Victoria. In D. Chappell, P. Grabosky, & H. Strang (Eds.), *Australian violence: Contemporary perspectives* (pp. 53–118). Canberra: Australian Institute of Criminology.

Pope, W. (1976). *Durkheim's suicide: A classic analyzed*. Chicago, IL: University of Chicago Press.

Pruitt, M., & Jackson, T. (1999). Perspectives on the divorce process: Parental perceptions of the legal system and its effect on family members. *American Academy of Psychiatry and the Law, 29*, 18–28.

Pruitt, D. G., & Rubin, J. Z. (1986). *Social conflict: Escalation, stalemate and settlement*. New York: Random House.

Qin, P., Agerbo, E., Westergaard-Neilson, N., Eriksson, T., & Mortensen, P. B. (2000). Gender differences in risk factors for suicide in Denmark. *British Journal of Psychiatry, 177*, 546–550.

Qin, P., & Mortensen, P. (2003). The impact of parental status on completed suicide. *Archives of General Psychiatry, 60*, 797–802.

Quinn, K. (2003). Justice for vulnerable and intimidated witnesses in adversarial proceedings. *Modern Law Review, 66*, 139–155.

Radford, L. (1992). Introduction. In J. Radford, & D. E. Russell (Eds.), *Femicide* (pp. 3–12). New York: Twayne.

Radford, J., & Russell, D. H. (Eds.), (1992). *Femicide: The politics of woman Killing*. New York: Twayne Publishers.

Rand, M., & Catalano, S. (2007). *Criminal victimization, 2006*. Bureau of Justice Statistics Bulletin, Department of Justice. http://ojp.gov/bjs/pub/cv06.pdf.

Ray, L. (2011). *Violence and society*. Thousand Oaks, CA: Sage.

Redwood (2013). http://www.theredwood.com/indexc.php?id=1&content=we%20can%20help%20you.
Rennison, C. (2003). *Intimate partner violence, 1993-2001*. Crime brief data. Washington, DC: Bureau of Justice Statistics.
Rennison, C., & Welchans, S. (2000). *Intimate partner violence*. Washington, DC: Bureau of Justice Statistics.
Repetti, R. L. (2001). Searching for the roots of marital conflict in uxoricides and uxorious husbands. In A. Booth, A. C. Crouter, & M. Clements (Eds.), *Couples in conflict* (pp. 47–56). Mahwah, NJ: Lawrence Erlbaum.
Resolution (2012). *Mediation assessment meetings are not working as they should*. www.familylawwek.co.uk,/siteaspx?i=edp6933.
Rhatigan, D. L., Street, A. E., & Axsom, D. K. (2006). A critical review of theories to explain violent relationship termination: Implications for research and intervention. *Clinical Psychology Review, 26*, 321–345.
Richards, L. (2009a). *Domestic abuse, stalking and honour based violence (DASH) 2009*. Created on behalf of the Association of Chief Police Officers (ACPO) and in partnership with Coordinated Action Against Domestic Abuse (CAADA). www@laurarichards.co.uk.
Richards, L. (2009b). *DASH (2009) frequently asked questions (FAQ's)*. Guidelines were created on behalf of ACPO in partnership with CAADA. www@laurarichards.co.uk.
Roberts, A. R. (1996). Battered women who kill: A comparative study of incarcerated participants with a community sample of battered women. *Journal of Family Violence, 1*, 291–304.
Roberts, N., & Noller, P. (1998). The association between adult association and couple violence. In J. A. Simpson, & W. S. Rholes (Eds.), *Attachment theory in close relationships* (pp. 166–188). New York: Guilford Press.
Rodgers, K., & MacDonald, G. (2000). Canada's shelters for abused women. *Canadian social trends, 3*. Toronto: Thompson. 248–252.
Roehl, J., O'Sullivan, C., Webster, D., & Campbell, J. (2005). *Intimate partner risk assessment validation study: The RAVE study, practitioners summary and recommendations-validation of tools for assessing risk from violent intimate partners*. Washington, DC: Department of Justice.
Rogge, R. D., & Bradbury, T. N. (1999). Til violence do us part: The differing roles of communication and aggression in predicting adverse marital outcomes. *Journal of Consulting and Clinical Psychology, 67*, 340–351.
Rosenbaum, M. (1990). The role of depression in couples involved in murder-suicide and homicide. *American Journal of Psychiatry, 147*, 1036–1039.
Rosenfeld, D. I. (2012). The high risk team model and GTS offender monitoring: Stopping DV in its tracks. *Domestic Violence Report, 17*, 31–48.
Ross, J. M., & Babcock, J. C. (2009). Proactive and reactive violence among intimate partner men diagnosed with antisocial and borderline personality disorder. *Journal of Family Violence, 24*, 607–617.
Roy, D. (2011). *An introduction to forced marriage in the South Asian community in the United States*. Manavi Occasional paper No 9. New Brunswick, NJ: Manavi.
Rudd, M. D. (2006). A test of the effectiveness of a list of suicide warning signs for the public. *Suicide and Life-threatening Behavior, 36*, 272–287.
Russell, D. E. (2001). Defining femicide and related concepts. In D. E. Russell, & R. A. Harmes (Eds.), *Femicide in global perspective* (pp. 12–18). New York: Teacher's College Press.
Ryan, A. (July 12, 2013). Statistics show that most British children will be born out of wedlock by 2016. *The Globe and Mail*, L4.
Safrath, B. A. (2013). *Difference between order of protection and restraining order, eHow contributer*. http://www.ehow.com/facts_5759194_difference-order-protection-restraining-order.html.

Sampson, R. (1989). The promises and pitfalls of macro-level research. *The Criminologist, 14* (pp. 1, 5, 10, and 11).

Sampson, R. J., Raudenbush, S. W., & Earls, F. (1979). Neighbourhoods and violent crime: A multi-level study of collective efficacy. *Science, 227,* 918–923.

Sanctuary (2013). *A say in the life: Domestic violence shelter.* http://sanctuaryforfamilies.org/index.php?option=com_content&task=view&id=351&Itemid-256.

Sander, F., & Goldberg, S. B. (1994). Fitting the forum to the fuss: A user-friendly guide to selecting an ADR procedure. *Negotiation Journal, January,* 49–68.

Sansome, R. A., Gaither, G. A., & Songer, D. A. (2002). Self-harm behaviors across the life-cycle: A pilot study of in-patients with borderline personality disorder. *Comprehensive Psychiatry, 43,* 215–218.

Sbarra, D. A., Law, R. W., & Portley, R. M. (2011). Divorce and death: A meta-analysis and research agenda for clinical, social and health psychology. *Perspectives on Psychological Science, 6,* 454–474.

Schechter, S. (1982). *Women and male violence.* Boston, MA: South End Press.

Schneider, A. K., & Mills, N. (2006). What family lawyers are really doing when they negotiate. *Family Court Review, 44,* 612–622.

Schneider, J. (1971). Of vigilance and virgins: Honor, shame and access to resources in Mediterranean societies. *Ethnology, 10,* 1–24.

Schneider, E. M. (1986). Describing and changing: Women's self defence work and the problem of expert testimony on battering. *Women's Rights Law Reporter, 4,* 16–21.

Schwartz, L. L., & Kaslow, F. W. (1997). *Painful partings: Divorce and its aftermath.* New York: Wiley.

Seedat, S., Stein, M. B., & Forde, D. R. (2005). Association between physical partner violence, posttraumatic stress, childhood trauma and suicide attempts. *Violence and Victims, 20,* 87–98.

Semin, G. R. (1980). Social psychology: A gloss on attribution theory. *British Journal of Clinical and Social Psychology, 19,* 291–300.

Sepp, S. D., Smith, T. D., Morse, J. Q., Hallquist, M. N., & Pilkonis, P. A. (2012). Prospective associations between borderline personality disorder symptoms, interpersonal problems and aggressive behaviors. *Journal of Interpersonal Violence, 27,* 103–124.

Serran, G., & Firestone, P. (2004). Intimate partner homicide: A review of the male proprietariness and self defence theories. *Aggression and Violent Behavior, 9,* 1–15.

Sev'er, A. (1997). Recent or imminent separation and intimate violence against women. *Violence Against Women, 3,* 566–589.

Sev'er, A. (2002). Flight of abused women, plight of Canadian shelters, another road to homelessness. *Journal of Social Distress and the Hopeless, 11*(4), 307–324.

Shackelford, T. (2001). Cohabitation, marriage and murder: Woman-killing by male romantic partners. *Aggressive Behavior, 27,* 284–291.

Shackleford, T. K. (2000). Reproductive-age women are overrepresented among perpetrators of husband killing. *Aggressive Behavior, 26,* 309–317.

Shaheen, K. A., Thakor, S., & Stewart, D. E. (2012). Turning points for perpetrators of intimate partner violence. *Trauma Violence Abuse, 13,* 30–40.

Shelters and Safehouses (2006). *Stop violence against women.* http://www1.umn.edu/humanrts/svaw/domestic/link/shelters.htm.

Sherif, M., & Hovland, C. I. (1961). *Social judgment: Assimilation and contrast effects in communication and attitude change.* New Haven: Yale University Press.

Sherman, K. (1992). *Policing domestic violence: Experiments and dilemmas.* New York: Free Press.

Sherman, L. W., & Berk, R. A. (1984). The specific deterrent effects of arrests for domestic assault. *American Sociological Review, 49,* 261–283.

Shorter, E. (1975). *The making of the modern family.* New York: Basic Books.

Showalter, C. R., Bonnie, R. J., & Roddy, V. (1980). The spousal homicide syndrome. *International Journal of Law and Psychiatry, 3*, 117–141.

Silverman, R., & Kennedy, L. (1993). *Deadly deeds*. Scarborough, ON: Nelson.

Silverman, R., & Mukerjee, S. K. (1987). Intimate homicide: Analysis of violent social relationships. *Behavioral Sciences and the Law, 5*, 37–47.

Simmel, G. (1955). *Conflict*. Translated by Kurt Wolff. Glencoe, IL: The Free Press.

Simon, T. R., Anderson, M., Thompson, M. P., Crosby, A., & Sacks, J. J. (2002). Assault victimization, suicidal ideation and behavior within a national sample of U.S. adults. *Suicide and Life-threatening Behavior, 32*, 42–50.

Singh, J. P. (2012). *Problems of India's changing family and state intervention*. Patna (Bihar), India: Department of Sociology, Patna University. Contact jpsingh1950@hotmail.com.

Sinha, M. (2012). Family violence in Canada, A Statistical Profile, 2010, *Statistics Canada*, 85-002-X, Juristat. Statistics Canada, "Homicide in Canada, 2011" (p. 11). http://www.statcan.gc.ca/pub/85-002-x/2012001/article/11738-eng.pdf.

Skogman, K., Alsen, M., & Ojehagen, A. (2004). Sex difference in risk factors for suicide after attempted suicide: A follow-up study of 1,052 suicide attempters. *Social Psychiatry Psychiatric Epidemiology, 39*, 113–120.

Skolnick, A. S. (1987). *The intimate environment: Exploring marriage and the family*. Boston: Little, Brown & Company.

Snider, C., Webster, D., O'Sullivan, C. S., & Campbell, J. (2009). Intimate partners violence: Development of a brief risk assessment for the emergency department. *Emergency Medicine, 16*, 1208–1216.

Snyder, R. L. (July 22, 2013). A raised hand: Can a new approach curb domestic homicide? *New Yorker*, 34–41.

Soloff, P. H., Lynch, G. G., Kelly, T. M., & Mann, J. J. (2000). Characteristics of suicide attempts of patients with major depressive episode and borderline personality disorder. *American Journal of Psychiatry, 157*, 601–608.

Spanier, G. B., & Casto, R. F. (1979). Adjustment to separation and divorce: A qualitative analysis. In G. Levinger, & O. C. Moles (Eds.), *Divorce and separation: Context, causes and consequences* (pp. 201–210). New York: Basic Books.

Spitzberg, B. (2002). The tactical topography of stalking victimization and management. *Trauma Violence Abuse, 3*, 261–288.

Stack, S. (1997). Homicide followed by suicide: An analysis of Chicago data. *Criminology, 35*, 435–453.

Stack, S. (2000). Suicide: A 15 year review of sociological literature, Part II: Modernization and social integration. *Suicide and Life-threatening Behavior, 30*, 163–176.

Stanley, B. (2008). Prospective predictors of suicide attempts in borderline personality disorder at one, two and two-to-five year follow-up. *Journal of Personality Disorders, 22*, 1123–1134.

Stark, E., & Flitcraft, A. (1996). *Women at risk*. London: Sage.

Statistics Canada (2009). *Violence against women…by the numbers*. http://www42.statcan.ca/smr08/2009/smr08_136_2009-eng.htm.

Statistics Canada (2011). *Homicide survey*. Ottawa: Centre for Justice Statistics.

Stensrud, A. (2005). *Toward a better understanding of the needs of shelter users: A consultation with shelter residents and workers*. Regina, Saskatchewan: PATHS.

Stets, J., & Straus, M. A. (1990). Gender differences in reporting marital violence and its medical and psychological consequences. In M. A. Straus, & R. J. Gelles (Eds.), *Physical violence in American families: Risk factors and adaptations to violence in 8,145 families* (pp. 151–166). New Brunswick, NJ: Transaction.

Stevenson, B., & Wolfers, J. (2000). *Til death do us part: Effects of divorce laws on suicide and intimate homicide*. Department of Economics, Harvard University. Manuscript.

Stewart, K. A., Thakor, S., & Stewart, D. E. (2012). Turning points for perpetrators of intimate partner violence. *Trauma, Violence & Abuse, 13*, 30–40.

Stone, L. (1992). *Broken lives: Separation and divorce in England 1660–1857*. New York: Oxford University Press.

Stone, M., Hurt, S., & Stone, D. (1987). Long-term follow-up of borderline patients meeting DSM III criteria. *Journal of Personality Disorders, 1*, 291–298.

Stout, K. D. (1989). "Intimate femicide": Effect of legislation and social services. *Affilia, 4*(2), 21–30.

Stout, K. D. (1993). Intimate femicide: A study of men who have killed their mates. *Journal of Offender Rehabilitation, 19*, 81–94.

Stover, C. S., Meadow, A. L., & Kaufman, J. (2009). Interventions for intimate partner violence, research and implications for evidence-based practice. *Professional Psychology, 40*(3), 223–233.

Straus, M. A. (1978). Measuring intra-family conflict and violence. *Journal of Marriage and the Family, 40*, 84–92.

Straus, M. A., & Gelles, R. (1990). *Physical violence in American families: Risk factors and adaptations to violence in 8,145 families*. New Brunswick, NJ: Transaction Publishers.

Straus, M. A., Hamby, S. L., Boney-McCoy, S., & Sugarman, D. S. (1996). The revised conflict tactics scales: Development and preliminary psychometric data. *Journal of Family Issues, 17*, 283–316.

Striving to Meet the Need (2008). *Summary of services provided by domestic and sexual violence programs in Oregon: DHS child welfare programs*.

Stuart, G. L., Moore, T. M., Hellmuth, J. C., Ramsey, S. E., & Kahler, C. W. (2006). Reasons for intimate partner violence perpetration among arrested women. *Violence Against Women, 12*, 609–612.

Stuckless, N., & Toner, B. (1998). *Sequential victimization: The influence of post-assault events on victims of violence*. Unpublished Social Sciences Humanities Research Council Postdoctoral Study. University of Toronto, Department of Psychiatry.

Sullivan, C., & Bybee, D. (1999). Reducing violence using community based advocacy for women with abusive partners. *Journal of Counselling and Clinical Psychology, 67*(1), 43–53.

Sullivan, C. M., & Bybee, D. I. (2000). *Using a longitudinal data set to further our understanding of the trajectory of intimate violence over time, final report*. Washington, DC: U.S. Department of Justice.

Tanay, E. (1976). *The murderers*. Indianapolis: The Bobbs-Merrill Co.

Tauchen, H., & Witte, A. D. (1995). The dynamics of domestic violence. *American Economic Review, 85*, 414–418.

Taylor, S. (1982). *Durkheim and the study of suicide*. London: Macmillan.

Tesler, P. H. (2008). *Collaborative law: Achieving effective resolution in divorce without litigation*. Chicago: American Bar Association.

Thernstrom, M. (August 24, 2003). Untying the knot. *The New York Times Magazine*, 38–44.

Thibaut, J., & Kelley, H. (1959). *The social psychology of groups*. New York: Wiley.

Thomas, S. (October 16, 2002). Ontario rise in spousal murders sign of things to come in B.C.—activists. *Vancouver Courier Newspaper*.

Thomas, W. I. (1966). The relation of research to the social process. In M. Janowitz (Ed.), *W.I. Thomas on social organization and social personality* (pp. 289–305). Chicago, IL: University of Chicago Press.

Tierney, K. (1982). The battered woman movement and the creation of the wife beating problem. *Social Problems, 3*(29), 207–220.
Tilley, N., & Pawson, R. (1997). *Realistic evaluation.* London: Routledge.
Timmermans, S. (2005). Suicide determination and the professional authority of medical examiners. *American Sociological Review, 70,* 311–333.
Tjaden, P., & Thoennes, N. (2000). Prevalence and consequences of male-to-female intimate partner violence as measured by the National Violence Against Women survey. *Violence Against Women, 6,* 142–161.
Torre, E., Chieppa, N., Imperatori, F., Jona, A., Ponzetti, D., & Usai, C. (1999). Suicide and attempted suicide in the province of Turin from 1988 to 1994: Epidemiological analysis. *European Journal of Psychiatry, 13,* 77–86.
Totman, J. (1978). *The murderess: A psychosocial study of criminal homicide.* San Francisco, CA: R &E Research Associates.
Totton, T. (2001). *Spousal violence after marital separation.* Ottawa: Canadian Centre for Justice Statistics. *Juristat, 21*(7).
Townsen, M. (2009). *Canadian women on their own are the poorest of the poor.* Canadian Centre for Policy Alternatives.
Trabold, N. (2007). Screening for intimate partner violence within a health care setting. *Social Work in Health Care, 45,* 1–18.
Trainor, C. (1999). Canada's shelters for abused women. *Juristat, 19*(6), 7.
Tutty, L. (1998). *The importance of follow-up programs for abused women.* Paper presented at the program evaluation and family violence research. Durham: University of New Hampshire.
Tutty, L., Bidwood, B., & Rothery, M. (1993). Support groups for battered women: Research on their efficacy. *Journal of Family Violence, 8*(4), 325–343.
Twenge, J. M. (1997). Attitudes towards women, 1970–1995: A meta-analysis. *Psychology of Women Quarterly, 21,* 35–51.
Unnithan, N. F., Huff-Corzine, L., Corzine, J., & Whitt, H. P. (1994). *The currents of lethal violence: An integrated model of homicide and suicide.* Albany, NY: State University Press of New York.
U.S. Bureau of the Census (1945). *Deaths from selected causes by marital status, by age and sex.* Washington, DC.
United States Census (2010), Department of Commerce, Washington DC.
Vallee, B. (1998). *Life and death with Billy.* Toronto: Seal Books.
van Wormer, K. (2008). The dynamics of murder-suicide in domestic situations. *Brief Treatment and Crisis Intervention, 8,* 3 (August).
Ver Steeg, N. (2003). Yes, no and maybe: Informed decision-making about divorce mediation in the presence of violence. *William and Mary School of Law, 9,* 145–206.
Violence Policy Center (2006). *American roulette: Murder-suicide in the United States.* Washington, DC.
Vites, K. A., & Sorenson, S. B. (2008). Restraining orders among victims of intimate homicide. *Injury Prevention, 14,* 191–195.
Walby, S. (1990). *Theorizing patriarchy.* London: Basil Blackwell.
Walby, S., & Myhill, A. (2001). Assessing and managing risk. In J. Taylor-Browne (Ed.), *What works in reducing domestic violence? A comprehensive guide for professionals.* London: Whiting-Birch.
Waldron, J. F. (2012). *Domestic violence and mandatory arrest: Influences on police officer actions.* El Paso, TX: LBF Scholarly Publishing LLC.

Walker, L. (1978). The battered woman and learned helplessness. *Victimology, 2*, 525–534.

Walker, L. (1979). *The battered woman*. New York: Harper and Row.

Walker, R. Logan, T. K., Jordan, C. E., & Campbell, J. C. (2004). An integrative review of separation in the context of victimization: Consequences and implications for women. *Trauma, Violence & Abuse, 5*, 143–193.

Wallace, A. (1986). *Homicide: The social reality*. New South Wales, Australia: New South Wales Bureau of Crime Statistics and Research.

Wallerstein, J. S., & Kelly, J. B. (1980). *Surviving the breakup: How children cope with divorce*. New York: Basic Books.

Wardle, L. D. (1994). *No-fault divorce and the divorce conundrum*. Paper presented at the Reuben, J. Clark Law School Family Law Symposium, Brigham Young University.

Weber, M. (1947). *The theory of social and economic organization*. Translated by Anderson, A. M., & Talcott Parsons. New York: Oxford University Press.

Websdale, N. (1999). *Understanding domestic homicide*. Boston: Northeastern University Press.

Weiss, R. (1975). *Marital separation*. New York: Basic Books.

Weiss, R. (1979). The emotional impact of separation. In G. Levinger, & O. C. Moles (Eds.), *Divorce and separation: Context, causes and consequences* (pp. 184–200). New York: Basic Books.

Welchan, L., & Hossain, S. (2005). Naming the crime: "Honour" rights and wrongs. In L. Welchan, & S. Hossain (Eds.), *Honour: Crimes, paradigms and violence against women* (pp. 1–21). London: Zed Press.

Wells, W., Ren, L., & DeLeon-Granados, W. (2010). Reducing intimate partner homicides: The effects of federally-funded shelter service availability in California. *Journal of Criminal Justice, 38*, 512–519.

West, D. J. (1966). *Murder followed by suicide*. Cambridge, MA: Harvard University Press.

Widyono, M. (2008). *Conceptualizing femicide. Strengthening understanding of femicide: Using research to galvanize action and accountability* (pp. 7–23). Washington, DC: World Health Organization Conference.

Wilbanks, W. (1984). *Murder in Miami*. Lanham, MD: University Press of America.

Wilson, M. (1985). Marital conflict and homicide in evolutionary perspective. In R. J. Gelles, & N. J. Bell (Eds.), *Sociobiology and the social sciences*. Lubbock, TX: Texas Tech University Press.

Wilson, M., & Daly, M. (1989). Marital conflict and homicide in evolutionary perspective. In R. W. Bell, & N. J. Bell (Eds.), *Sociobiology and the social sciences*. Lubbock, TX: Texas Tech University Press.

Wilson, M., & Daly, M. (1992). Till death do us part. In J. Radford, & D. Russell (Eds.), *Femicide: The politics of woman-killing* (pp. 83–98). New York: Twane.

Wilson, M., & Daly, M. (1993). Spousal homicide risk and estrangement. *Violence and Victims, 8*, 3–16.

Wilson, M., & Daly, M. (1994). Spousal homicide. *Juristat*. Cat. 85–002. Ottawa: Centre for Justice Statistics, Statistics Canada.

Wilson, M., & Daly, M. (1996). Male sexual proprietariness and violence against wives. *Current Directions in Psychological Science, 5*, 2–7.

Wilson, M., & Daly, M. (2001). Lethal and non-lethal violence against wives and the evolutionary psychology of male sexual proprietariness. In R. E. Dobash, & R. P. Dobash (Eds.), *Rethinking violence against wives* (pp. 199–230). Thousand Oaks, CA: Sage.

Wilson, M., & Daly, M. (2002). The evolutionary psychology of couple conflict in registered versus de facto unions. In A. Booth, A. C. Crouter, & M. Clements (Eds.), *Couples in conflict* (pp. 3–26). Mahwah, NJ: Lawrence Erlbaum.

Winstock, Z. (2013). *Partner violence: A new paradigm for understanding conflict escalation*. New York: Springer.

Winstock, Z., & Eisikovits, Z. (2007). Motives and control in escalatory conflicts in intimate relationships. *Children and Youth Services Review, 30*, 287–296.

Wiseman, R. (2010). *The honour killings debate in Canada: A discussion paper prepared for the Sheldon Chumir Foundation for Ethics in leadership*. Toronto.

Wolfgang, M. E. (1958). *Patterns of criminal homicide*. Philadelphia: University of Philadelphia Press.

Wolfgang, M. E. (1962). Victim-precipitated criminal homicide. In M. Wolfgang, l. Savitz, & N. Johnson (Eds.), *The sociology of crime and delinquency* (pp. 388–396). New York: Wiley.

World Health Organization (2008). When love kills: Strengthening understanding of femicide. In Conference held in Washington DC, April 14–16. Convened jointly with PATH, Inter-Cambios and the Research Council of South Africa.

World Health Report (2002). *World report on violence and health*. In E. G. Krug, L. L. Dahlberg, J. A. Mercy, A. B. Zwi, & R. Lozano (Eds.). (Geneva).

Wyder, M., Ward, P., & De Leo, D. (2009). Separation as a risk factor. *Journal of Affective Disorders, 116*, 208–213.

Wyder, M., Ward, P., & De Leo, D. (2009). Separation as a suicide risk factor. *Journal of Affective Disorders, 116*, 208–213.

Yang, M., Wong, S. C. P., & Coid, J. (2010). The efficacy of violence prediction: A meta-analytic comparison of nine risk assessment tools. *Psychological Bulletin, 136*, 740–767.

Yllo, K., & Straus, M. (1984). Patriarchy and violence against wives: The impact of structural and normative factors. *Journal of International and Comparative Social Welfare, 1*, 16–29.

York Region Violence Against Women Coordinating Committee (2009). *Mapping violence against women services in York region*. http://www.yrvawcc.ca/site/pdfs/Mapping%20Report%20-%20final.pdf.

Author Index

Note: Page numbers followed by "*f*" indicate figures; "*t*" tables; "*b*" boxes.

A

Adams, J. S., 18, 67
Adler, J. S., 24, 86–87, 106–109, 114, 117–118, 120
Agnew, R., 49–50
Albrecht, S., 169
Aldridge, M. L., 25, 31–33
Allen, N. H., 23–24
Alsen, M., 132
Anderson, D., 78–79, 83–84, 156
Anderson-Block, K., 68
Anderson, D. K., 5, 10–11, 160, 163–164, 169–170
Arendell, T., 3, 9, 82–83, 88–89, 95, 150
Asher, S. J., 1–2
Aston, C., 31–32, 34, 41
Atkinson, J. M., 19–21
Aubert, V., 79
Axsom, D. K., 10

B

Badkhen, A., 159
Baechler, J., 19–21, 131
Bancroft, L., 23–24, 76–77
Bandura, A., 117
Banks, I., 16, 24
Bankstron, W. B., 56, 82, 89, 91
Barber, C. W., 16
Barker, L., 1, 55
Barnard, G. W., 51
Barraclough, B., 16, 39, 132
Beh, S. L., 38
Belknap, J., 56
Bennett, M. D., 153, 155
Bergman, B., 134–135
Berk, R. A., 139–140, 147–148
Berkowitz, L., 117
Bernal, M., 132
Bernard, J., 3–4, 9, 94
Bernard, T. J., 49–50, 59–60
Bhargava, N., 77
Black, D., 23–24, 78, 86–87, 103–104
Blair-West, G. W., 132
Block, C. R., 8–9, 15, 32–33, 36, 42–43, 47, 49–50, 54–59, 91–92
Bloom, B. L., 1–2
Bograd, M., 94
Boles, S. M., 113–114
Bonnie, R. J., 25–26
Bourget, D., 39, 55, 60–61
Bowker, L. H., 58, 60
Bowlby, J., 118, 123–124
Bradbury, T. N., 10, 79, 97
Braver, S. L., 82–83, 90
Breault, K. D., 36
Brismar, B., 134–135
Broadhurst, R. G., 38
Brodsky, B., 24, 132–133, 135
Browne, A., 15, 25, 32, 45–49, 51, 54, 58–60, 134
Browne, K. D., 25, 31–33, 160
Browning, J. J., 111–113
Brownridge, D. A., 31–33
Burch, T. K., 77
Burns, S., 7
Buss, D. M., 25–26, 63, 64, 70–73, 78, 82, 86, 94, 137
Butts, J., 36, 38
Buzawa, E. S., 147
Buzawa, C. G., 147

C

Campbell, J. C., 15, 23–24, 32–33, 36, 67, 69, 80, 112–114, 139–141, 144, 158, 161–162, 165, 182–186
Cantor, C., 129–134
Caputi, J., 23–24
Carcach, C., 38–39, 114
Carnevale, P. J., 79, 81
Casto, R. F., 150
Catalino, S., 139–140
Cavan, R., 16, 24
Cavanagh, K., 36, 66–67, 75–76, 93
Chan, C. Y., 38
Chaucer, G., 94
Cherlin, J., 1–2, 8
Chimbos, P., 55, 59–60, 68, 92
Choice, P., 81
Christakos, A., 36
Clarkin, J., 131–132
Coleman, D. H., 94
Conner, K. R., 132–133
Coon, M. H., 104
Cooney, M., 74

Cooper, M., 23–24, 100, 119–120
Coser, L. A., 61, 82
Costa, P. T., Jr., 59–60
Crawford, M., 36–37, 39, 102, 112–113
Crimmins, S., 81, 134
Cross, S. E., 9
Cummings, E. M., 97

D

Daly, M., 9, 14, 24–25, 34–38, 43, 47–48, 52, 55–56, 58, 61, 64–68, 72, 76, 78, 84, 86, 91–93, 96, 99–101, 103–104, 119–120, 128–129
Danigelis, N., 121, 124, 126–127, 129, 136–137
Davies, M., 134
Davies, P., 97
Dawkins, R., 64
Dawson, M., 15–19, 31–32, 34, 36
Dee, T. S., 56, 88–89, 95
DeKeseredy, W., 32–33, 47, 56
De Leo, D., 31–32, 41, 129–131
DeLeon-Granados, W., 157, 165–167
DeMaris, A., 10
Demo, D. H., 78
Denney, J. T., 127–129
Diserood, D., 132
Dobash, R. E., 31–32, 36, 66–67, 73–76, 84, 93–96, 101–102
Dobash, R. P., 17–18, 25–26, 47, 50, 66–67, 73–76, 84, 93–96
Dollard, J., 108–109, 116–117
Douglas, J. D., 19–21, 137
Dunford, F., 148
Duntley, J. D., 26, 64, 70–71, 86, 137
Durkheim, E., 19–21, 108, 121–130, 136–137
Durrant, R., 25, 72–73
Dutton, D. G., 24–26, 36, 39, 55–56, 102–103, 111–113, 118, 123–124

E

Earls, F., 45–46
Easteal, E. W., 48, 53, 55, 59, 61
Easteal, P. W., 38, 18–19, 25, 31–32, 37–39, 47, 51
Eaves, D., 23–24, 100, 119–120
Edwards, J. N., 78
Eisikovits, Z., 85
Elias, N., 86
Eliason, S., 25
Elliott, D. S., 148
Ellis, D., 3–5, 23–25, 33, 47, 56, 70, 78–79, 81, 83–84, 89–90, 101–102, 115, 117–120, 143–144, 147, 150–152, 156, 161, 184, 187

Emery, R. E., 83, 89–90
Ettlinger, R. W., 137

F

Ferraro, K. J., 148
Fine, M. A., 79, 97
Firestone, P., 23–24
Fisher, R., 152
Flitcraft, A., 134–135
Flordah, P., 137
Flynn, S., 16, 54–55, 87
Foucault, M., 94–95
Frances, A., 131–132
Fry, D. P., 72, 78
Fryer, M., 131–132

G

Gabriel, T., 7
Gagne, P., 39, 55, 60–61
Garcia, L., 25, 31–33, 36
Gartner, R., 15, 36–37, 39, 102, 112–113
Gauthier, D. K., 56, 82, 89, 91
Gavigan, S., 95
Gelles, R., 26, 78, 86
Gillespie, C., 86–87
Gillespie, M., 118
Gillis, A. R., 87–88
Glass, N., 69
Godbole, A., 114
Goetting, A., 45, 51, 55, 112–113
Gold, M., 123–124
Goldberg, S. B., 83
Golding, J. M., 134–135
Gondolf, E. W., 80
Goode, W. J., 81
Gottman, J. M., 153, 155
Gould, S. J., 64
Goussinsky, R., 25–26, 81, 107
Grabosky, P. N. P. N., 38–39, 114
Graham, K., 54–55
Grant, B. C., 49–50, 52, 55
Gulliver, P., 83–84, 156
Gunderson, J. G., 111
Guttmacher, M. S., 67–68

H

Hagerty, K. D., 149
Hall-Smith, P., 36
Hamby, S. L., 81
Harper, D. W., 17–18, 103–104
Harris, E. C., 16, 39, 132–133

Hassan, R., 130
Hawton, K., 132–133
Hearn, V., 86–87, 118
Hedeem, T., 90
Hegerl, U., 132
Heider, F., 104
Hengeveld, M., 102
Henry, A. F., 86–87, 104, 108–109, 116–118, 122–124, 137
Hetherington, E. M., 8–9
Hirsch, C. S., 16, 132
Hirsch, T., 102
Hobbes, T., 79
Hoffman, K., 78
Holmes, T. H., 1–2
Hossain, S., 74
Hotton, T., 16, 31–32, 34–37, 68–69
Hovland, C. I., 47
Huer, L. B., 87
Hughes, S., 153, 155
Huizinga, D., 148
Humphrey, J. A., 24
Hunnicutt, G., 74–75
Hurt, S. W., 131–132
Hurwitz, E. L., 25, 31–33, 36

I

Ide, N., 41–42
Isacsson, G., 132
Iyengar, R., 148–149

J

Jackson, T., 83, 150
Jacobs, S., 25, 45, 50, 60, 134
Jacobson, G. F., 8–9
Jensen, V., 45, 50, 55, 60
Johnson, H., 15–16, 21, 23, 31–32, 34, 68–69, 74, 96
Johnson, M., 1–2, 5, 80
Jones, A., 45, 47
Jordan, C. E., 32–33
Jurik, N. C., 55

K

Kaighobadi, F., 65
Kalmuss, D. S., 81
Kandiyoti, D., 70, 77, 78
Kaslow, F. W., 1–2
Katkin, D. M., 49–50, 59–60
Kay, M., 159, 162–163
Kellerman, A. I., 19, 55

Kelley, H., 94–95
Kelley, H. H., 104
Kelly, J. B., 21, 23
Kennedy, L., 55, 80–81
Kerry, G., 24, 36, 39, 102–103, 112, 119
Kemmelmeier, M., 104
King, D., 77
Koenrdraat, F., 102
Kolves, K., 40–41, 130–131, 133–135
Kowalski, M., 37–38, 80–81, 134
Koziol-McLain, J., 9, 19, 24, 39, 69–70
Kposowa, A. J., 31–32, 36, 40, 129, 136–137
Kruk, E., 1–2
Kulwicki, A., 74
Kurz, D., 3, 10, 36, 83

L

Lakoff, G., 1–2, 80
Landenburger, K., 5
Large, M. N., 16
Law, T. C., 8–9, 43
Lecomte, D., 132
Leon, A. C., 132–133
Leone, J. M., 135
Levi, K., 81, 134
Lewontin, R. C., 64
Liem, M., 16, 24, 38, 102–103, 105–106, 113, 119, 132
Linehan, M., 131–133
Lofland, J., 49
Logan, J., 30, 39, 150, 168
Logan, J. K., 32–33
Logan, T. K., 32–33, 90
Lund, L. E., 24, 31–32, 38

M

MacCharles, T., 22–23
Madsen, L., 9
Mahoney, M., 23–25, 60, 96
Makin, K., 22–23
Malone, K. M., 132–133
Maris, R. W., 124
Marsiglio, W., 74
Marzuk, P. M., 16, 24, 102, 132
McCrae, R. R., 59–60
McFarlane, J., 36, 134–135
McGirr, A., 132–133
Medina-Ariza, J., 36, 66–67
Megargee, E., 59
Mercy, J. A., 56, 134
Merton, R. K., 29

Messing, J. T., 144, 167–168, 180–181, 184–187
Miller, N., 117
Mills, N., 90
Milroy, C. M., 16, 24, 31–32, 38–39
Miner, E. J., 92
Miotto, K., 113–114
Mnookin, R., 96, 150
Moamai, J., 39
Montgomery, S., 157
Moracco, K. M., 36, 38
Mortensen, P. B., 132
Morton, E., 23–24, 38–39, 116
Mosiciki, E. K., 132
Mouzas, J., 134
Mukerjee, S. K., 104
Myhill, A., 140

N

Newman, G., 51
Nieuwbeerta, P., 16, 38, 102
Noller, P., 111–112, 114, 119
Nye, J., 7

O

O'Connell, D., 82–83
O'Connor, G. O., 8–9
O'Sullivan, C. S., 69
Odoms, T., 97
Ogle, R. S., 25, 45, 49–50, 59–60, 134
Ojehagen, A., 132
Okun, L., 5
Oquendo, M. A., 132
Oyserman, D., 104

P

Palermo, G. B., 24, 102
Palmer, S., 24
Parradine, K., 148
Patton, W., 152
Paymar, M., 22, 94
Pearson, J., 90
Pence, E., 22, 94
Penrod, S., 87
Pinchevsky, G. M., 45–46
Pinker, S., 72, 76, 86
Pleck, J. H., 74
Polk, K., 17–18, 100–102
Pope, W., 121, 124, 126–127, 129, 136–137
Porter, B., 29–30
Portley, R. M., 43

Portuges, S. H., 8–9
Postulart, M., 38, 102
Pottie-Bunge, V., 31–32, 34, 41
Pruett, M., 83, 150
Pruitt, D. G., 79, 81, 155

Q

Qin, P., 132

R

Radford. L., 14, 31–32
Rahe, R.H., 1–2
Rand, M., 139–140
Raudenbush, S. W., 45–46
Ray, L., 148–149
Rennison, C., 31–32
Repetti, R. L., 43
Rhatigan, D. L., 10
Rich, C. L., 132
Richards, L., 145–146
Roberts, D. W., 24, 38, 80, 102, 132
Roberts, N., 114, 119
Roddy, V., 25–26
Roehl, J., 182–186
Rogge, R. D., 10, 79, 97
Rosenbaum, M., 39
Rubin, J. Z., 155
Runyan, C. W., 15, 23–24
Russell, D. E., 14–15, 23–24, 31–32
Ryan, A., 7

S

Sakinofsky, I., 9, 18–19, 33, 78
Salem, P., 90
Saltzman, L. E., 56, 134
Sampson, R., 45–46, 60, 95–96, 117–118
Sander, F., 83
Sansome, R. A., 132–133
Saunders, D. G., 5, 10–11
Sbarra, D. A., 43
Schechter, S., 59
Schneider, A. K., 90
Schneider, E. M., 59
Schneider, J., 70
Schwartz, L. L., 1–2
Seedat, S., 134–135
Semin, G. R., 106
Serran, G., 23–24
Sev'er, A., 36, 76
Shackleford, T. K., 86

Shaheen, K. A., 58
Sherif, M., 47
Sherman, L. W., 139–140, 147–149
Short, J. F., 86–87, 108–109, 116–118, 122–124, 137
Shorter, E., 108
Showalter, C. R., 25–26
Silverman, R. A., 55, 80–81, 86–87, 104, 118
Simmel, G., 23, 79, 82, 86–87
Simon, T. R., 134–135
Singh, G. K., 36
Skogman, K., 132
Skolnick, A. S., 8
Slator, P., 130
Smorodinsky, S., 24, 31–32, 38
Snider, C., 69
Snyder, R. L., 141–143, 162
Soderberg, P., 72, 78, 86
Soloff, P. H., 132–133
Soria, C., 25, 31–33, 36
Spanier, G. B., 150
Stack, S., 24, 38–39, 85–87, 92, 105–106, 109–110, 117–118, 130
Stark, E., 134–135
Stets, J., 23
Stewart, D. E., 58
Stone, L., 87–88
Stone, M., 131–132
Stout, K. D., 15, 80
Straus, M. A., 23, 78–79, 81, 86, 94–96
Street, A. E., 10
Stuckless, N., 9, 18–19, 23, 33, 78, 81, 83
Sugarman, D. S., 81

T

Tardiff, K., 16, 102, 132
Taylor, S., 19–21, 121, 124–125, 131, 136–137
Tesler, P. H., 82
Thakor, S., 58
Thernstrom, M., 4–6
Thibaut, J., 94–95
Thomas, W. I., 9
Thonnes, N., 90
Tierney, K., 158
Tilley, N., 147
Timmermans, S., 137
Torre, E., 130–131

Totman, J., 45, 51
Trabold, N., 147

U

Unnithan, N. F., 104–105
Ury, W., 152

V

Ver Steeg, N., 90
Vera, H., 51
Voight, L., 17–18, 103–104

W

Walby, S., 74, 140
Walker, L., 5, 10, 25, 32–33, 59, 111
Wallace, R., 5, 36, 47, 53, 55, 57–58
Ward, P., 31–32, 129–130
Wardle, L. D., 96
Watson, K., 36
Weber, M., 122–123
Websdale, N., 36
Webster, D., 69
Weghorst, S. J., 66
Weiss, R., 1–3, 8
Welchan, L., 74
Welchans, S., 31–32
West, D. J., 24, 39, 102
White, S. W., 1–2
Widyono, M., 15
Wilbanks, W., 52, 66
Wilkinson, J., 148
Williams, K., 15, 31–32
Wilson, M. 9, 14, 23–25, 34–38, 43, 47–48, 52, 55–56, 58, 61, 64–66, 78, 81, 91–93, 96, 99–104, 119–120, 128–129
Winstock, Z., 79, 85–86, 119
Witte, A. D., 147
Wolfgang, M. E., 51, 66–67, 109
Wright, E. M., 45–46
Wyder, M., 31–32, 40–41, 129–131
Wynne, R., 55

Y

Yassour-Borochowitz, D., 25–26, 81, 107
Yllo, K., 95–96

Subject Index

Note: Page numbers followed by "f" indicate figures; "t" tables; "b" boxes.

A

Adversarial process, 5–7, 11
Affidavits, 83–84, 89
Aggravating effects, 9–10
Anomic suicide, 122
Appeals suicide, 125, 131
Arguments, 134
Arrest
    effect on femicide, 175, 182–183
    mandatory arrest, 148–149
    non-mandatory arrest, 148
    offender at the scene, 148
    offender who fled the scene, 148
    warrant arrests, 148
    warrantless arrests, 148–149
Attachment/frustration aggression, 108–109
Attribution theory, 104–106

B

Battering process
    definition, 50
    homicidal process, 134
    suicide, 134
Behaviour control, 103
Better alternative to a negotiated agreement (BATNA), 156
Borderline personality disorder (BPD), 123–124, 131
Borderline personality theory, 110–114

C

Causal mechanisms, 57t, 116, 116t, 135t, 146t
Centers for Disease Control and Prevention (CDC), 1
Coercive controlling violence (CCV), 22
Collaborative process, 5–7
Collective efficacy process, definition, 45–46
Communication patterns
    dysfunctional, 114
    functional, 111–112, 114
Communication skills, 153–154
Community property, 88–89
Conflict process
    as bad/boiling blood, 79
    definition, 78
    intensity, 79
Conflict resolution, 49, 52
    arguments, 80
    cost-benefit ratio, 85–86
    dynamics, 84–86
    escalation, 85–86
    intimate partner femicide, 84, 91t
    ladder, 152
    sensitivity to harm ratio, 85–86
    theory, 78–84, 114–115, 133
    training, 151–152
Conflict resolution tactics
    adversarial, 82–83
    collaborative, 82
Conjugal group, 121–122
Coordinated Action Against Domestic Abuse (CAADA), 146

D

Danger assessment process, 69
Dangerousness hearing, 142
Deductive theory, 63
Density
    family, 122
    household, 127
Depression, 131–132
Desertion process, 65
Divorce regimes process, 88
Divorce, definition, 2
Domestic Abuse, Stalking, and Harassment (DASH), 139, 145–146
Domestic context-specific theory, 86
Domestic society, 121–122
Domestic violence courts (DVCs), 171–174
Domestic Violence Death Review Committees (DVDRCs), 37
Domestic Violence High Risk Team (DVHRT) model, 139, 141–143
Domestic violence-MOSAIC (DV-MOSAIC), 183–184
Domestic violence types
    coercive controlling, 21–22
    situational couple, 21, 23
    violent resistance, 21–22

E

Egoistic suicide, 121–122
EMERGE, 76–77
Empirical generalization
　definition, 29
　and explanation, 30
Encapsulation
　conflict resolution theory, 49
　definition, 49
Escalation, 130, 134
Estranged husbands/wives, 35
Evolutionary psychological theory, 63–64, 99

F

Family group, 121–122
Family honour killings, 70, 74, 77
Fate control, 103
Femicide, 14–16
Femicide adaptation theory (FAT), 71
Femicide ideation, 71–73
Femicide prevention models, 146t
Frustration-aggression theory, 108–109, 117
Fundamental attribution error (FAE), 153–154

G

Gender inequality, 47, 50
Grounds for divorce, 2, 7–8

H

His/her metaphor process, 3–4
Homicide, 13–14

I

Infidelity, 65
Intimate partner femicide
　definition, 36
　following separation, 36–37
　relative frequency, 31t
Intimate partner femicide-suicide
　definition, 38
　following separation, 38–42
　relative frequency, 31t
Intimate partner homicide
　definition, 34–35, 47
　following separation, 36–37
　relative frequency, 30, 31t
Intimate partner suicide
　definition, 40
　following separation, 40–41
　gender differences in, 34t
　relative frequency, 31t

L

Law enforcement interventions, 139–156
Lethal domestic violence
　continuum/separate categories, 24–27
　definition, 13
　femicide-suicide as "extended suicide", 23–27
　femicide-suicide and premeditation, 16–21
　intimate partner femicide, 14–16
　intimate partner femicide-suicide, 16
　intimate partner homicide, 13–14
　intimate partner suicide, 13
　lethal and non-lethal domestic violence, 24–27
　officially reported violent crimes, 14
Legal separation, 2–3

M

Male batterers, 47
Male partner violence, 9–10
Male sexual proprietariness (MSP), 64
Mandatory arrest, 148–150
Mandatory information Program (MIP), 150
Marital property, 88–89
Marital status, 1–2, 11
Marital status transitions, 2
Married-registered and common law, 3, 7
Maryland Lethality Assessment Program (LAP), 139–141, 143
Masculinity theory, 106–107
Mediation Information and Assessment Meetings (MIAMs), 151
Micro-social context, 124–125
Monitoring process, 142
Morbid amorous jealousy, 102
Motives, 65–67

N

National Violent Death Reporting System (NVDRS), 30
Negative sentiment override (NSO), 153–154
Non-mandatory arrest (Not cited in the text)
NVivo analysis, 101

P

Paternity uncertainty, 65
Patriarchal bargain, 78
Patriarchal domination, 74
Patriarchy theory, 48, 73–75
Penal control, 103
Personality theory, 110–114
Phase separations, 5
Possessiveness, 100–101

Prediction, 139–140
Prevention, 166–167
Preventive detention, 142, 144
Principled negotiation skills (PN), 154–155
Protective effects, 9–10

R
Relational system, 123–124
Residence, 77
    patrilocal, 77
    separate, 82
    together, 81–82
Resolve conflicts, 79–80
Routine activities model, 49

S
Screening, 145–146
Selection process
    natural selection thinking, 72–73, 92
    self-selection, 81
Self defence, 46–47
Self-help theory, 45
Separation-instigated violence (SIV), 23
Separation process, 3–7
    agreements, 3
    and divorce proceedings, 9–11
    rational decision, 17
    source of stress, 1–2
    violence as cause of, 2, 7–9
Sexual jealousy/possessiveness, 64, 70
Sexual proprietariness, 56
Shelters
    history, 158–159
    international need for, 159
    types, 159
    users, 160
Situational couple violence (SCV), 23
Social integration-regulation theory, 121–125
Social interaction theory, 50
Social judgment theory, 47
Social separations, 3
Sociological social control theory, 103
Specific design features, 93
Spousal sex ratio of killings (SSROK), 32–33
Stateless location, 45–46
Strain theory, 49–50
Structural level-macro (Not cited in the text)
Suicide
    anomic, 122
    appeals, 125, 131
    egoistic, 121–122

T
Typical intimate partner homicide, 48

U
Ultimate conflict resolution tactic, 52
Unwilling separations, 9
US States, 76–78, 93
Utility, 8–9

V
Validity, 8–9
Victim precipitated, 51
Violent, 103, 111–112
Violent resistance (VR), 22